S0-ADM-641

LIVING ABROAD IN
NICARAGUA

RANDALL WOOD & JOSHUA BERMAN

Contents

WELCOME TO NICARAGUA

Forget everything you thought you knew about Nicaragua. As this nation's turbulent history fades even farther into the past, the unique, offbeat allure of Central America's largest and least-visited nation has caught the world's attention once again – this time for more appealing, positive reasons than the specter of civil conflict. Nicaragua is a place where, even in the 21st century, time clicks by a bit more slowly than you may be used to; where the sun is warm, the breeze blows year-round, and where the basic things in life – like family, friends, and time to sit out under clear, starry skies – are more important than normal North American concerns like office politics, mortgage payments, and credit card bills.

Nicaragua is an illumined land of sandy shores, cloudy forests, volcanic peaks, and a vibrant people who take life one day at a time. Nicas (as they call themselves) enjoy each other's company in a way the "developed" world seems to have forgotten,

Take it easy with a view of the shore.

© JOSHUA BERMAN

and if you find their enthusiasm contagious, you are not alone. Recently, while seated among an eclectic gathering of Nicaraguan artists, Dutch hikers, British language instructors, and Colombian agronomists, an American friend remarked, "Nicaragua has such an incredible ability to bring people together." Twenty-five years ago, such a group probably would have been gathered in this Matagalpa restaurant in solidarity with the revolutionary government; today, their reasons are infinitely more personal as they pursue dreams as different as the paths that led them here. Yet, these *extranjeros* (foreigners) have one thing in common: They have discovered that living in Nicaragua is safer than it is in most American or European cities — that it is exceedingly affordable, constantly inspiring, and an adventure unto itself.

Whether you discover Nicaragua in the context of a semester program, building brigade, or community service trip; as a researcher, economist, or entrepreneur; whether you come to work, explore, set down roots, or retire, Nicaragua has something

Volcán Concepción on Ometepe

© JOSHUA BERMAN

to offer you. This country's astonishing beauty begins with its broad diversity in geography and ecology – volcanoes, mangrove swamps, rich agricultural fields, and Caribbean pine forests – and continues with its charismatic architecture; from rustic, red-tiled villages and stately colonial-era towns to parks, plazas, and cathedrals that will keep you reaching for your camera. Most important are the six million Nicaraguans themselves, a rousing and vivacious people who have lived through difficult times and, despite past and current differences (including an enormous gulf between rich and poor), are fiercely proud of their common Nicaraguan heritage.

Foreigners who make even the slightest effort to communicate will find most Nicas to be fun-loving and eager hosts – quick with a smile, a joke, and a hot cup of coffee. They love to laugh, to give each other nicknames (you'll get yours, too; just wait), and to argue about sports and politics. Many Nicaraguans have family overseas, particularly in Miami, Houston, and Los Angeles, and have a more well-informed opinion of the United States than you may expect. And though they are aware of – and sometimes aspire to – some aspects of North American culture, most Nicaraguans have not forgotten what is important in life: that

Stretch your budget by enjoying fresh produce from local markets instead of imported luxuries.

© RANDALL WOOD

you work in order to live and not the other way around, that children and the elderly are to be nurtured and kept close, not dropped off in day-care centers and put into old folks' homes, and that who you are and how you behave is more important than what you own or where you work. Above all, Nicaraguans' intense history has taught them that life is short and should be lived fully, among family and friends.

We have both experienced this sentiment in personal ways; Nicaragua has changed us. Never mind the adventures, the great stories, and the albums of brightly colored photographs; seeing the world through another culture that has suffered mightily but retains the resilience, the strength of spirit, and the proud sense of self to build and grow is a life-changing experience. We both admire the Nicaraguan people and the way they see the world. After a couple of years in Nicaragua, life "back home" seemed immeasurably altered – things that were once important to us were no longer a priority, and other things we thought little of became more important.

We encourage you to pack the essentials for your journey: patience, a sense of humor, an unhurried spirit, and the willing-ness to experience things that are new to you. We encourage you

Diriamba's exuberant Festival of San Sebastián

© RANDALL WOOD

to keep an open mind, live with curiosity and compassion, and be willing to accept what you cannot change. Whether you make Nicaragua your next home or not, you will return with far more than you left with, and probably will look at the world differently as a consequence.

We both balance lives spent sometimes in Nicaragua and sometimes elsewhere, but we never fail to return to Nicaragua with a sense of coming home. If this book does no more than share with you the pride and solidarity we feel with the Nicaraguan people, we have succeeded. But we hope to do much more. We hope this book will help you determine if this country is right for you. And if it is, it can give you the information you need to cut through the red tape, set up your life, and buy or rent a home or apartment that matches what you're looking for.

The rustic end of Little Corn Island has varied lodging.
© RANDALL WOOD

INTRODUCTION

Is Nicaragua right for you? The first thing to consider is that, despite so much recent hype, an extended or permanent stay in Nicaragua is a bold and major lifestyle change. It would be wrong—and seriously misguided—to expect living in Nicaragua to be remotely similar to more traditional warm-weather retreats, like Florida or Costa Rica, for example. There are as many challenges as there are opportunities here, and the process of determining whether Nicaragua is your cup of tea should not be taken lightly. *Moon Living Abroad in Nicaragua* is a tool to assist you with that process; eventually, however, the questions you ask are your own, as is the responsibility of being prepared.

Start with, *"Why* am I moving to Nicaragua?" If your first answer has to do with something you read in a real estate brochure, flashy magazine article, or get-rich-quick scheme you found online, then you've got some more research to do.

© JOSHUA BERMAN

NICARAGUA

Caribbean Sea

Cabo Gracias a Dios

Bismuna
Punta Gorda
Laguna Bismuna
Laguna Pahra
Santa Marta
Tuapi
Puerto Cabezas (Bilwi)
Ulang
Wawa
Waspám
Yulú
Laguna Karatá
Wouhnta
Miskitos Cays
Kukalaya
Laguna Wouhnta
Little Corn Island
Big Corn Island
Susun
Bambana
Kukadoya
Prinzapolka
Guerrera Cays
Tyara Cays
Pearl Cays
Costa de Miskitos
Siuna
Makantaka
Barra de Río Grande
Tasbapauni
El Empalme
Makantaka
Matagalpa
Bella Vista
Pearl Lagoon
Costa de
Bosawás Biosphere Reserve
Cordillera Isabella
San Pedro del Norte
Sierra Amerrisque
Siquia
Mico
Tierra Dorada
Bahía de Perlas
El Bluff
Isla del Venado
Bluefields
Bahía de Bluefields
Monkey Point
Rama
Escondido
Bahía de Punta Gorda
La Gran Reserva Biológico Río Indio-Maíz
Bocay
Río Coco (Wangki)
Tuma
Grande
Cordillera Chontaleña
Wiwilí
San José de Bocay
Lago de Apanás
Juigalpa
San Miguelito
San Carlos
Los Chiles
Upala
HONDURAS
Concordia
La Concordia
Jinotega
Matagalpa
Cordillera Dariense
Sébaco
Boaco
San Benito
Tipitapa
Peñas Blancas
Lago Cocibolca
Isla de Ometepe
Solentiname Archipiélago
Cañas Dulces
COSTA RICA
Campamento
Dipilto
Ocotal
San Francisco del Norte
Somoto
Estelí
Masaya
Granada
Isla de Zapatera
Cordillera y Jalapa
Managua
Jinotepe
Nandaime
Rivas
La Cruz
Guaimaca
Danlí
Las Manos
El Espino
Guasaule
Estelí
Lago Xolotlán
El Crucero
Masachapa
Casares
San Juan del Sur
La Venta
Comayagua
PAN-AMERICAN HWY
Tegucigalpa
Chinandega
Cordillera Los Maribios
León
Poneloya
Corinto
El Tránsito
PACIFIC OCEAN
Puerto Cutuco
Punta San José
Potosí
Golfo de Fonseca
Estero Real
Estero Padre Ramos
Punta Ñata
EL SALVADOR
La Esperanza
San Miguel

© AVALON TRAVEL PUBLISHING, INC.

40 mi
40 km

Ultimately, you'll face the most important and potentially challenging aspect of living in Nicaragua: its poverty. Although a few upscale resorts and gated communities have recently sprouted in the southwest corner of the country, nowhere in Nicaragua will you be sealed off from the harsh, everyday realities of one of the poorest countries in the hemisphere. For many foreign visitors, this is their reason for coming—to import goodwill, skills, and knowledge to people who have not had the opportunities we in the United States, Canada, and Europe take for granted. These well-intentioned souls will find plenty of work to do, though creating sustainable solutions to poverty rather than more dependency is a far greater challenge than learning how to take a bucket bath or use a latrine. Will you know how to make a meaningful difference?

Business-minded immigrants believe the answer lies in investment, jobs, and the trickle-down effect. They figure they can help the economy and turn a small profit at the same time. Perhaps you are one of these, restaurant blueprints in hand or images of a long-dreamed lakeside bed-and-breakfast flitting through your head. You'll find your own set of trials and tribulations, from a short-changing contractor to an unexpected beachfront-turned-swamp in the rainy season, to the classic bureaucratic nightmares so common in Latin America—all of which you'll bear with your slowly improving Spanish language skills. Are you ready for such tests?

Even foreigners who arrive with no motive loftier than taking a break from the rat race, or even retiring from it, will be pushing their normal comfort zones. Basic services like electricity and water fail sporadically throughout Nicaragua. The recently privatized telephone service is improving, but at times the nation's entire telecommunications network gets saturated and there's nothing you can do but relax and wait. Some highways are smooth, but most roads are bumpy and uncomfortable, the drivers aggressive and reckless, and traffic snarls between Managua and Granada are the norm. Can you roll with such inconsistencies?

Then there is the Nicaraguan administrative and legal system. Your every run-in with the petty officials that demand and process your paperwork, from getting a driver's license to paying your taxes, will exasperate you and make you long for home, where everything seems to just *work* better. Do you have the patience?

Though we had no idea what to expect when we first moved to Nicaragua in 1998, it ended up being a perfect fit, and we have never stopped thanking our lucky stars for the different ways in which this place has affected our lives. Maybe you will be similarly enchanted; maybe you won't. Discovering if Nicaragua is right for you means asking all the questions above and more. It means reading this book and others, and above all, it means flying south and taking a gander. Research what you're getting into: Take a Spanish course, talk to Nicas, and chat up the expatriates who have made Nicaragua their home. Walk the streets, ride the buses, visit the markets, sample the food, and see the sights. Whether or not you decide to stay, this experience—and at least some part of Nicaragua—will remain with you for life.

The Lay of the Land

COUNTRY DIVISIONS

Nicaragua is divided into 15 units called *departamentos* and two vast autonomous regions on the Atlantic coast known as the North and South Atlantic Autonomous Regions (RAAN and RAAS). In the north, Jinotega, Matagalpa, and Nueva Segovia are famed for rolling mountains and deep valleys of coffee, pine forest, and fields of vegetables. Of these, Jinotega is the largest and wildest, and includes not just the Bosawás wilderness reserve, quite possibly the wildest and most remote corner in Central America, but scores of remote areas accessible only on foot or horse.

More toward the center of the country, Estelí is cowboy country, but more famous for its broadleaf tobacco plantations. From there, as you head eastward through rough and wild Boaco and Chontales the farms grow bigger and the people more hardy. Both *departamentos* are renowned for their production of milk and cheese (so much so that Boaco's motto is "the rivers are made of milk and the mountains are cheese"). Elsewhere, Nicaraguans place bets on whether Boaco and Chontales's cattle population is greater than its human population. Beyond Jinotega in the north and Chontales in the center, Nicaragua's rough mountains diminish and the landscape flattens into the pine savannas that characterize the Atlantic coastline.

Well over half of Nicaragua's population is clustered along the Pacific coast in the hot, fertile *departamentos* of Chinandega, León, and Carazo. Both Chinandega and León live in the shadow of the mighty Maribios mountains, whose volcanic soils have made this area Nicaragua's agricultural powerhouse. Only the breeze off the Pacific cools down this region, known for higher temperatures and starry nights.

South of Managua, the capital, the departments of Carazo and Rivas are pressed between the broad Lake Cocibolca and the Pacific Ocean. Carazo is cool and pleasant and boasts a small coffee industry of its own, though a good part of the sugarcane grown in Nicaragua is produced in this region, as are many of the nation's vegetables for the local markets. Rivas is cattle country like Boaco and Chontales, but the area is better connected to the rest of the country and feels less like the outback, especially since a good highway runs straight through Rivas to the Costa Rican border.

The Río San Juan is one of the areas that is most difficult to reach, and its startling beauty therefore goes underappreciated. The *departamento* of Río San Juan was named after the river that makes up its southern border, but it incorporates some of Nicaragua's most important environmental reserves along the Costa Rican border.

Lastly, the capital, Managua, together with the *departamento* that encompasses it, is the single most populous region in Nicaragua. One in two Nicaraguans lives in Managua, especially as a result of four decades of urbanization caused by immigrants looking for better lives in the city. Managua has swelled to accommodate them all, and continues to sprawl toward the south as new neighborhoods are expanded, renovated, or hacked out of the farmland that separates Managua from Masaya.

The departments, in turn, are divided into a total of 145 municipalities. The two autonomous regions elect their own officials, not necessarily according to the same election schedule as the rest of the nation. Nicaragua's three largest cities are Managua, León, and Granada, followed by Estelí, Masaya, and the remaining department capitals. A Nicaraguan *departamento* is the equivalent of a county in the United States, at least territorially, but geographically and socially each different *departamento* has a social climate of its own, and Nicaraguans associate strongly with their *departamento*.

GEOGRAPHY

At 128,000 square kilometers (49,000 square miles), Nicaragua is about the size of New York state, and its northern boundary with Honduras is the widest point in the Central American isthmus. Nicaragua's favorite nickname for itself—"The Land of Lakes and Volcanoes"—is a good indicator of what to expect, especially on its Pacific side, where most of the population resides amid the country's most striking physical features. Eastward from the northern cities of Jinotega and Matagalpa, the land rises in a vast expanse of cloud forest, then grows flatter and more tropical as it approaches the Caribbean, finally dissolving into barrens of white pines and marshland before reaching the ocean. The southern border with Costa Rica is formed by the Río San Juan, which receives most of the central highlands' rainfall and is lined with protected tropical forest and cattle ranches.

WHAT NICARAGUA HAS TAUGHT ME

Though it'll take some time to settle into your new Nicaraguan lifestyle, once you do, you'll discover two things: that you appreciate things you'd have never anticipated and that an old dog *can*, in fact, learn new tricks. The following responses were taken from a survey of U.S. volunteers who had just spent more than two years living in Nicaragua. "When I first arrived in Nicaragua," said one respondent, "I wasn't sure what to expect. I've found myself astonished, elated, taken aback, lonely, comfortable, excited, and unsure. I guess the only constant is that I never stopped learning."

THINGS I'VE LEARNED

- How to dance salsa with a great partner.
- To say "I'll come by this weekend" instead of "I'll be there Sunday at 3:30 P.M."
- That rain is a universally understood reason for being late or taking the day off.
- How to have a pretty good conversation with someone without really having any idea of what they're talking about.
- Nica slang words, like *turqueado, en carcajadas, coolazo, ahuevado* (beaten up, cracking up with laughter, super-cool, and bummed out).
- That although Nica men sing, dance, and write poetry, real men definitely do *not* carry umbrellas.
- That dogs have just as much right to mosey into restaurants, stores, and churches as people.
- That chewing-gum is a perfectly acceptable form of giving change.
- That ketchup goes well on sandwiches, rice, and spaghetti.

Principal Ecosystems

Nicaragua's varied topography and uneven rainfall distribution, not to mention the presence of tropical reefs, volcanoes, and volcanic crater lakes, result in a phenomenal diversity of terrain and ecosystems. This can be easily appreciated during any road trip through Nicaragua, as you watch prairie grasslands melt into rolling hills into near-desert into craggy mountain ranges whose peaks are draped in cloud forest. You can burn your feet on an active volcano's peak and cool your heels in ocean surf the same day. Nicaragua's higher peaks are isolated ecosystems in their own right and home to several endangered as well as endemic species, and the streams, rivers, and two very different coastlines furnish myriad other distinct ecosystems. In general, the land can be divided into four ecological zones.

- That part of daily life revolves around buying and drinking liquids in plastic bags.
- That if you tell me your neighbor's name and how far you live from the nearest church, I'm pretty sure I can find your house.
- That happiness has more to do with what you have, and less to do with what you think you "need."

THINGS I'VE LEARNED TO LOVE
- Feeling chilly in 74 degree weather.
- The respect little boys have for their mothers.
- Waking up at 6 A.M. on a Sunday morning to Bonnie Tyler's "Total Eclipse of the Heart" on my neighbor's radio.
- Sound effects when people tell stories, like "baah, pra, plam, ahh-hhhh-la."
- Warm beans in a bag.
- Walking barefoot on a freshly mopped floor.
- Yellow and fuchsia flowers against a cobalt blue sky.
- The taste of *cuajada* (a soft cheese) and the texture of *quesillo* (another type of soft cheese).
- The windy season.
- *Tajadas* (fried plantain strips) with *bastante ensalada y chile* (lots of salad and hot sauce).
- How patiently people explain things to me, even though it must get very annoying.

– Special thanks to *¡Va Pue!*, Jean Walsh, and Chris Romano

Pacific Dry Forest: The lowlands of the Pacific coast, specifically the broad, flat strip that borders the Pacific Ocean from sea level to approximately 800 meters (2,600 feet) in altitude, are a rain-stressed region dominated by thorny, rubbery species. The region typically receives less than 2,000 millimeters (80 inches) of rain per year. Both trees and non cactus-like plants in this ecosystem shed their leaves in the middle of the dry season in preparation for the rain to come, and often burst into flower in April or May.

Upland Pine Forest: With the exception of the slopes of several Pacific mountains, namely San Cristóbal and Las Casitas in Chinandega, and Güisisíl in Matagalpa, the majority of Nicaragua's pine forests are found in the north near Jalapa and Ocotal. Pines particularly thrive on poor, acidic soils, which erode easily if the area is logged.

Lower Mountainous Broadleaf Forest: Nicaragua's higher peaks are cloud covered for most of the year and home to a cool, moist biosphere, rich in flora and fauna. Most of these areas are the more remote peaks of Matagalpa and Jinotega, like Kilambé, Peñas Blancas, Saslaya, and Musún. It's easier to enjoy this ecosystem on the beautiful and easily visited peaks of Volcán Mombacho (near Granada) and Volcán Maderas (on Ometepe).

Caribbean Rainy Zone: The Atlantic coast receives rain throughout nearly 10 months of the year, and the humidity hovers around 90 percent year-round. Most of the Atlantic coast is covered with tropical forest or even lowland rainforest, with trees that often reach 30 or 40 meters (100 or 130 feet) in height. In the north along the Río Coco are the remains of Nicaragua's last extensive pine forests *(Pinus caribaea),* presently subject to intensive logging by national and international concessions.

Lakes

Nicaragua's two great lakes are unique in Central America. The smaller of the two, Lake Xolotlán (or Lago de Managua), borders the capital city and is biologically dead after decades of unrestrained industrial dumping and a century of untreated human sewage. Lake Cocibolca (or Lago Nicaragua) is another story. Cocibolca (the name means "Sweet Sea") is just smaller than the island of Puerto Rico and is 160 kilometers long down the middle. It's well-loved for its radiant sunsets, but it's also clean and swimmable and full of fish (except where Granada spews effluent on a small spot of its northwest shore). Sometimes it reflects the surrounding scenery on a mirror surface, but it's also big enough to kick up some serious waves when the wind picks up, making for exciting ferry rides to La Isla de Ometepe.

Volcanoes

Nicaragua's 40 volcanoes form part of the famed "Ring of Fire" that circles the entire Pacific Ocean, and each has its own personality. Low-lying Volcán Masaya is one of the few volcanoes on earth you can peer right down into and even, from time to time, see glowing lava; you might also catch a glimpse of its unique "crater parakeets," which make their nests in the sulfurous folds of the crater's inner wall. Volcanes Momotombo (rising from the shallow northwest waters of Lake Managua), Telica (just outside of León), and San Cristóbal (just outside of Chinandega) are equally active, and all have been known to belch up smoke or tremble a bit from time to time. Volcán Cosigüina, the peak farthest to the north, is extinct as far as anyone knows, but in January 1835, when it blew its top, it covered the surrounding area for 250 kilometers in every direction with a devastating layer of ash and burning pumice. Like most volcanoes mentioned above, Cosigüina's summit and parts of its slopes are protected as a wildlife reserve, with numerous hiking trails and campsites that only your local guide knows about.

Of course a discussion of Nicaragua's volcanoes is incomplete without paying tribute to La Isla de Ometepe, a beatific island formed by a pair of volcanoes—one active and hot (Concepción), the other dormant and filled with rainwater (Maderas). The fertile runoff of both has fused them at their bases, providing land for thriving banana and coffee plantations, numerous other agricultural projects, small fishing communities, and an increasing number of delightful—and rustic—guesthouses.

Beaches

Nicaragua's sandy, largely unspoiled Pacific coastline is certainly one the biggest draws for the current wave of foreign speculators. The historic port of San Juan del Sur is a low-key fishing town turned expat hangout on a peaceful and protected crescent bay. North and south of San Juan del Sur, the waves get bigger and the beaches emptier, each separated from the next by a rocky outcrop or stretch of forest—or in some areas, by some newly constructed resort or housing development. The dark-sand stretches of Nicaragua's northwest coastline are just as tranquil, but even more remote and less developed. Nicaragua's remote "Atlantic coast," as it is known, actually consists of 645 kilometers (400 miles) of wild Caribbean oceanfront, most of it inaccessible and backed by brackish swamps; there are a number of white-sand exceptions, however, including the Corn Islands and several isolated clusters of cayes, or small islands.

FLORA

Nicaragua's variety of ecosystems and its position at the biological crossroads between North and South America and between the Atlantic and Pacific Oceans have blessed it with an astonishingly broad assortment of wildlife. Of the world's known 250,000 species of flowering plants, an estimated 15,000–17,000 are found in Central America. It is estimated that Nicaragua is home to some 9,000 species of vascular plants, many of which are thought to be of medicinal value. Nicaragua is also a fantasyland for orchid lovers, especially in the northern highlands and atop the higher volcanoes. But while a few areas are relatively well protected, little effort has been made to protect the rest, where the majority of the land set aside by the government continues to experience intense pressure from the agricultural frontier and the scattered human settlements within the confines of the reserves. As tourism develops and becomes a viable incentive for protecting the forest, things may change.

Trees

The *madroño (Calycophyllum candidissimum)* is the national tree of Nicaragua. The hills south of Sébaco form the southern limit of the pine family found on the continent; south of Nicaragua the pines are outcompeted by other species. As of 2002, Nicaragua had a forest area of 5.5 million hectares (13.6 million acres), the majority of which is broadleaf forest, followed by pine forest *(Pinus caribea* and *P. oocarpa)*. At altitudes greater than 1,200 meters (4,000 feet) the forests also include *P. maximinoi* and *P. tecunumanii*. A full 2.5 million hectares (6.2 million acres) of forest are considered commercial timber forest. Though the forests are often privately owned, the exploitation of forest products is under the control of the Nicaraguan government.

FAUNA

Nicaragua is home to a great deal of exotic wildlife, much of which—unfortunately—you'll only see for sale on the sides of the highways and at intersections in Managua, where barefoot merchants peddle toucans, reptiles, ocelots, parrots, and macaws. This is a considerable, largely unchecked problem, more so because, of the animals that are captured for sale or export in Nicaragua, 80 percent die before reaching their final destination. To view fauna in their natural habitat involves getting out there, being very, very quiet, and looking and listening. Most critters are shy and many are nocturnal, but they're out there. To date, 1,804 vertebrate species, including 21 species endemic to Nicaragua, and approximately 14,000 invertebrate species have been defined. However, Nicaragua remains the least-studied country in the region, and it is thought that excursions into the relatively unexplored reserves of the north and northeast will uncover previously undiscovered residents of the planet.

Mammals

There are 176 mammal species (including sealife) known to exist in Nicaragua, over half of which are bats or small mammals, including rodents. Nicaragua has at least three endemic mammal species, two of which are

© DANIELLE VAUGHN

All three of Nicaragua's primate species have been sighted throughout the Los Guatuzos Wildlife Refuge.

associated with the Caribbean town of El Rama—the Rama squirrel *(Sciurus richmondi),* considered the tropical world's most endangered squirrel due to reduced habitat, and the Rama rice mouse *(Oryzomis dimidiatus).*

Nicaragua is also home to six big cat species, but there's no guarantee they'll be around for long. All six are listed as endangered, most seriously of all the jaguar and puma. Both were once common, but they require vast amounts of wild land on which to hunt. The Pacific region of Nicaragua, home to extensive agriculture for so many consecutive years now, is most likely devoid of big felines, with the possible exception of isolated communities on the higher slopes of some forested volcanoes like Mombacho. In the Atlantic region, small communities of cats eke out their survival in the dense forests of the southeast side of the Bosawás reserve. These species are unstudied and untracked, and are presumably preyed upon by local communities. Better off than the pumas and jaguars are smaller felines like ocelots and *tigrillos* trapped in the central forests, the latter of which are notorious chicken killers in rural farming communities.

There are three kinds of monkeys in Nicaragua: the mantled howler monkey *(Alouata palliata),* known popularly in Nicaragua as the *"mono congo";* the Central American spider monkey *(Ateles geoffroyii);* and the white-faced capuchin *(Cebus capucinus).* Of the monkeys, the congo is the most common. One thousand individuals roam the slopes of Mombacho alone. You can also find them (or at least hear their throaty, haunting cries) on La Isla de Ometepe and in the mountains of Matagalpa, particularly Selva Negra. Howler monkeys are able to project their voices an incredible distance; you can easily hear them several kilometers away. They eat fruits and leaves and spend most of their time in high tree branches. The white-faced capuchin is most frequently found in the forests in southeastern Nicaragua and parts of the Atlantic coast. It is a threatened species, but more so is the spider monkey, whose population has nearly been eliminated.

Aquatic Life

Nicaragua is home to a wide variety of both saltwater and freshwater species of fish, due to its two large lakes, two ocean coastlines, and numerous isolated crater lakes. Among Nicaragua's many saltwater species are flat needlefish, wahoo, three kinds of sole, spotted eagle rays, the Gill's sand lance, two kinds of moray, croakers, triggerfish, hogfish, eight kinds of perch, sea bass, and a dozen species of shark, including the world's only freshwater shark.

Among the freshwater species are needlefish, grunts, introduced tilapia, catfish, mojarra, and snook. Some species of cichlid found nowhere else in the world swim in Nicaragua's varied crater lakes.

At least 58 different types of marine corals have been identified in the Atlantic, specifically in the Miskito Cays, Corn Island, and the Pearl Cays. Nicaragua's most common coral species include *Acropora pamata, A. cervicornis,* and *Montastrea anularis.* Brain coral *(Colypophylia natans)* and black coral *(Antipathes pennacea)* are common. Studied for the first time in 1977 and 1978, the shallow reefs of the Pearl Cays contain the best coral formations in the nation, but they are currently threatened by the enormous sediment load discharged by the Río Grande de Matagalpa.

The manatee *(Trichechus manatus)* is an important species currently protected by international statutes. In Nicaragua it can occasionally be found in the Caribbean in the mouth of the Río San Juan and in the coastal lagoons, notably in Bluefields Bay. In 1993 the freshwater dolphin *(Sotalia fluviatilis)* was first spotted in Nicaragua and is most commonly sighted in Laguna de Wounta. The northern range for the freshwater dolphin was previously thought to be limited to Panama.

Birds

As a result of its prime location along the Central American biosphere corridor, along which many thousands of species migrate annually with the seasons, Nicaragua teems with birdlife. To date 676 species of birds in 56 families have been observed here, the more exotic of which you'll find in the mountains of the north and east, and along the Atlantic shore. Nicaragua has no endemic species of its own but hosts 87 percent of all bird species known. The most exotic species known to reside in Nicaragua is also its most elusive, the quetzal *(Pharomacrus mocinno),* known to inhabit highlands in Bosawás, Jinotega, and Matagalpa, especially along the slopes of Mt. Kilambé, and in Miraflor in Estelí.

Nicaragua's elegant and colorful national bird, the *guardabarranco*

(Momotus momota), is more easily found than you'd think. The "guardian of the stream" (as its Spanish name translates) can be found catching small insects in urban gardens in the capital. It is distinguished by its long, odd-shaped, iridescent tail, which it carefully preens to catch the eye of the opposite sex.

The *urraca* is a bigger, meaner version of the North American blue jay, with a dangly black crest on the top of its head. It's one of the larger of the common birds in Nicaragua and can frequently be found in treetops scolding the humans below. Though *urracas* are everywhere, a particularly sizable population patrols the slopes of Ometepe's twin volcanoes and another is found in the Isletas by Granada. Also in the Isletas, look for the brightly colored oropendolas *(Psarocolius wagleri)*, which hang their elaborate, suspended bag-nests from the treetops around the lakeshore.

CLIMATE

Nicaragua is pinched between the 11 and 15 degree north latitude marks, so it's decidedly tropical, even by Central American standards. If you're used to the mountain breezes of San José, Costa Rica, Nicaragua will seem hot to you. If you're used to the frigid Januaries of New York, it will seem like heaven. The weather is warm enough year-round to go swim in the ocean, and only in the mountain towns of Jinotega and Matagalpa does it ever feel "cool," but even there, the temperature can climb into the 90s (°F) at midday.

In general, expect temperatures of 27–32°C (81–90°F) during the rainy season, and temperatures about 3°C (5°F) warmer than that during the dry season. The coolest months are without a doubt January and February. April and May are the most uncomfortable months, when the tension before the rainy season begins is palpable, and some days it's just too hot to move.

Nicaragua's tropical climate experiences two distinct weather patterns the Nicas call "summer" *(el verano)* and "winter" *(el invierno)*. Summer is what northerners would call the dry season: It's hot, rains almost not at all (this prolonged drought is one of the country's most serious economic liabilities), and boasts clear, starry nights. The length of the summer season varies according to region, the north having a longer and drier summer than the south and east. In Estelí, summer can last from December to May, while in Rivas it might be from January to April, and in Bluefields or along the Río San Juan it might only be March and April. The rest of the year is what Nicas call "winter" and what northerners would call the wet season. During this wonderful time of year, bright blue morning skies gradually moisten until cloud cover towers into thunderheads. Not long after lunchtime, the first fat raindrops fall. The rains typically last until late afternoon, after which the air is cool and refreshing and everyone comes outside to walk and chat. This is when Nicaraguan farmers try to coax out of the ground a crop of white corn and red beans in succession.

Social Climate

Nicaragua's six million inhabitants are unfailingly proud to call themselves Nicaragüenses (*"¡por Gracias de Dios!,"* or "by the grace of God," as the song by Carlos Mejia Godoy goes). They're generally open and talkative, famous for their hospitality, curious about foreigners—and not afraid to ask questions.

No Nica is more than a generation removed from the countryside. They rise early to beat the heat, work hard, and relax with friends in the afternoon. The concept of working on weekends or holidays is anathema, and overtime is an insult, not an opportunity. That's not to say Nicas aren't industrious. They are ingenious and thrifty, and among your neighbors you will find hard-working farmers, seamstresses, cattle ranchers, and fishermen. In general, most Nicas are friendly and warm, and will welcome you in as one of their own—if you let them.

DEMOGRAPHICS

Nicaragua remains Central America's least densely populated country. The 5.2 million inhabitants enjoy more land on which to make their homes. This is changing dramatically as Nicaragua's higher-than-average birth rate is leading to something of a baby boom. Half of Nicaraguans live in Managua, the lively and chaotic capital, and another quarter live in the rest of Nicaragua's major cities combined. The rest live quiet bucolic existences in the many small villages that characterize the countryside throughout the north.

Volcanic activity is responsible for Nicaragua's rich expanses of soil along the Pacific coast, and as a consequence, that's where most of the people have made their home. If you drew two lines from north to south to divide the nation into three parallel bands, about 80 percent of the population would be living in the western third, along the volcanic chain known as the Maribios ("giants" in Nahuatl). Nicaragua's largest and most populous cities are found in this area, from León and Chinandega in the northwest to the capital, Managua, sitting by a lake of the same name, and southward to Masaya, Granada, and Rivas.

The two biggest cities outside the sprawling, difficult-to-manage capital are León and Granada, and not surprisingly, they are two of Nicaragua's most popular destinations for travelers and would-be residents. Both are painted in rich terra cotta colors, with strict building and zoning laws to ensure the preservation of the colonial style and heritage. Unassuming front doors open onto verdant garden patios, around which are set the sitting rooms and dormitories of the houses. Though their politics are diametrically opposed, the lifestyle is unhurried and languorous in both León and Granada, probably because of the heat, and few folks are so pressed for time they can't stop to chat.

The Atlantic coast is a land unto itself, isolated from the rest of the nation by bad or nonexistent roads and a culture gap, which is closing as more mestizos emigrate from the west. This area was once a British colony, so the people speak English and Creole (in addition to a few tribal dialects), have ancestors going back to the African slave trade, and generally think of themselves as a Caribbean nation that just happens to be bound to Latin America.

Northern Nicaragua is where the country's poorest subsistence farmers eke out meager livings growing corn and beans or raising cattle; others work on tobacco and coffee plantations. The soil is poorer than along the Pacific, worsened by practices that have led to erosion and the occasional landslide.

Nicaragua in essentially a young nation. Half of Nicaragua is younger than 20 years old, which means that to the majority of Nicaraguans, the Sandinista revolution of 1979 is ancient history, and the war is just a childhood memory. Four out of seven young Nicaraguans tend to be boys, but Nicaraguans in their 40s are the ones who fought the revolution or the counterrevolution that ensued in the 1980s, and women outnumber men in this age group by about five to three (many women recall in the 1980s when the discos were full of women because no man went for fear of being drafted into the military by the recruiters that hung out there).

NICA ATTITUDES TOWARD FOREIGNERS

Foreigners are no longer the oddity they once were in Granada's central plaza or on León's cathedral steps. The result of a near-constant stream of *extranjeros* (foreigners) in some parts of Nicaragua is bound to be a certain coolness on the part of Nicaraguans—and an increased eagerness of beggars and scam artists. Stray just a few blocks from the main tourist circuit, however, and you'll find the fresh, smiling curiosity with which Nicas have been greeting newcomers for decades.

Nicaraguans are surprisingly approachable, and a chance meeting is an opportunity for both parties to try out their broken Spanish and English. What's more, Nicaraguans know better than anyone that the views of a nation's people are not necessarily reflected by the policies of their government, so don't expect any animosity or misplaced blame for historical events. The word "gringo" is a harmless moniker for foreigners—unless, of course, it is preceded by a qualifier like *"pinche"* (cheap). Likewise, *"chele"* (pronounced CHEH-ley), along with its diminutive forms, *chelito* and *chelita,* just means "light-skinned," and if you listen to the physically inspired nicknames Nicas use for each other, you'll know it is nothing more than a friendly, descriptive term that they are equally prone to use amongst themselves. We've often heard a loud *"oye, chelito"* and turned with a smart remark only to find out the call had been directed to another Nicaraguan!

Expect lots of questions from your new Nicaraguan friends and neighbors. The United States and Europe are off-limits to many Nicaraguans due to immigration laws, but many Nicas have friends or family who have made the trip (either legally or *mojado*) and provide some connection to these places. In addition, Nicas are avid consumers of U.S. cable television and have much interest in North American culture and lifestyle—and many misperceptions. To give you an idea of the cultural divide and the incredibly candid curiosity of Nica culture, here are a few actual questions that we and our expat friends have been asked by sincere, inquisitive Nicaraguans:

- "Is it true that if Americans stop working the government pays them anyway?"
- "Do people get married on a contract, like for six months?"
- "When you were in college, was it like *Beverly Hills 90210?*"
- "Most American women look like the ones on *Baywatch,* right?"
- "The United States, is that near Miami?"
- "I have a cousin in Los Angeles, *se llama* Nelson. Do you know him?"
- "Is it true that in *los Estados* no one knows how to cook and all the food comes in cans?"
- "In your country, is everyone as fat as you are?"
- "Is it true a woman's last name disappears when she gets married?"

Keep in mind that the urban Nica living a relatively cosmopolitan life-style, possibly with a cousin or two in Miami, will have a more informed perspective than the average Nicaraguan campesino in the mountains. And for that matter, keep in mind that your questions to Nicas might sound just as funny to them as these questions do to you.

HISTORY, GOVERNMENT, AND ECONOMY

Nicaragua's turbulent history, eventful political theater, and developing importance in the new global economy continue to attract and intrigue a unique set of international visitors and immigrants from around the world. Most tend to agree with author Patrick Marnham's 1985 assessment that Nicaraguan politics are concerned "more with the rivalries of competing clans and families than with the world struggle between Marx and Capital." Indeed, such rivalries began hundreds of years before the Sandinistas' social experiment and continue through today's political shenanigans—decades after the end of the Contra War. That's not to say the Sandinista revolution wasn't based on lofty egalitarian ideals; it was. But rhetoric and implementation are different beasts, and modern Nicaragua is a place where the words "equality for all" offer little consolation in the face of one of the most grossly inequitable economies in the region.

It goes without saying that a basic understanding of these things—of recent Nicaraguan history and current affairs of state—is essential if you

© JOSHUA BERMAN

are considering making this your new home. What follows is a step in that direction, with an emphasis on "basic." A more thorough understanding of Nicaragua's exceptional background begins in the *Resources* section of this book, followed by a visit to your library and, most importantly, a trip to Nicaragua, where talking politics with the locals will teach you more than any book or website.

History

PRE-COLONIAL YEARS

The first human signs in modern-day Nicaragua were left by a Caribbean tribe known as Los Concheros (the shell collectors), who inhabited—or frequently visited—the Atlantic coast around 8,000 years ago. Agriculture began around 5,000 years ago with the cultivation of corn. Pottery making followed about 2,000 years later.

Sometime in the 13th century, the Chorotega and Nicarao people, under pressure from the aggressive Aztecs in Mexico, fled south through the Central American isthmus, led by a vision of a land dominated by a great lake. Their dreams fulfilled, the Chorotegas settled near Lake Cocibolca and around the volcanic crater lakes of Masaya and Apoyo, and the Nicaraos made their home farther south along the Cocibolca shoreline and La Isla de Ometepe.

COLONIALISM

Cristóbal Colón, a.k.a. Christopher Columbus, first set eyes on Nicaragua in July of 1502, on his fourth and final trip to the Americas. Searching for a navigable passage through the landmass, Columbus skirted Nicaragua's "Mosquito Coast," then continued on to South America without noticing the outlet of the Río San Juan. Seventeen years later, Spanish conquistadors returned and engaged the local caciques (tribal leaders), Nicarao and Diriangén, in a brief battle, giving the Spanish a hint of the Nicaragüenses' warrior spirit.

Francisco Hernández de Córdoba arrived soon after with the royal duty of establishing Spain's first settlements in the new land. Córdoba formed Granada alongside the Chorotega communities on the banks of Lake Cocibolca, and, pushing farther inland, he created León on the western shores of Lake Xolotlán (Lago de Managua). Nicaragua remained a part of Spain's overseas possessions for the next 300 years under the governance of the colonial capital in Guatemala.

KEY DATES IN RECENT NICARAGUAN HISTORY

1502	Christopher Columbus cruises the coast of Nicaragua.
1524	Francisco Hernández de Córdoba founds León and Granada.
1610	León is relocated to its present location.
1633	The English first establish contact on the Atlantic coast.
1740	First English settlements appear on the Atlantic coast.
1811	Popular uprisings begin against Spanish rule.
1821	Act of Central American Independence is signed in Guatemala.
1823	Central America receives independence from Spain.
1838	Nicaragua separates from the Central American Union.
1850	First German immigrants arrive in Nicaragua.
1855	William Walker arrives in Nicaragua with his mercenaries.
1856	Walker proclaims himself president of Nicaragua.
1875	Coffee economy begins to grow at a fast pace.
1894	José Zelaya "annexes" the Atlantic coast, gaining control from the English.

INDEPENDENCE AND THE BIRTH OF A RIVALRY

Central America won independence from Spain in 1821 and for a short time remained united as the five provinces of the Central American Federation. The belief that Europe would act militarily to repossess the former colonies convinced the United States to declare the Monroe Doctrine in 1823, declaring the New World off limits to further European interference. This was the beginning of two centuries of U.S. political domination in Latin America. The Central American Federation was short-lived, however; when Nicaragua withdrew in 1838, the remaining states opted to become independent republics as well and the federation dissolved.

After several years of complete anarchy in the new Nicaraguan nation, in which the two primary cities, León and Granada, operated as independent city-states, a national government was finally agreed upon in 1845. At the time, Nicaragua's principal exports were cacao, indigo, and cattle, the sale of which allowed the landed and merchant classes to accumulate considerable wealth—on the backs of the Native Americans and landless farmers, of course, who worked the farms and ranches as indentured servants. At the same time, the aspiring bourgeoisie, influenced by the

1914	Chamorro Bryan Treaty grants the United States exclusive right to build a canal through Nicaraguan territory.
1927	General Augusto C. Sandino takes to the hills of Ocotal.
1930	Nicaragua cedes the islands of San Andrés and Providencia to Colombia.
1931	Earthquake destroys Managua.
1933	Anastasio Somoza García becomes head of National Guard.
1947	First of three Somozas becomes president of Nicaragua.
1956	Sandinista (FSLN) guerrillas begin training in the mountains.
1972	Earthquake destroys Managua.
1979	Sandinista revolution overthrows "Tachito" Somoza.
1981–1990	Contra War takes place.
1990	Violeta Barrios de Chamorro wins the presidency.
1996	Arnoldo Alemán becomes president.
1998	Hurricane Mitch devastates much of the north.
2000	Daniel Ortega and Alemán sign *El Pacto*.
2001	Enrique Bolaños becomes president.

liberal teachings of the universities in León and by the American and French revolutions, sought to liberate the poor working classes of their feudal labor obligations, making their labor available to all at market prices. The landed class, mostly based in Granada and loyal to the aristocratic system that favored them, resisted. The León Liberals–Granada Conservatives split was responsible for over 100 years of ensuing civil war and continues into modern political party rivalries.

Early U.S. Intervention

Except for the audacious takeover of Nicaragua by a deluded American adventurer and his army of thugs (William Walker in the mid-1800s), most U.S. intervention has come from direct economic and political interests, often concerning Nicaragua's long history of unrealized transcontinental canal plans. U.S. Marines saw considerable action on Nicaraguan soil in the late 19th and early 20th centuries, protecting North American corporate interests, taking sides in the ongoing Liberal vs. Conservative battle, and helping out with more than one U.S.-backed regime change.

In 1925, as the Liberals and Conservatives sought a power-sharing arrangement, one of the Liberal generals, Augusto Cesar Sandino, who was opposed to the pact, fled with his men to the northern mountains to start a guerrilla war in opposition to the continued presence of the United States in Nicaragua. The U.S. military tried unsuccessfully—for seven years—to flush Sandino from the mountains, so in 1933, Washington tried a new approach. Withdrawing troops from Nicaragua, the United States formed a Nicaraguan military unit called the National Guard, placed a young Anastasio Somoza García at its head, and handed power to them and the new president, Juan Bautista Sacasa.

Despite propaganda painting him as a common outlaw, Sandino enjoyed overwhelming popular support in Nicaragua's northern mountains and had achieved two of his goals—the removal of both U.S. armed forces and the Conservative oligarchy from power. Sandino represented a major threat to Somoza's political and military ambitions, and in February of 1934, after signing a truce, Sandino was assassinated on the streets of Managua. The assassination was followed by a government-sponsored reign of terror in the northern countryside, destroying cooperatives, returning lands to their previous owners, and hunting down, imprisoning, or killing Sandino's supporters.

THE SOMOZA ERA

The formation of the National Guard paved the way for its leader, General Anastasio Somoza García, to seize control of Nicaragua in 1937 and begin an enormously wealthy and powerful family dynasty that would permanently reorient and completely control Nicaraguan politics for the following 42 years. So formidable was the rule of the Somoza family that many Nicaraguans and foreigners alike refer to the nearly continuous succession of three Somoza presidents as one all-powerful "Somoza." The Somozas were wily politicians with a near-genius for using existing political conflicts to their personal advantage; they were expert practitioners of a favorite trick of Latin American dictators, *continuismo,* in which a puppet leader would be elected but resign shortly afterward, handing the power back to the Somozas and putting on a show of "democracy" to the world. Five such presidents were "elected" during the Somozas' reign, not one of which lasted longer than three years. The Somozas maintained a strong grip on the national economy as well (much to the dismay of merchants in Granada) by manipulating the government licensing mechanisms and importing contraband for local markets with the complicity of the National Guard. If there was money to be made anywhere in Nicaragua, the Somozas took notice and squeezed out the competition. It is said that by the late 1970s the Somoza family owned everything in Nicaragua worth owning.

Anastasio Somoza Debayle, a.k.a. "Tachito," was a graduate of the West Point Military Academy (1946) and the third and most avaricious president of the Somoza dynasty. At the time Tachito became president, the nascent FSLN (Frente Sandinista de Liberación Nacional) opposition movement, which had named itself after its hero and martyr, General Augusto Sandino, was gaining attention through attacks and kidnappings in northern Nicaragua. Over the next decade, the Sandinistas would prod Tachito into becoming the most relentless and cruel president the nation had ever seen. The Sandinistas (see sidebar, *The Sandinista Revolution*) finally forcefully ousted him in 1979 via a revolution that inspired most of the world.

THE NEW DEMOCRACY

After 11 years of rule, the Sandinistas lost the 1990 elections and peacefully handed the reins of the nation to Violeta Barrios de Chamorro. Doña Violeta (as she is affectionately known) had no formal political affiliations or training, but her charismatic ability to reconcile and unite ushered Nicaragua into its new era. She attempted to rebuild the nation as though it were a shattered family, which to some degree, it was. Her administration made great gains in reestablishing diplomatic and economic ties with the rest of the world. Chamorro ended the draft, reduced the army, and brought both the army and the police force under civil control. She began the difficult process of demobilizing and disarming the Contras and initiated a new agrarian reform, aiming to reassign formerly expropriated lands. Today, the issue of land ownership is still bitter and contested in many regions of the country.

The elections of 1996, run without the massive international funding that characterized previous elections, were rife with abnormalities, near-riots, and disorder. Even so, Nicaraguans turned out in record numbers and elected Managua's slippery Liberal mayor, Arnoldo Alemán, over Daniel Ortega. It was a scandalous beginning to a scandalous presidency. A lawyer by training, Alemán was a political conservative and hard-core capitalist with a sworn aversion to all things Sandinista and a professed admiration for the Somozas, whose proclivity for political manipulation and capacity to accumulate personal fortune Alemán imitated. His economic program courted foreign investment and promoted exports at the expense of a social safety net. Politics returned to the back room, where endless scandals of kickbacks, insider deals, and frenzied pocket-filling embarrassed and infuriated the nation. The net worth of Alemán, a one-time Miami used-car salesman, rose from

THE SANDINISTA REVOLUTION

Guerrilla groups inspired by Fidel Castro and opposed to the Somoza dictatorship began training in clandestine camps in the 1950s and coalesced a decade later with the formation of the **Frente Sandinista de Liberación Nacional (FSLN),** whose basic tenet was that dictatorships could never be reformed – only overthrown. FSLN leaders' ideology was an inspired combination of Marxism and the anti-imperialist beliefs of Augusto Sandino.

The first Sandinista insurrections in the early 1960s were quickly crushed, but they legitimized the FSLN among radical university students and city dwellers. As a result, the Sandinistas' military strength and daring escalated rapidly through the 1970s in spite of several bitter defeats at the hands of the National Guard. Somoza's heavy-handed attempts to silence this growing opposition only served to stoke the fire beneath him. Trade unions, student organizations, and popular movements – private, secular, and religious – all threw their weight behind the insurgency, and in July 1979, the Sandinista command offensive, encouraged by an increasingly militant popular attitude, won complete control of Nicaragua.

The exuberance of military victory quickly faded as the new leaders struggled to convert revolutionary fervor into support for the new nation they wanted to build. The sweeping economic, political, and social reforms of the Sandinista revolution made Nicaragua a real-time social experiment, and the entire world – particularly the United States – looked on with fascination and fear.

In their zeal to "defend the revolution at all costs," the Sandinista leaders ran into opposition from all sides – from the business community; from Somoza's former cronies, who missed their days of wealth and privilege and were enraged by the policy of confiscation; from the former members of the National Guard, who had regrouped outside of Nicaragua, becoming the nucleus of the *contra-revolucionarios* (Contras); and lastly, from the United States. President Ronald Reagan seized on the Communist tendencies of the Sandinista leadership and made Nicaragua the "backyard" focal point of his Cold War policy; he launched a political, economic, and military program designed to strangle the Sandinistas out of power and replace them with something more amenable to the economic interests of North America. This desire to remove the Sandinistas was not North America's alone – many moderate Nicaraguans felt betrayed by the Sandinistas, who, they felt, had imposed a Marxist-Leninist regime on the nation without their approval and had simply replaced one political elite with another. Thus the U.S.-financed Contras were just the military arm of a multifaceted opposition that soon led to yet another Nicaraguan regime's downfall.

By the close of the 1980s both the Contras and the FSLN were exhausted and broke. More than 50,000 young Nicaraguans were dead and buried. The ruined Sandinista economy could no longer support a prolonged war of attrition, while the collapse of the Soviet Union had decimated the primary source of funding. The Contras had suffered severe military setbacks, received mixed messages from their patrons in Miami and Washington, and had little hope of a military victory. The Iran-Contra scandal in the United States, in which the American public became aware that arms were being secretly and illegally sold in the Middle East to raise money for the Contras, ended all further funding for Reagan's "Freedom Fighters." The moment was propitious for a peace initiative, supplied by Costa Rican president Oscar Arias and culminating in the 1990 elections. To the surprise of the FSLN leaders, the Nicaraguan people overwhelmingly voted them out of office. The revolution had ended.

The Sandinistas have since reinvented themselves as a legitimate opposition political party, and have been strong participants in municipal and presidential elections ever since. However, in spite of their continued support from their traditional base – the poor and disenfranchised – they have been unable to place their longtime leader, Daniel Ortega, back in the presidency. Most Nicaraguans still remember all too well the civil war, chronic shortages of basic goods, and the military draft that plagued the 1980s. Also unforgivable for many was an event now known as *"la piñata,"* in which a lame-duck Ortega administration in the late 1980s looted the state of everything it could, from office equipment to fancy Managua homes, keeping the best of it for themselves. In the eyes of many Nicaraguans, it was the final abandonment of every ideal the revolution had ever claimed to stand for.

Today, many consider the FSLN to be completely usurped by the egotistical ambitions of Daniel Ortega; he was a strong contender in the 2001 presidential election, though Ortega's campaign downplayed the use of the word "Sandinista" and concentrated on his own personality instead: Banners read not "¡FSLN!" but "¡Daniel!"

Ortega will run again in 2006, and he retains the ability to draw enthusiastic crowds of supporters, not because of any particularly strong policy platform but because he and Arnoldo Alemán have systematically unraveled the political patronage system to their benefit in the years since *El Pacto,* a miserable agreement in which Ortega and Alemán agreed to divide the government power between them and single-handedly set Nicaraguan democracy back by decades. How well Ortega is able to maintain his position will depend on his continued ability to crush the young and well-educated potential FSLN leaders who would dethrone him.

© RANDALL WOOD

The Sandinista Revolution changed the nation.

US$20,000 (when he took office as mayor of Managua) to US$250 million (when he was voted out of the presidency in 2001). He has since been indicted for his crimes, thrown in prison, then relegated to "house arrest," where, inexplicably, he manages to continue his political "career."

Enrique Bolaños, Alemán's nondescript vice president, came to power in 2002 on an anticorruption platform. His pledge to clean house resonated with Nicaraguans fed up with Alemán's abuses, and they elected him over Daniel Ortega with a 56 percent majority. But despite good intentions, Bolaños was unable to overcome the powerful party dynamics that have maintained the Nicaraguan political elite in power for centuries. The Liberal party (Partido Liberal Constitucionalista), which had brought Bolaños to power, was bloated with corruption, and by attacking it Bolaños destroyed the political support he needed to be an effective leader.

Today's Nicaragua enjoys relative stability and peace, allowing an ever-increasing number of outsiders to discover its natural beauty and charm. At the same time, continued corruption and political shenanigans keep Nicaragua watchers and investors ever-wary.

Government and Politics

Nicaragua boasts the rare distinction of having experienced three radically different systems of government in as many decades: A 40-year dynastic dictatorship essentially capitalist in nature but overwhelmingly monopolized by the Somoza family, which ran the nation like a family farm, fell to Marxism/Leninism in 1979, which was itself replaced by capitalism and a neoliberal open market. The ramifications of these changes are still being felt and analyzed. In hindsight, nothing is clear. Nicaraguans rose up in protest to the abuses meted out by the Somoza dynasty, but the socialist state run by the Sandinistas was economically disastrous from the start and in blatant opposition to the character of many Nicaraguans, even in the countryside. But capitalist reforms in the 1990s took well over a decade to have any impact at all, and even today some older Nicaraguans look fondly back to the Somoza era as a time when "things were better."

ORGANIZATION

The Republic of Nicaragua is a constitutional democracy that gained its independence from Spain in 1821. In addition to the national government, there is a parallel government responsible for the administration of

© RANDALL WOOD

"¡Salve a ti, Nicaragua!"

the two autonomous regions of the Atlantic coast, which elect their own leaders separately from the rest of the nation.

Branches of Government

Nicaragua's government is divided into four branches: The executive branch consists of the president and vice president. The judicial branch includes the Supreme Court, subordinate appeals courts, district courts, and local courts, plus separate labor and administrative tribunals. The Supreme Court oversees the entire judicial system and consists of 12 justices elected by the National Assembly for seven-year terms. Many consider the judicial system ineffective and plagued by party interests and manipulations by the rich, but it does have some points in its favor, including an approach that attempts to reduce crowding in jails by having the aggressor and the aggrieved meet to strike a deal. For minor offenses, this is an effective tactic. There is no capital punishment in Nicaragua, and the maximum sentence is 30 years.

The legislative branch consists of the Asamblea Nacional (National Assembly), a chamber in which 90 *diputados* (deputies) representing Nicaragua's different geographical regions vote on policy. The *diputados* are elected from party lists provided by the major political parties, though defeated presidential candidates that earn a minimum requirement of votes automatically become lifetime members, and by law, former presidents are also guaranteed a seat.

The fourth branch of government is unique to Nicaragua: The Consejo Supremo Electoral (Supreme Electoral Council, or CSE) consists of seven magistrates elected by the National Assembly for five-year terms. The CSE has the responsibility of organizing, running, and declaring the winners of elections, referendums, and plebiscites. Electoral reforms put in place in 2000 allowed the FSLN and the PLC the new ability to name political appointees to the council, politicizing the CSE to the extreme, a move that has led to a perceived reduction in the transparency of the Nicaraguan government as a whole.

Elections

The Nicaraguan people vote for their president and *diputados* every five years. The president cannot run for consecutive terms. Until Bolaños enacted legislation preventing it in 2004, former presidents were eligible to run again; now they are not (stay tuned for the inevitable next salvo in this battle).

THE CONSTITUTION

The present constitution, written in 1987 by the FSLN administration, was amended in 1995 to balance the distribution of power more evenly between the legislative and executive branches. The National Assembly's ability to veto was bolstered and the president's ability to veto reduced. It was revised again in 2000 to increase the power of the Supreme Court and the comptroller-general's office, which supervises all government expenditures.

Civil Liberties

Among Latin American societies the people of Nicaragua enjoy unequaled freedom, and owe it largely to the Sandinista revolution. Most notable is their nearly unparalleled freedom of speech, a right guaranteed by the constitution and exercised with great vigor by Nicaraguans of all persuasions. The repression, censorship, and brutality of Somoza's dictatorship ended within the recent memory of many Nicaraguans, and they do not take the freedom they enjoy in the 21st century for granted. There is no official state censorship of the media in Nicaragua, though there have been occasional governmental attempts to exert influence through subtler means, such as the embargo of government-sponsored ad revenue of newspapers that seem overly critical.

The constitution additionally guarantees freedom of religion, freedom of movement within the country, freedom of foreign travel, emigration and repatriation, and the right to peacefully assemble and associate. Domestic and international human rights' monitors are permitted to operate freely and interview whomever they wish.

The Nicaraguan constitution prohibits discrimination in all forms, including discrimination by birth, nationality, political belief, race, gender, language, religion, opinion, national origin, or economic or social condition. In practice, however, there are many social forms of discrimination,

A GUIDE TO NICARAGUAN POLITICAL PARTIES

The concept of the modern Nicaraguan political party seems to be more for organizational convenience than any real conviction of principles. Nicaraguan politicians change from one party to another as necessary to suit their own ambitions, and smaller parties continually coalesce into alliances that later fracture into new arrangements. Infighting and division have been an integral part of the Nicaraguan political scene since its inception.

In the 19th century things were relatively simple: The Conservatives more strongly supported the Spanish crown and were organized around Granada, and the Liberals supported independence and were centered in León. A century later, the **Frente Sandinista de Liberación Nacional** (FSLN or simply "the Sandinistas") formed in response to decades of brutality at the hand of the Somoza dictators and represented something indeed revolutionary in Nicaraguan politics. After gaining power in 1979, the FSLN's popularity subsequently declined, and no fewer than 20 political parties rose to oppose them. Doña Violeta Chamorro formed her UNO coalition from 14 of them. In 1996, the number of parties swelled to 35, all of which participated in the elections on their own or as one of five coalitions. So in 2000, Ortega and Alemán enacted new legislation as part of their dirty little gentlemen's agreement to prohibit such a free-for-all and to make entry more difficult for smaller political parties. In reality this was simply a way to prevent newcomers from muscling in on their turf.

Three parties were represented in the presidential election of 2001 and continue as the major players in Nicaraguan politics: the FSLN, the right-leaning **Partido Liberal Constitucionalista (PLC),** and the **Partido Conservador Nicaragüense (PCN),** the last being the moderate-right representatives of the old Conservative party. The Sandinistas (and their anti-PLC coalition, **La Convergencia**) battled the right-wing PLC-dominated **Alianza Liberal,** which ultimately won the election.

In early 2006 the landscape complicated further: José Antonio Alvarado was running with Enrique Bolaños' incipient **Alliance for the Republic (APRE)** coalition, made up of moderate PLC dissidents, and Vice President Rizo threw his hat in the ring with the support of the PLC. Eduardo Montealegre split from the PLC, and Herty Lewites, the popular Sandinista mayor of Managua, split from the FSLN, representing major threats to the nation's strongest political parties. Look out for all of the aforementioned names in the future – even if they're representing different constituencies by the time you read this. In a land of few opportunities, politics is the best business in town, and everybody wants a piece of the pie.

including a *machista* society that, in addition to imposing a double standard on women, also associates lighter-skinned people with the aristocracy and darker-skinned people with the labor force, regardless of whether
that's the case.

Nicaraguans are permitted to form labor unions, though intimidation
by employers, especially of foreign-owned maquiladoras (assembly plants,
the worst of which are called "sweatshops") is all too common. Nearly half
of the workforce, including much of the agricultural labor, is unionized.
The trade unions receive much international support from labor groups
overseas, who often step in on behalf of Nicaraguan laborers in disputes
in the free trade zones.

The Economy

Two successive governments have had to jump-start the Nicaraguan
economy from an essential stand-still: the Sandinistas, who picked up
the shattered remains upon ousting Tachito, and Doña Violeta, who had
to recover from the war and a decade of socialism. Her administration
made dramatic progress, reducing the foreign debt by over half, slashing
inflation from 13,500 percent to 12 percent, and privatizing several hundred state-run businesses. The new economy began to expand in 1994
and these days is growing at just over 4 percent, despite several major
catastrophes, including Hurricane Mitch in 1998, which decimated
agricultural production.

Nevertheless, Nicaragua remains the second poorest nation in the Western hemisphere with a per capita GDP of US$780, and its external debt
ratio—nearly twice the gross national product—is a serious constraint to
growth. Unemployment is a pervasive problem: More than half the adult
urban population scrapes by in the informal sector (selling water and goods
at the roadside, for example), and population growth is probably going to
keep it that way. High demand for jobs means employers can essentially
ignore the minimum wage requirement, especially in the countryside,
where agricultural laborers typically earn as little as US$1 a day, insuffi-
cient for survival even by Nicaraguan standards. Nearly 600,000 people
face severe malnutrition.

Nicaragua has an economy almost entirely based on agricultural export
of primary material, though in recent years tourism and several nontraditional exports have gained in importance. Export earnings are US$700
million and rising: Agricultural programs in 2000 and 2001 that helped

DEBT, THE HIPC, AND FOREIGN AID

For years, Nicaragua has been one of the most highly indebted nations of the world. When Somoza fled the country, he took the capital reserves of the banks with him, leaving behind US$1.6 billion of debt. The Sandinistas, through a combination of gross economic mismanagement, extensive borrowing (primarily from Eastern bloc nations), the U.S. economic embargo, and high defense expenditures augmented the national debt by a factor of 10, nearly half of which was in arrears. By 1994 Nicaragua had the highest ratio of debt to GDP in the world, a challenge every successive administration has had to deal with. Germany, Russia, and Mexico were the first nations to forgive Nicaraguan debt entirely.

Propitious to Nicaragua's future economic growth was its inclusion in the Highly Indebted Poor Countries (HIPC) debt relief initiative in 2000. Inclusion in the initiative means Nicaragua will be exonerated from the majority of its international debt upon compliance with an International Monetary Fund (IMF) and World Bank program, but that program mandates several austerity measures, debt restructuring, and the opening of its economy to foreign markets. More hotly contested is the mandated privatization of public utilities, including the telephone system (privatized in 2002) and municipal water distribution. City water systems have not yet been privatized, and the issue is extremely controversial with those who consider water a basic human right rather than a commodity. Central to the HIPC initiative is Nicaragua's continued effort toward macroeconomic adjustment and structural and social policy reforms, particularly basic health and education.

increase Nicaragua's ability to export beef and milk give hope that exports will rise in the latter part of the decade. Traditional export products include coffee, beef, and sugar, followed by bananas, shellfish (especially lobster tails and shrimp), and tobacco. New nontraditional exports are on the rise as well, including sesame, onions, melons, and fruit.

AGRICULTURE

Nicaragua is, above all, an agricultural nation—a third of its gross domestic product is agriculture-based, and agriculture represents the fastest growing economic sector, at 8 percent growth per year. However, much of the new land put into agricultural production is opened at the expense of the forests, the indiscriminate harvesting of which has a negative overall effect on the environment and water supply. Agriculture employs 45 percent of the workforce. Outside of the small, upscale producers who export to international markets, the majority of Nicaraguan agriculture is for

WELCOME TO NICARAGUA

domestic consumption, and much of that is subsistence farming. Drought years often require importing of basic grains.

Subsistence farmers typically grow yellow corn and red beans. The choice of red beans over black and yellow corn over white is cultural and presents additional challenges to farmers, as red beans are more susceptible to drought (and less nutritious) than black beans or soybeans.

The Sébaco Valley is an agriculturally productive area and the primary source of wet rice for local consumption; it's also widely planted with onions. Extensive irrigation of rice plantations caused the water table in the Sébaco Valley to drop over three meters in the 1990s, and the area is infamous for its high pesticide use. Jinotega's cool climate is a major source of fruit and vegetable production, including cabbages, peppers, onions, melons, watermelons, squash, and tomatoes.

The Coffee Economy

There's no underestimating the importance of coffee to the Nicaraguan economy. Coffee is produced on more than 100,000 hectares of Nicaraguan land, contributes an average of US$140 million per year to the economy, and employs more than 200,000 people, nearly a third of the agricultural workforce (13 percent of the national workforce). Nicaragua exports its beans primarily to Europe, North America, and Japan—to the tune of

© JOSHUA BERMAN

The forest canopy remains lush and full over this small, shade-grown coffee farm.

1 million 100-pound burlap sacks every year. These beans are roasted and ground (usually abroad) to produce 11 billion pounds of java.

In addition, because most Nicaragua growers produce full-bodied Arabica beans at altitudes of 900 meters and higher, the quality of its crop is recognized the world over. The June 2004 issue of *Smithsonian* magazine reported Nicaragua as "the 'hot origin' for gourmet coffee, with its beans winning taste awards and its decent wages for many small farmers a hopeful beacon for a global coffee market under siege." It also declared Nicaragua a country where "the goals of a better cup of joe, social justice and a healthier environment are nowhere more tightly entwined." This translates into higher prices brought in by the organic and fair trade certification movements, which have been crucial as Nicaragua struggles to emerge from the worst crash in the global coffee economy in a century.

INDUSTRY

Industrial production in Nicaragua reached its zenith in 1978 under Anastasio Somoza, who encouraged industrial expansion in Managua at the expense of the environment, especially Lake Xolotlán. Investment policies of the time exonerated industries from the need to worry about environmental protection. Industry—and agro-industry—has been underdeveloped in the years since the revolution. There is a small amount of production for domestic and regional markets, including cement processing, petroleum refining, and a small amount of production of plastic goods. Another aspect of Nicaragua's export industry is the steadily increasing number of Zonas Francas (free trade zones) near Managua, Sébaco, Masaya, and Granada, where tens of thousands of Nicaraguans are employed in foreign-owned maquiladoras, or barnlike assembly plants.

TOURISM

As global tourism continues its rise around the world, cash-happy foreign visitors—mainly from North America and Europe—are widely hoped to be a sustainable solution to Nicaragua's economic woes. At present, tourism represents the third-largest source of foreign exchange. Public Law 306 provides a 10-year tax break to newly constructed tourist facilities that meet certain criteria. Since the mid-1990s, investment in tourism has skyrocketed, notably in Managua, Granada, and San Juan del Sur. During his campaign, President Enrique Bolaños pledged to augment tourism with luxury cruise ships and large international hotel and resort chains up and down the Pacific coast, a vision that has to some extent begun to be realized.

PEOPLE AND CULTURE

Most visitors agree that Nicaragua's greatest strength lies in the exuberance, tenacity, and charm of its people. While investments, retirement opportunities, or the search for a simpler lifestyle may draw you to Nicaragua, it is *los Nicaragüenses* who will convince you to stay.

Nicaraguans now number nearly 6 million and, by some estimates, will reach 10 million before 2030. Nicaragua is a young country (more than half of its population is younger than 16 years old), and all those new mouths to feed are putting severe constraints on the nation's ability to address its poverty and environmental issues. Not surprisingly, that drives lots of Nicaraguans overseas in search of a better lifestyle. Of these, nearly 700,000 have wound up in Costa Rica, where they form the working-class labor force of the construction and farm sectors (Nicas like to boast that without Nicaraguan labor, Costa Rica's coffee harvest would be exactly zero). Another half a million Nicaraguans have emigrated to the United States, particularly Miami, Texas, and California, where they tend to live in nondescript communities and keep a low profile.

© RANDALL WOOD

Ethnicity and Class

Nearly every Nicaraguan is descended from some mixture of Spanish and indigenous (mostly Nahuatl and Chorotega) ancestry. Nicaragua has experienced less influence by other European nations than South America has; during the 1950s and 1960s European immigrants tended to land in Argentina and Peru, not Central America.

MESTIZOS

The word "mestizo" refers to anyone of mixed Spanish-indigenous blood, and mestizos count for the overwhelming majority (more than 90 percent) of the population. The process of *mestizaje* (mixing) began 500 years ago, when the first Spanish conquistadors settled in Granada, and continues with the latest wave of *extranjeros* (foreigners) to reach Nicaraguan shores. Lighter-skinned mestizos often call those whose indigenous physical characteristics are more pronounced *"indios."* The word has a slightly negative connotation, used also for anyone who is not worldly or is otherwise perceived as ignorant, backwards, or inferior (which, incidentally, is how Costa Ricans view all their northern Nica neighbors, regardless of subtle skin color differences).

ATLANTIC COAST CULTURES

Nicaragua's Atlantic coast, which formed part of the British Empire for the better part of a century, has a decidedly different ethnic makeup than the rest of the country, despite steadily increasing immigration of mestizo Nicas. Known in its early, pirate-marauding days as the "Mosquito Coast," the land surrounding Puerto Cabezas and Bluefields (and the nearby handful of Caribbean islands) was home to populations of slaves (escaped, freed, or still working) of African and Caribbean origin. They mixed

© RANDALL WOOD

Costeños (coastal inhabitants) on Nicaragua's Atlantic side are more Caribbean than mestizo.

freely with the coastal natives, so that today's Atlantic coast population includes people who speak English and have darker skin and curlier hair. As a result, if you ask the majority of Nicaraguans where they're from, they'll tell you "Nicaragua," while Costeños will say, "the Atlantic Coast," occasionally adding, "of Nicaragua." They really do consider themselves a culture apart, and even refer to mestizo Nicaraguans as "the Spanish."

Nicaragua's few remaining pockets of indigenous populations form small but proud, separate communities, mostly on the Atlantic coast and up the Río Coco. They include Miskitos, Mayangna, Rama, and Garífuna, each with a distinct language, culture, and history.

ECONOMIC CLASS STRUCTURE

Economists rate Nicaragua as one of the most unequally advantaged societies in Latin America (Brazil is the most unequal). That means a relatively small elite sector controls the lion's share of economic resources while an overwhelming majority remains poor. Nicaragua's tiny middle class continues to shrink while the number of people who get by on less than US$2 per day rises inexorably. The typical expat falls economically squarely in the middle: not as garishly rich as Nicaragua's privileged, but certainly not poor, by any definition. The same goes for the class of Nicaraguan nouveau riche returning from years of exile in Miami with savings accounts, some worldly goods, and lots of plans. More than one economist has identified this class as one of the most prominent elements of socio-economic change in 21st century Nicaragua, a role that the conscientious investor or retiree will undoubtedly share.

Religion

Catholicism is still the dominant religion in Nicaragua: Over 80 percent of Nicaraguans describe themselves as Catholic, though levels of observance very widely. Various Evangelical Protestant sects are steadily encroaching on the Catholic church's statistics, and on the Atlantic coast the Moravian church still enjoys lots of influence. Unlike in South America, the Jewish population in Nicaragua is minuscule and nonpracticing; the only synagogue was dismantled and sold during the 1980s. Structured religion is more important to the older generation these days, it seems, with many young couples taking a lackadaisical view about official marriage bonds. And while Nicaraguans generally accept people as they are, avowed atheists remain incomprehensible.

Nicaragua was notably one of the centerpieces in the fascinating phenomenon of Liberation Theology, a belief system that took root in the 1970s throughout Latin America by exploring the relationship between theology and social activism, particularly as it related to social justice and human rights.

The Arts

Creative and art-loving visitors won't be disappointed by their time in Nicaragua. Likely, you'll find yourself just as inspired by the natural and cultural landscapes as the many communities of Nicaraguan artists across the country. From Managua's galleries to Matagalpa's crafts cooperatives, from Masaya's *folkloricos* to the primitivist painters of the Solentiname archipelago in the south end of Lake Cocibolca, Nicaragua offers worlds of ingenuity to explore.

LITERATURE

Along with painting, pottery, theater, music, and crafts, the Sandinista government strongly encouraged literature during the 1980s, and the Sandinistan Ministry of Culture stayed busy instituting poetry workshops and publishing magazines and books, even in the midst of civil war. The man in charge of this effort, Father Ernesto Cardenal, is today an internationally acclaimed author, widely translated into English. Likewise accessible is Gioconda Belli, whose work evokes the sensuality of her country's land and people, and who was named one of the 100 most important poets of the 20th century. Dozens of other Nicaraguan authors, young and old, grace the shelves of the many bookstores in Managua's university neighborhoods, though you'll find that most everyday Nicaraguans are not avid readers, and lending libraries are few and far between (providing a fantastic niche that more than one expat has filled in his/her adopted community).

Invariably, for any discussion of Nicaraguan literature one must go back 100 years to Nicaragua's literary giant, Rubén Darío, who set the stage for his nation's love affair with poetry by producing a style unprecedented in Spanish literature. Poet, journalist, diplomat, and favorite son of Nicaragua, Darío is the icon for all that is artistic or cultural in the country. Today, his portrait graces the front of the 100 córdoba bill, his name is on most of the nation's libraries and bookstores, and his sculpted likeness presides throughout the land. His reputation is even bigger than that, though; throughout the world of Spanish language literature Darío is recognized as a master.

© RANDALL WOOD

"Awake, sweet love of my life," sing Managua's mariachi crooners.

MUSIC AND DANCE

Nicas like their music and they like it loud!—whether it's blaring merengue at six in the morning, trite American pop on an afternoon bus, thumping Mexican *rancheras* in the bar all night long, or, more commonly, all at the same time, clashing at maddening volumes. Music makes up a huge part of the Nicaraguan soundscape. Search beyond the more obvious sound pollution in public spaces, however, and you'll discover the wonderful world of traditional Nicaraguan folk music, from revolutionary anthems to the ubiquitous and cheerful wooden sounds of the marimba.

And where there is music, there is dance. Look for traditional folk presentations, or *folkloricos,* of costumed youngsters in Masaya and the surrounding pueblos, or find swinging, gyrating rumps in hundreds of *discotecas* across the land. While Managua has the greatest number and variety of dance clubs, every city and many small pueblos have popular discos as well, at least on weekends. And when the disco's not open, Nicas crank the music and dance on their patio, in the living room, or on the sidewalk in front of their home—*no importa.* Merengue and salsa are the most popular steps, and Nicaragua has a handful of nationally famous party bands who play both covers and originals, and who are on a constant, year-round tour of the country's countless fiestas.

VISUAL ARTS

To get a broad view of what is produced in Nicaragua, visit either the *artesanía* market in Masaya or Managua's Mercado Roberto Huembes; then strike out on your own tour of Nicaragua to visit the various sources of each style of art, where you can usually find the artist at work in his or her home. Although the brightly colored primitivist paintings of southern Nicaragua and the Solentiname archipelago are the most easily recognized of the country's visual arts, there is plenty more to see, including a few internationally traded sculptors and painters. Managua has numerous galleries, some quite hidden away, and León and Granada boast excellent museums. Many of the famous Sandinista murals of the 1980s have been painted over, but many remain, especially in the northern cities, and a new generation of less politicized muralists is being trained in Estelí. For ceramics, you'll end up in living room studios in San Juan de Oriente (near Masaya) and in a number of northern villages around Estelí and Ocotal. To find the famous white soapstone carvings, travel north to San Juan de Limay.

Customs and Etiquette

It's tempting to generalize Nicaraguans as "Latinos," as if all Spanish speakers south of the Río Grande could be lumped together into one homogenous unit. In reality, if you put a Nicaraguan, a Mexican, a Honduran, and a Bolivian in the same room, they'll be able to talk for hours about what makes them similar but can spend just as much time discussing how they are different. Latin culture does share some things, like the Catholic religion and relaxed sense of time, but from there it's better to discard what you expect from "Latinos" and accept Nicaraguans for who they are—a proud population of *"pinoleros"* (a self-imposed nickname that describes their supposed love for a sweet corn drink, *pinol*) whose attitude, outlook, and way of life are completely distinct from those of any other Latin American nation.

Nicaraguans are an affable and vivacious people who have lived through exceptionally sad and violent years and continue to endure amidst an increasingly divisive gap between rich and poor. They have high aspirations for their society, a strong love for their immediate and extended families, and the ability to enjoy life in spite of tough economic circumstances. In addition, Nicas are generally open and talkative, and extremely hospitable.

NICARAGUAN BEHAVIOR

After the initial impact of the heat and colors starts to ebb, after you've become somewhat accustomed to dusty, trash-strewn scenes of poverty amidst the tropical Nicaraguan landscape, after you've begun interacting with Nicaraguans on more than a superficial level—only then will you

SHOCK AND AWE: ADJUSTING TO NICARAGUAN CULTURE

When the initial excitement of your big move begins to wane and the day-to-day adventure of life in Nicaragua (i.e., stepping outside your door) seems more difficult than thrilling, it's time to relax and take a deep breath. Feelings of anxiety, confusion, irritability, disgust, and even physical illness are all normal when adapting to a new land and its people. Then again, so are feelings of joy, exhilaration, contentment, and rapture. Label-lovers will delight to know there is a name for your condition: It's called "culture shock," and it even has four defined phases through which you can track your progress. They are: (1) honeymoon, (2) shock, (3) negotiation, and (4) acceptance or assimilation.

Of course, the experience is not that simple, especially that holy grail of assimilation, which, if attained, is continually interrupted by slides back into the first three stages – even years after settling in Nicaragua. Although a few expats may in fact achieve the peaceful harmony of total cultural integration, while others permanently stall out in the bitter purgatory of cynicism, the most common response is to swing wildly between the two: a love-hate roller coaster that makes up no small part of life in a foreign country. In fact, it is this unpredictable and capricious journey that attracts so many, um, interesting type-A personalities to the expat lifestyle.

In addition, it is common when adapting to a new set of cultural values to find yourself believing that one way of life – either your own or the Nicaraguan – is somehow "better" than the other. This may seem ridiculous right now, basking in the luxury of your liberal, open-minded foresight; but when you're in the thick of it, you may very well be tempted to reject

begin to notice the subtle cultural quirks in this strange new land. Whether you've been adopted into an extended family of poor campesinos or you find yourself behind barbed-wire fences in Managua, where your interaction with Nicas is limited to your security guards and chauffeurs, you *will* be confronted with the peculiarities of Nicaraguan culture (which to Nicas, of course, are not nearly as peculiar as your own brash habits). If you've traveled and lived in other Latin cultures, the following behaviors will be less of a surprise than if you haven't. Regardless, knowing what to expect will help ease the transition—as will a humble attitude, the desire to learn, and (if we haven't mentioned it already) the calm ability to laugh at yourself.

Confianza

Reaching a high level of comfort, trust, and openness with another individual—or among a group of individuals—is known in Latin America as

one culture as more or less "civilized" than the other. Resist this. The answer lies in finding a personalized balance that acknowledges both your own and Nicaraguan customs, a process that is at once transforming, satisfying, and downright exasperating.

So how do you do it?

The first rule is to remember where you come from: Recognize your background as unique, communicate with friends and family back home, and allow yourself to feel sad about leaving them. Then move on: Get outside, meet your neighbors, and develop a routine that involves both physical activity and mental relaxation. Go for walks, lift weights, read books about Central America, do yoga and meditation, surf, whatever it takes. Next, sign up for Spanish class and study hard: Read *La Prensa* every morning, carry a notebook and dictionary everywhere you go, and practice speaking as much as possible; not only will your new language skills make the practical parts of life in Nicaragua easier, but the triumphs of the learning curve will result in crucial morale boosts as you struggle forward.

The more ways you find to integrate yourself into the community, the better you will feel and the more quickly you will find Nicaragua becomes your home. Our friend "Marco from Masaya" joined the local basketball team while he was an expat there and learned, among other things, that his Spanish skills weren't necessary but raw basketball skills were, as the locals enjoyed learning from him and testing his ability to keep up. After a couple of games he was already one of the team.

Lastly, accept that this is all going to take time: learning Spanish, making friends, feeling grounded, and fitting in. Like we said, it's a wild ride − enjoy every minute of it.

having *"confianza"* with one another, and it is just as important for making friends as it is for doing business, teaching, or succeeding in development work. Little things you do (e.g., wearing inappropriate clothing or throwing a temper tantrum in public) can damage your *confianza* with Nicaraguans, but they won't confront you directly about it; instead, their behavior will become perceptibly cooler, something commonly called "saving face."

Conversation and Saving Face

Nicaraguans go to great lengths to avoid embarrassing you or being embarrassed, which they call "having *pena*" (pronounced PEY-nah). This concept of "saving face" is a bold departure from the direct way in which most North Americans communicate. If you can visualize a North American speaker talking in a straight line, right to the point, try to imagine Nicaraguan conversation as vaguely circular, spiraling inward to where the point is to be made, but often stopping just short of the center. It is up to you to have the sensitivity to the speaker, and to the subject at hand, to know what is being implied. Speaking this way avoids the risk of losing *confianza* with someone, especially if there is accusation or criticism implied in the message. Direct and open criticism, no matter how well-intentioned or constructive, may very well result in a severed relationship, as your former Nica acquaintance or employee disappears in order to save you both the embarrassment of seeing each other again.

On a similar note, one must be careful not to directly allude to inequality in money matters. For example, instead of saying "I'm buying!"—which implies, "I have more money than you!"—one simply says, "I invite you" *(te invito),* and then orders (conversely, an invitation out automatically implies that the inviter is picking up the tab). This sensitivity can cause problems during business transactions, where Nicas are content to let the details of the matter remain unspoken, while North Americans demand a clear agreement of amounts and terms, if not a written contract.

Finally, be aware that when asking a Nicaraguan for directions, rather

MEETING, GREETING, AND SAYING GOODBYE

Some of the terms of address you learned in high school Spanish class or elsewhere in Latin America do not necessarily apply in Nicaragua. Nicas are far less formal than other Latinos, especially with their use of the casual second person, or **"vos,"** with family members and friends. "*El voceo*," as it is called, is employed in place of *tú* and has its own set of verb conjugations and accent stresses, which are especially different in the command form. **"Usted"** remains the preferred third person term of respect, used at the very least with officials, elders, and professionals. Even for peers, stick with "*Usted*" until someone calls you "*vos*," which is a sign they want to treat you with *confianza* (trust). The concept of "graduating" from "*Usted*" to "*vos*" is novel to most foreigners, who do not differentiate between the formal and the informal, but you'll get used to it.

Nicaraguans use *don* (rhymes with the English "bone") and *doña*, two colonial terms of respect for men and women, respectively, and you can expect to both hear and use them on a daily basis. The terms, which were once reserved exclusively for landowners and the aristocracy, are now attached to a person's given name, as in Don Carlos and Doña María, and are used to show deference to the elderly, the important, and the wealthy, as well as to the poor, to avoid belittling them in conversation.

In addition, practitioners of certain professions enjoy being addressed by their titles, often dropping their given names entirely, even with friends. So you can expect to be introduced to people known simply as

than admit, "Sorry, Señor, I don't know where that is," he or she may instead invent an answer or point you in any direction, gracefully sparing you both from great *pena*. Same goes for bus schedules—an accepted method is to ask three or four people what time your bus leaves, than take the average and hope for the best. Another simplification in your new life is not having to deal with exact physical distances—any length of land or highway between 50 meters and 1,000 kilometers can be conveniently referred to as *"allí no más,"* which means, "just over there."

Personal Space and Privacy

Americans in particular, but most European cultures as well, have a concept of personal space that is much more rigorously defined than in Latin America. Nicas greet each other with hugs and kisses, and like to touch your arm to emphasize their points as they talk to you.

This concept of shared space flows right into the issue of privacy, which, save for in the bathroom and shower, is virtually nonexistent in Nicaraguan

---

"la doctora," "el ingeniero," or *"la abogada."* When you, the lawyer, enter a room full of Nicaraguan colleagues, the introductions go like this: *"Abogado, abogado, abogado, abogado."*

As for physical greetings, Nicaraguan tradition dictates that men may kiss women on the cheek, but only if invited. Women will typically signal that this is appropriate by turning their cheek slightly as you greet. If they extend their hand it is for shaking, not kissing. Men traditionally extend their hands for a stiff handshake, occasionally grasping your elbow or shoulder with their free hand as you shake as an additional gesture of warmth and friendliness. Sometimes, Nica men will continue to hold your hand in theirs after the shaking has ended. It's a bit of a strange feeling. A simple tug will extract you, but to be polite, maintain eye contact as you pull your hand away.

Note that in Nicaragua you are expected to end a conversation by formally asking permission to leave, although it usually comes out more as a statement than a question. Pause a second, then say *"con permiso,"* to politely end the engagement and exit. Your partner will reply, *"suyo,"* meaning permission is granted. Also note that while *"¡Adiós!"* does indeed mean "goodbye," it is also commonly used as a greeting when passing someone in the street, in which case it is loudly slurred and sung, usually through a wide smile, as *"Ah-yoh!"*

Don't stress over terms of address, greetings, and departures. Overall, in spite of the traditions and (by North American standards) the formality, Nicas are easygoing, expect you not to understand their ways, and will forgive your occasional gaffs.

"¡Hasta luegito!"

culture. People doing a homestay in a Nicaraguan household will notice this immediately, even if they are given the rare luxury of a private room that locks (which, for security reasons, is to be expected during homestays set up through Spanish language schools and other programs). For example, if you are relaxing by yourself, reading a book or writing a letter, you might be asked *"Está triste?"* ("Are you sad?"). And why suffer the lonely sound of silence when you can blast every radio and television in the house at once? This will surely fill the otherwise depressed, empty space with *alegría* (happiness)!

Clothing and Hygiene

Nicaraguans, regardless of economic status, take great pride in their personal appearance and wouldn't think of stepping out in torn or dirty clothes, barefoot, or without bathing—and neither should you. Many North Americans are used to a culture that values comfort over class (just take a look at all the people on your Nica-bound flight dressed in sweatpants, tank tops, and flip-flops). But in Nicaragua, style comes first, and cleanliness is essential. Even in the north, during the cold months when the water from the well is frigid, children bathe every morning and go off to school in neat, pressed school uniforms and polished shoes. While people wear their old clothes into the fields to work, or out back while they're doing chores, in public they take great pains to be clean and presentable. Our first few months living in Nicaragua we were frequently faced with the question, "Is it true that because the weather is so cold in your country you only bathe twice a year?" But after bumping into some particularly unkempt backpackers, the root of the misperception became clear. As an *extranjero* you are afforded some license to act and dress a little crazily—Nicas will chalk it up to your not knowing any better. But a freshly shaved chin and crisply pressed shirt sleeve will open a lot of doors for you when doing business in Nicaragua, even if your "business" is nothing more than applying for a driver's license or buying a bag of milk.

Table Manners

Nicas enjoy good food, good drink, and good times, and that pretty much precludes dainty table manners. So grab that greasy chicken leg with two hands, shovel down that *vigorón* from its banana leaf wrapper while the shaved cabbage spills down your shirt, and chase it with long swigs of a cold drink—straight from the bottle or plastic baggie. If you're too careful at the dinner table, the signal is all too clear you're not pleased with the meal. There are limits of course, so keep an eye on your dining companions for what's appropriate and what's not, but while you're carefully picking at your fried cheese and sweet plantains, the guy next to you has finished his meal, pulled his shirt up with one hand, and is happily rubbing his belly with the other. If you'd like to get a laugh out of your Nicaraguan hosts or waiters, after you've finished your plate tell them, *"Barriga llena, corazón contenta"* ("Belly full, happy heart").

Gender Issues

In one area of Nicaraguan society—the roles of men and women— Latino stereotypes can hold true, especially *machismo.* On the men's part, this involves a schizophrenic balancing act between defending the honor of one's sister, daughter, or mother, while treating other women as expendable objects of desire—thus the cat-calling, whistling, and leering. Nicaraguan women endure constant unsolicited attention, and you can expect the same—particularly the sing-song shouts of *"Adios amorrr,"* often accompanied by a sleazy, staccato *"Tss-tss."* Uninterested or unimpressed Nica women ignore the comments and whistles entirely, refusing to dignify them with a response. Traveling with a male companion sometimes, but not always, diminishes the attention, since some cat-callers actually think they are flattering you. *Machista* ideas also result in shocking rates of male infidelity; don't be surprised to hear Nica men boasting of their exploits, but feel free not to humor them either.

On a positive note, physical harassment, assault, and rape are far less common in Nicaragua than elsewhere in Latin America, so you are more in danger of being annoyed than attacked. Sexual violence, when it does occur, typically involves alcohol, so take the same precautions you would anywhere to avoid dangerous situations.

LOVE AND MARRIAGE

The Catholic church's sway over family life is diminished but not vanquished these days, and the Sandinistas empowered Nicaraguan women to a degree the rest of Latin America envies this day. So where love and marriage are concerned, in Nicaragua you *can* have one without the other, and many young Romeos and Julietas do just that. But many families remain staunchly traditional in matters of the heart and retain the strict (supervised) courtship, white wedding, and family-raising routine of generations past. Modern times and the influence of television, the decline of the traditional family, and other factors have led to a society in which many couples raise families without marrying, and lots of men have extra-marital affairs and father illegitimate children, often disappearing when it's clear the mistress is pregnant.

If you find yourself bound to Nicaragua by romance, you aren't alone. An exotic, fine-looking foreigner like yourself can expect to receive plenty of attention from members of the opposite sex in Nicaragua. If the romance of living in Nicaragua for you involves actual romance, you ought to keep in mind a few things.

First, dating *(jalando)* in Nicaragua is more of a formal courtship procedure than you may be used to (though the more cosmopolitan and well-traveled your partner is, the less such formalities will be followed). Your first several meetings will most likely be chaperoned events. Men dating Nicaraguan women can expect their date's friends, siblings, or cousins to tag along, and women dating Nicaragua men can expect a polite and but pointed interview with his mother. For both men and women, if and when you are invited home to meet the parents, expect long waits in the *sala* and equally long and confusingly indirect inquisitions about your occupation, prospects, and intentions.

It's easy to marry in Nicaragua, and involves no more than your passport, birth certificate, and a trip to the local notary public. But with marriage comes an implicit agreement that you will help financially support your spouse's family, and often the entire extended family. The church wedding often follows, as it is highly important to many Nicaraguan traditional families but optional in the eyes of the law. If on the other hand your intention is casual romantic companionship, be careful to respect your partner's culture, which is to say, take time to understand the ramifications of what you are getting into. If it is obvious that you and are partner are sleeping together—whether or not you are actually living under the same roof—you are said to be *viviendo juntos,* or living together, which means things are serious. You as a foreigner won't notice the change in perception but know that your partner's reputation is at stake from that moment on.

If you do decide to tie the knot, or *casarse,* and have any desire to bring your spouse back to your country, your first stop should be at your embassy website's consular section. The fact that you are married does not guarantee your spouse a visa back home, and the process will take a background investigation, lots of paperwork, and several weeks. Note that trying to obtain a fiancé visa or green card for someone through a phony relationship is illegal and punishable by law.

Wedding Etiquette

If you are invited to a Nicaraguan wedding, get ready to get down! This is a great excuse to go out and buy that guayabera you've been eyeing at the market; this formal/informal button-down shirt, accompanied by pressed pants and real leather shoes, is totally appropriate, as is any other nice, tucked-in shirt or simple dress, though Nicaraguans like to dress up and suits are increasingly common. Bring a card and small gift, which can be monetary or material, and plan on leaving it in the general pile at the door to the reception. Don't be surprised if your gift goes unacknowledged, as this is a face-saving custom. The ensuing reception is where you'll see Nicaraguans at their exuberant finest—enjoying lots of homemade foods and drinking prodigious amounts of alcohol and dancing like nobody's watching. In poorer areas, your camera will be much appreciated, and if you take pictures of the festivities, making copies for the host is the least you can do.

SEXUAL EXPLOITATION

As a poor country, Nicaragua is increasingly vulnerable to predatory foreigners eager to sexually exploit young Nicaraguan men and women—or worse, boys and girls—who will do anything to feed themselves, their children, and their families. Disparaged as "sexpats" and "the dead pecker brigade" by the rest of the community, pedophiles can be found in the bars and streets of San Juan del Sur and Granada, where they leverage their thick bank accounts and exotic, foreign status to prowl for barely legal lovers. When such individuals are ready to "settle down," they basically purchase young girls from desperate parents, often for peanuts. If this occurs between two consenting adults, fine; love and marriage is a complex thing and who are we to judge? But when the youngest victims are chosen purely for their desperation, it is not okay, and depending on their age, it is illegal. This is the slimy white underbelly that pervades many of the world's expat communities. Its existence elsewhere in the world is, of course, no excuse for condoning it in Nicaragua. In addition to the suffering it causes to both victims and perpetrators, it will inevitably lead to resentment and anger against all foreigners.

ABORTION

Except for some cases of therapeutic abortion to protect the life of the mother in extreme circumstances, abortion is illegal in Nicaragua. This, of course, only means that the tens of thousands of abortions that do occur take place in clandestine and unsafe conditions. Ipas, a North Carolina–based international NGO that works to promote reproductive rights and reduce deaths and injuries of women from unsafe abortion worldwide, estimates that around 32,000 abortions are carried out and some 6,700 women seek medical services for abortion-related complications in Nicaragua every year. The topic came to a head in 2003 over the case of a nine-year-old rape victim whose parents sought an abortion to protect her life and who was promptly excommunicated by the Catholic church. The Nicaraguan Bishops' Conference and several right-wing Liberal party members used the event to decry *all* forms of abortion; Bishop Abelardo Mata called abortion an "abominable crime … even when it is disguised by pseudo-humanitarian extenuating circumstances by classifying it as therapeutic."

GAY AND LESBIAN CULTURE

Though officially illegal—according to both Nicaraguan law and the Catholic church—gay and lesbian communities are prevalent in Nicaraguan society and generally tolerated. Kept mostly in the closet (except for the transvestite prostitutes of Managua), the "dominant" partner of a gay male Nicaraguan relationship often considers himself straight, while reserving the word *maricón* (queer) for his "submissive" partner. Another facet of *machismo* is widespread homophobia, expressed in a great deal of humor and ribbing between Nicaragua men. Even popular songs, advertisements, and other public entertainment sometimes use gay-bashing as a topic for a good laugh. Lesbians seem to be less tolerated than gay men and are rarely mentioned, even in the aforementioned joking around.

Gay men and lesbian travelers or expatriates should not feel threatened in Nicaragua provided they maintain a modicum of discretion. Managua and some of the larger towns boast a few openly gay clubs, and same-sex couples may be able to find gay and lesbian communities willing to help orient them to the local scene.

PLANNING YOUR FACT-FINDING TRIP

No amount of reading or research will prepare you for a move to a foreign country like packing a bag and making a reconnaissance trip. Learning what to expect from Nicaragua begins with immersing yourself in its sights, sounds, smells, tastes, and touches—all of which will, more than any guidebook or website, teach you volumes about this unique country and its inhabitants. As one of our expatriate friends living in Managua said, "Nicaragua is not a snapshot. It is a movie. You must know its recent past to understand its present."

Yes, this means reading books about Nicaraguan history before and during your trip, but ultimately, such an academic approach will only put you in touch with a couple of isolated authors. Meeting Nicaraguans—the stars of the movie and your potential hosts and neighbors—is the next crucial step. Consider this as you move about the country and make attempts to come into contact with more than just your hotel staff. Nicaraguans' stories are often fascinating; how was their family affected by recent decades?

© RANDALL WOOD

What is their outlook on the future? What do *they* think is important for you to know about Nicaragua?

What's more, journeying to Nicaragua with a mission other than mere recreation, a trip that is in fact the first step of a major life decision, is its own experience, a truly exceptional way to travel.

Preparing to Leave

WHAT TO BRING
Luggage

Everything you bring to Nicaragua should be sturdy, water-resistant (where possible), and replaceable. Your luggage will be more useful to you if it's lightweight and small enough that you can carry it on your back. Wheeled luggage is all but useless once you leave the Managua airport; use a small duffle bag or backpack instead. Take a combination luggage lock with which you can secure your bags—just to keep honest people honest. An additional small daypack will be invaluable for carrying a guidebook, notebook, and water bottle as you conduct your legwork.

Clothing

Choose clothing that is lightweight, light-colored, and breathable. Nicaragua is tropical, after all, and the noon sun will feel less penetrating if you are properly dressed. Only in the mountains in December or January will you need something as substantial as a flannel shirt (unless you decide to take in a movie in one of Managua's glacially cooled cinemas). Otherwise, plan on keeping the sun off your skin—beginning with a broad-brimmed hat or at least a ball cap. For super-lightweight traveling, two to three changes of clothing should be more than enough (laundry services are available in any hotel), but if you plan to do any business with officialdom, a nice outfit (clean khakis, button shirt, and real shoes) should also be part of your wardrobe. Otherwise, keep it simple. Choose a comfortable pair of shoes in which you can walk all day.

Nicaraguan men wear pants and shirts, leaving their shorts only for in the house or in the fields. Women enjoy a bit more freedom in how they dress. When we first landed in Nicaragua, our female colleagues were told to stick to long dresses with sleeves, and preferably dresses that hung below the knee. But it became clear soon enough that their Nicaraguan counterparts were far less conservative than that, and before long the long dresses got packed away. Foreign women should understand that in the wake of dubbed U.S. television programs like *Baywatch* and *Dukes of Hazzard,* they are fighting the stereotype of being sexually and morally loose, and should dress no more provocatively than they feel comfortable with. The more skin you show, the more attention you'll attract. No such parallel stereotype exists for foreign men.

At the beach, Nicaraguans are far more conservative than their Brazilian colleagues. It's rare to see a thong or a g-string at the beach, and many Nicaraguan women prefer one-piece bathing suits. In no cases do Nicaraguan women go topless on the beach, and foreigners who do so are crossing a line.

A final word about clothing. Nicaraguans typically dry their clothing by hanging it from barbed wire fencing or clotheslines. Your clothes will have to survive hard scrubbing, harsh detergent, and a bright tropical sun that will bleach the colors out of your favorite things. You can prolong the destruction by hanging your clothing the way Nicas do: inside out, so the colors last longer. But besides that, get in the habit of giving your old clothing away and replacing it, just like everyone else does.

Footwear

Most foreigners stick to open sandals, which is generally acceptable for day-to-day business, even though the majority of Nicaraguan men wear carefully polished, closed leather shoes. Slip-on rubber flip-flops (called *chinelas*) are for indoors or the bathroom only. Women are okay with nice sandals or open shoes anywhere. Bring some closed-toe light hiking boots if you plan on any volcano climbs or hiking.

Equipment and Paperwork

Bring a notebook small enough to carry in your pocket or daypack; you may feel swamped with information as you explore Nicaragua, and making a conscientious effort to record your thoughts, the results of your research, and answers to your questions in one place will be indispensable once you're back home trying to make sense of all you've learned. For that matter, before you even step foot on Nicaraguan soil, organize your thoughts on the first pages and try to spell out exactly what you are going there to learn. We're not being pedantic: You'd be surprised how many visitors to Nicaragua explore the country for two weeks and return home only to realize they never found answers to their important questions, like whether you can get ESPN in your home (yes, you can). If you're not a note-taking kind of person, consider a pocket tape recorder.

Though nearly every first-aid concern you would need (and then some) is available in Nicaraguan pharmacies, a small custom kit is a good idea. Carry some ibuprofen, sunblock, aloe gel for sunburns, moleskin for blisters, and a bandage or two, just enough to keep you moving through the more common traveler's problems. Ear plugs are essential for early-morning roosters and merengue music.

A small camera is useful, not just to record Nicaragua's beauty but to allow you to document street scenes, housing types, and so on, again, with the goal of recording what you learn long enough to get home and make sense of it (Did houses in Granada have steel bars on the windows?). Most travelers carry digital cameras these days, but many parts of Nicaragua still lack the facilities with which to download and print your pictures. If you leave your laptop and photo software at home, make sure to bring enough storage media (chips, discs, etc.) to record the number of photos you anticipate taking until you get home. If you take an old-fashioned film camera you will be able to develop your pictures in country, but waiting till you are home will ensure better quality.

Lastly, smart travelers take photocopies of their important documents (passport, driver's license, important phone numbers, etc.) and keep them in a money pouch they maintain under their clothing. And remember; that money pouch is only a secret as long as no one ever sees you pull it out. Keep your large bills there and keep enough cash for a day's travels in your wallet.

MONEY MATTERS
Currency and Exchange

Nicaraguan currency is the córdoba, abbreviated as C$. In January 2006, the official exchange rate was just over 17 córdobas to the dollar, but the Central Bank of Nicaragua has established a sliding peg exchange rate, which means the rate gets just a little bit worse (for Nicaraguans) every day. Check the day's exchange rate at the Central Bank's website (www.bcn.gob.ni).

Because the córdoba's value changes from day to day, you'll find many prices quoted in U.S. dollars, as are most prices throughout this book. You can expect just about anyone to accept your dollars (banknotes, not coins) in payment, though you'll probably be given change in córdobas. The disadvantage to paying for things in dollars is the on-the-fly calculation of the day's exchange rate, which more often than not leaves you with a lousy deal, so get in the practice of working with—and thinking in—córdobas, even if paying with dollars.

You can exchange money in any bank during normal business hours (many are closed during lunch hours); prepare to show your passport. Official money changers have stalls near some of the main tourist markets. Black market *(mercado negro)* money changers typically operate with impunity on a fixed street corner in most cities and towns and give perfectly acceptable rates (and have more convenient business hours than the banks). Please see the *Finances* chapter for more information.

How Much Cash to Bring

How much you'll spend depends largely on how well you'd like to live while you're exploring Nicaragua. Backpackers intent on stretching their cash out as long as possible can eat, sleep, and recreate for US$20–30 a day or less. Though Nicaragua's nicer and more luxurious hotels can cost US$50–70 a night (or more) in places like Granada and León, clean and comfortable digs are easily found for US$15–30; for three decent but not extravagant meals per day (with a few drinks), US$30 a day is sufficient.

Renting a vehicle to facilitate exploration (and to experience nerve-wracking traffic experiences) cranks up expenses considerably. Budget at least US$40 per day—plus gasoline, which as of January 2006 was running at US$4 per gallon. Hiring a car with driver costs around US$60–80 per day.

With the exception of certain banks in Managua (e.g., Bancentro), currencies other than U.S. dollars are not accepted. Your credit card will come in handy for bigger and more cosmopolitan hotels and restaurants, which will alleviate the need to travel with large amounts of cash, but you can't make credit card purchases just anywhere, so don't count on living off your charge card as you travel. ATMs are increasingly more common, in both banks and gas station mini-marts. Bottom line? US$1,000 cash for a 10-day trip is more than sufficient, allowing for some shopping, organized tours, and a few splurges. Cautious travelers would bring half that and replenish at ATMs, or carry travelers checks as a backup (in Managua and major cities you can change U.S. dollar travelers checks, but outside of big cities they are useless).

WHEN TO GO

Most tourists plan their trip around both their vacation schedules and the most pleasant part of Nicaragua's dry season, and you'll likely do the same. However, if at all possible, think about seeing Nicaragua during its not-so-nice months as well, especially if you plan to live and do business there year-round. The difference between rainy and dry seasons can be quite drastic in some areas, especially where unimproved access roads swing between dust clouds and mud baths.

Climate and Seasons

December and January are the coolest and most refreshing months, with good, clear weather, starry skies at night, and warm, enticing days. Up in the mountains north of Estelí the temperature might drop to a brisk 16°C (60°F), but along Lake Cocibolca, in the capital, and on La Isla de Ometepe, nights during this time period are still a balmy 22°C (70°F), and throughout the country, daytime temperatures are around 32°C (88°F). This is Nicaragua is at its best: Summertime, or *el verano* (dry season) is mostly verdant, crisp, and colorful.

But February–May, temperatures slowly climb until you are stewing in your own sweat, and the damp, heavy air begs for the release of a thundershower that never comes. By April, daytime temperatures are frequently 41°C (105°F) with little relief at night, as temperatures linger around 25°C (75°F). Your opinion of just how hot Nicaragua is might be radically readjusted during this period, especially when the sun-baked dust settles into every nook and cranny of your body and home. On or about May 15, the long-awaited first rains fall, and Nicaragua enters its wet season *(el invierno)*, which lasts until November (in the more arid north and west) or December (in the lusher southeast). The rains let up only once, for approximately

CELEBRATIONS AND FIESTAS

It might be fun to time your visit in order to experience one of Nicaragua's greater celebrations, as that's when Nicaraguans really strut their stuff. Or, depending on your personality, you might find the altered transportation schedules and the masses a hassle and wish to avoid them altogether. Either way, the airlines that serve Nicaragua are well aware of when expatriate Nicas living in the United States like to return home for family time and celebration, and at these times you can expect airfares to nearly double in price.

Christmas is one of these times. The Christmas celebrations begin almost a week before the December 25 and nothing truly returns to normal until after January 7. That's not to say you won't be able to get around, but expect a higher demand for hotel rooms and the like, and prepare to have very little luck at all with the authorities. Banks are open, but government agencies operate on a limited schedule if they're open at all.

Semana Santa (Holy Week), however, is an even bigger event than Christmas. The week that precedes Easter Sunday is an important and much-loved holiday, when every Nica that can finds his or her way to the beach for some fun in the sun. At the very least, Wednesday, Thursday, and Friday before Easter are completely lost days, but many Nicas take off Monday and Tuesday as well and make a long vacation out of it. During this period even bus service slackens,

and even the banks reduce hours, while government officials, if you can find them, will deal with you between clenched teeth. You are keeping them from the beach and will be made to suffer for it.

Additional city-specific festivals happen throughout the year with great amounts of local pride and traditional revelry. Participating in these events is a memorable and enjoyable experience. Every city has its own patron saint, and that saint is celebrated annually in an event as lavish as the locals can afford; the most elaborate festivals often involve bands and parades and food throughout the night. But some cities have other festivals as well; Masaya is the most jubilant, with well over a dozen festivals throughout the year. To catch a taste of the local flavor, plan your trip around the following fiestas.

Granada puts on a gastronomy, folklore, and handicraft festival every year the third week in March, and celebrates the Assumption of Mary on August 15. **Managua** puts on its patron saint festival twice: on August 1, when the patron saint is paraded down from a hillside chapel to a small church on the eastern side of the capital, then again on August 10 when it is paraded back up. **Estelí** puts on a lively festival of "Mariachis and Mazurkas" (the mazurka is a traditional dance) the third week in August. On **Ometepe** there's an Equestrian Rally November 3-5, and November 12-18 Altagracia celebrates its patron saint, San Diego de Alcalá.

two weeks in mid-August. This *canícula* signals the harvesting of the first crop and the planting of the second, and is typically a two-week period of bright sunny skies and no rain whatsoever.

Arriving in Nicaragua

Unless you overland it through Mexico and the rest of Central America, Managua's International Airport will be your *bienvenida* (welcome) to the Land of Lakes and Volcanoes. At the airport you can rent a vehicle, meet your tour guide, or catch buses north or south. Managua's fancier hotels offer bus service from the airport, and a few hotels in Granada will send a taxi, but be sure this is arranged beforehand—otherwise the waiting airport taxis will gouge you for all that you allow them.

SHORT-TERM VISAS

Every visitor to Nicaragua must possess a passport valid for six months beyond the date of entry. Upon entering the country, most visitors will be granted an automatic three-month tourist visa and pay US$7. But visitors from certain countries require a visa in advance of arrival. These include: Afghanistan, Albania, Bosnia-Herzegovina, Colombia, Cuba, Haiti, India, Iran, Iraq, Jordan, Lebanon, Libya, Nepal, Pakistan, the People's Republic of China, the People's Republic of Korea, Somalia, Sri Lanka, and Vietnam. Longer visas are also granted for special purposes like work, study, and similar reasons, but their requirements are more stringent and some—like the student visa—require a substantial deposit beforehand equivalent to a round-trip first-class ticket (just to make sure you don't for some reason decide to abandon your "internship" and stay around longer than you're welcome). For that reason, most students usually just arrive on tourist visas and avoid the hassle (and the no-interest loan).

It's improbable that your fact-finding trip would last longer than three months, but travelers who require an extension to their three-month tourist visa can do so (with some effort) by visiting the **Office of Immigration** (Dirección General de Migración y Extranjería, 1.5 blocks north of the *semáforos de Tenderí,* tel. 244-0741, open Mon.–Fri. 8:30 A.M.–noon and 2–4:30 P.M.) in Managua. The extension will not be automatically granted, and the risk of being asked to provide onerous documentation or pay fees usually drives tourists across the border to Costa Rica or Honduras, where they enjoy some lunch and then re-enter Nicaragua, earning a cool new three-month tourist visa.

TRANSPORTATION

Traveling between cities by public bus is the best way to get a sense of what Nicaragua is like—and what being Nicaraguan is like—but if you are on a limited timeframe, it is not the most efficient way to go. In that case, several companies rent vehicles at the Managua airport, where you can strike a deal for a short-term or several-week rental. You can also choose to hire a car and driver through your hotel or real estate agency to facilitate getting around (see the *Travel and Transportation* chapter).

Sample Itineraries

Here are a few suggestions for planning a fact-finding trip of varying lengths; we've focused on the two areas most popular with foreigners—Granada and San Juan del Sur—and also included a side trip to La Isla de Ometepe, so that you can determine on your own if it will be the next big hot spot. Even if you decide Ometepe is still too risky for investment, a visit will give you a wonderful experience to write home about. Most tourists skip Managua if they can, but you should give it at least a day or two, more if you think you might end up working there.

ONE WEEK

If you only have a week (a work week and two weekends), you should certainly rent a vehicle or driver in order to cut down on travel time and facilitate exploration up and down the Pacific coast. Your time might look like this:

Days 1-3: Land in Managua and transfer directly to Granada. Spend at least the day you arrive plus two more exploring Granada and nearby destinations (Volcán Mombacho, Laguna de Apoyo, the Pueblos Blancos), and perhaps the Isletas. In Granada you are already smack-dab in the center of the nation's second hottest real estate market, so chat up some of the expats lingering around the restaurants and hotels. Likewise, take an afternoon to visit the real estate agents whose offices are located around the park. They will give you an idea of the Granada market and what to expect, plus answer some of your questions about the intricacies of purchasing property. But mostly, walk the streets of Granada to get an idea of what it would be like to make this your next home. If you're feeling pressed for time, rent a horse carriage from the park and have the driver go up and down the city streets between the park and the lake. Don't miss the open-air market just south of the park, the city's movie theater, or the lakeshore.

You will have an easier time getting a feel for the lay of the land in the comparatively small areas of Laguna de Apoyo and Volcán Mombacho. It's important to drive there to see with your own eyes what the landscape is like and just how quiet the area is, but you can ask questions about properties and lifestyle from the real estate agents in Granada.

Days 4-6: Drive south to San Juan del Sur. Spend a full day in town, then an additional day or two exploring in your rented or hired car up and down the coast. The beach bars along the water are a logical jumping-off point for your day. Every expat in town winds up at one sooner or later, but the Gato Negro bookstore is another popular place for expats. The real estate agents throughout town list properties on the boards outside their front doors, but more important is the chance to talk to them about what properties are costing these days, as the market is changing so rapidly. If you need some down time, purchase one of the national newspapers *(La Prensa* or *El Nuevo Diario)* and relax at the water's edge for awhile. This is a great time to browse the classified ads to get a feel for the job market. You won't find a job for yourself, more likely than not, but you'll get an idea of what salaries are like in Nicaragua.

Days 7-8: Drive your vehicle onto the ferry to Ometepe for a visit to the island. Or, leave your vehicle on the docks at San Jorge (you can pay for a supposedly guarded parking space there, but it's still a bit risky). In two days you can get a sense of Moyogalpa and Altagracia, the two principal towns, but you won't have time to do much more than that. If you're considering trying to settle on the island, though, getting a feel for the relative calm and isolation is important, as is learning what the ferry trips back and forth between your home and the rest of the world are like.

Day 9: Return to Managua and spend an afternoon exploring the restaurants and services available (and not available). Managua, like most Central American capitals, can be awfully overwhelming, and if you require more time here (i.e., you're considering accepting a job), then forget the Ometepe side trip. Managua is best experienced from the back seat of a taxi. Tell the driver you'd like to see the *zona rosa* (the fun area) and sit back and enjoy not having to deal with traffic. Most of what's fun in Managua is found in two or three compact areas, so it's feasible to cruise all three of them in an hour or two, then come back for dinner to explore more in depth. Your best bets for eating are all located in the Carretera Masaya area by the big hotels, but don't be afraid to branch out.

TWO WEEKS

The extra week in Nicaragua will make a profound difference in your ability to determine how best to make Nicaragua your next home, so if there is any way at all you can arrange a longer stay in country, do so. Spend your additional time investigating either the places in which you are more thoroughly interested or the rest of the country to see what the nontraditional options are.

Days 1-5: Land in Managua and depart directly for Granada. You can now spend three full days in town chatting up the other expats, taking tours with real estate agents, and soaking in the lifestyle. Spend two days (as in the one-week itinerary) visiting the Pueblos Blancos and Laguna de Apoyo. The pueblos are numerous, and each one is a little different, so take a lap through each and stop to explore where you feel more excited about the surroundings. At the least, don't miss Catarina, whose view of the Laguna de Apoyo is unsurpassed; as such, Catarina is the most interesting of the Pueblos Blancos for expats. In Granada, you've got more time to get a feel for the city, so make sure to visit one of the small supermarkets to see whether or not your favorite foods are available. If you've gotten an idea of which properties are for sale within the city limits, this is your best chance to come back at night or in the early morning to determine whether the neighborhoods are safe enough and quiet enough for your liking.

Days 6-8: Head for La Isla de Ometepe (it may take most of a day to get there), followed by a few nights at one of many unique accommodations. Altagracia is worth the better part of a day but certainly not a full day, and you can use it as a base to fan out along the coastline. Same goes for Moyogalpa. Balgüe, on the north flank of Volcán Maderas, is one of our favorite places to really soak in the island atmosphere, and the folks that run the Finca Magdalena know the island better than just about anybody, so it's a good opportunity to ask questions about where they do their shopping, how often they return to the mainland, and what it's like when the weather is bad.

Days 9-12: Transfer to San Juan del Sur and visit the coastline villages (and properties) north and south of San Juan del Sur proper. You'll need a good vehicle for this, and it's most enlightening if you travel with a real estate agent, who can tell you a little more about new developments and properties being opened to the market.

Days 13-14: Give Managua a little more time. It will be your base for supplies, doctors, and the like, so drive around enough to get a feel for what it really means to rely on Nicaragua's capital. A smart day trip would be to the hospital just to look around and get a sense of the facilities available, but you also now have time to take in a cultural performance—a dance presentation or something similar—or just explore some more. You've got enough time to visit the Huembes market to look for handicrafts and gifts, plus get an idea of what kind of clothing and shoes you can pick up here. Specifically, people with shoes bigger than a size 10 can find out whether they'll have trouble finding shoes their size.

Second-Week Alternative Itinerary

If you're not sold on Nicaragua's main hot spots and think life in the countryside might suit you, spend your first eight days as though you were on the one-week tour above, then spend your second week as follows.

Days 8-10: Travel to León and visit the area around the city and Poneloya, León's popular Pacific beach area. León is very much like Granada but relatively immune from the ongoing real estate boom, so if Granada is "too has-been" for you, this is your refuge. Start with a relaxing breakfast somewhere in the vicinity of the park, the cultural ground zero for the city. Then explore the streets around the market or simply take a walking tour of Leon's dozens of remarkable churches as a pretext for walking the city streets. Hint: Start early, as León at midday gets hot. If you're lucky you will be in town for one of León's raucous and exciting baseball games. If you make León your home, baseball will be a large part of your entertainment, so check out a game and cheer for the locals—not at the expense of some time on one of León's popular beaches, though. Poneloya and Las Peñitas are a quick drive from León and will be an important refuge for you during the warmer months, so see what kind of beach experience awaits you and ponder it over an ice cream cone.

Days 11-12: Drive from León east and north, spending a night each in Estelí and Matagalpa. Both offer a lifestyle very unlike the rest of the country—rougher, wilder, with a bit of a "frontier" taste, which you'll only sense if you spend a night there. In Estelí, browse the shops along the main street south of the cathedral, and go make a phone call from the ENITEL office, just to see what it's like to call from a common phone instead of having one in your own home. You might not be tempted to mess around with public transportation if you are traveling on a tight two-week schedule, but just for fun, stop by the bus terminal in Estelí to see how the locals get around and to get a sense of the energy that pervades these hubs of intercity transport.

Days 13-14: Return to Managua, take a quick tour, and catch your flight home. After bouncing around the countryside, you might be happy just to have a warm shower and good restaurant food, but if you've got the energy, pass by the National Museum downtown, or at least gaze at the wreckage of the old cathedral.

ONE MONTH

A full month gives you more time not just to sample Nicaragua's geographical regions but to investigate the intricacies of the various government bureaucracies and travel with enough leisure to grow more familiar with the Nicaraguan people, who will dramatically strengthen your decision one way or another. Consider spending your time according to the following proportions, unless you fall in love with one particular geographical area and want to concentrate your time there.

Now is your chance to really absorb the Nicaraguan experience, so don't be afraid to get out there and explore. That doesn't necessarily mean heading off into the bush, but rather take your more relaxed schedule and use it to get to know the local pattern of life. Go to a church service in a town like Granada or León, go to a movie in a city like Estelí, and get your hair cut at some local barber. Get in the habit of reading the newspaper during your sojourn, to learn about local politics and the frenzied pontificating that accompanies every political party's latest pronouncement. Then head to a restaurant to argue about it with the local expats. In places like Granada and San Juan del Sur visit the bars and restaurants where you *don't* see the expats hanging out, since you probably won't be insulating yourself from the Nicaraguans in a hermetically sealed expat environment.

In a month you can actually find the time to fly out to the Atlantic coast and witness the different culture out there. Take advantage of the time to dive or snorkel and chat with the locals. You will find a handful of expatriates even on Little Corn Island and north of Bluefields. Ask questions about their lifestyle, what they miss from home, and what they enjoy having gotten away from. Similarly, in Managua you can take the time to look into buying a vehicle, get in the habit of listening to the news on the radio, and maybe even try your hand driving around the city.

Days 1-6: Granada remains the most important city to get to know from a potential expat's point of view, so start your exploration here. In six days you have got two or three good days to walk the streets, chat with the real estate agents about properties, and talk up the locals over a cold beer. But you've also got a full day to drive out to Laguna de Apoyo and go for a swim, a full day to hike Mombacho or have a real estate agent drive you out around the surrounding countryside, and a full day to visit either Masaya or the Pueblos Blancos.

Days 7-11: Once you've gotten familiar with Granada, concentrate on the area around San Juan del Sur, where many expats are looking for a little piece of the coastline. Because this is the second epicenter of the expat community, take the time to get to know it well. In your rented vehicle you can spend a full day or two exploring the developments north of town and a full day or two exploring the developments south of town. Take along a bag lunch from any San Juan del Sur restaurant or even your hotel, or just pick something up at the market on your way out of town. Because you've got the time, you can stop to linger at any of the ongoing developments to check out the view, the lots, and even the construction.

Days 12-16: Make the Atlantic coast your next focus. This is a remote enough area that you really can't check it out on the tighter itineraries, but given a month (or even three weeks!) it's worth exploring. From San Juan del Sur, drive back to Managua and return your rental car—you won't be needing it from this point on. Spend the night there and take the morning flight to Corn Island. Two days on Corn Island and two or three on Little Corn Island will give you a good feel for Nicaragua's Caribbean and hopefully help you figure out whether you can tolerate being that far away from "everything." Return from the Atlantic coast on the morning flight and hop a bus to León.

Days 17-23: León and the northwest are less traveled than the south of the country, at least by folks looking for homes, but León is your second-best bet if you are looking for something colonial. Try to spend at least two days in León visiting the markets and walking the streets to see what's for sale in the supermarkets and what kind of entertainment to expect from the city. From there, hop on a bus to the beach towns of Poneloya and Las Peñitas; you can spend a day in each relaxing on the beach and enjoying the coastline. Return to León and take the bus to Estelí to begin exploring the north.

Days 24-27: Estelí is a great place to begin appreciating the rugged character of Nicaragua's mountain country. You'll find far fewer foreigners up here, but understanding how people live outside of the more popular Granada and San Juan del Sur region is important. Perhaps you'll gain an appreciation for the relative luxuries available in the capital and Granada. From Estelí it's easy to catch a bus farther north to smaller cities like Ocotal and Somoto, but a much more enjoyable itinerary is to catch one of the many buses to Matagalpa and from there catch a bus to Selva Negra, the country's most popular mountain resort hotel. Selva Negra is worth two days at least, and you can easily spend a third hiking the numerous trails around the hotel. Otherwise, spend a day in the city of Matagalpa before heading back down to the capital, which will seem sweltering after your body has gotten acclimatized to the cool mountain air of Matagalpa and Estelí.

Days 28-30: On your last days in the country, really explore Managua. Stay one night each in a different hotel, spend an afternoon shopping for gifts in the Huembes market, enjoy a show or a dance one evening and go to a disco the next, enjoy a movie or visit a café to see how the young people spend their time, and make sure to wander around the shopping centers to get a feel for prices in the luxury class. If you get sick of the city you can always pop out to the surrounding countryside for some exploration. The folks who run your hotel will have plenty of suggestions for you.

Practicalities

The following list of hotels, restaurants, and things to see will help you get around the country and keep your belly full, and we've tried to give you our top-pick recommendations in each area. However, as Nicaragua's tourism scene staggers forward in spurts of growth and improvement, things are constantly changing, and any list attempting to capture it should be considered an incomplete snapshot at best. Remember, you're on a research trip, so think like a guidebook writer and ask about the latest developments (hotels, restaurants, services) in town. Not only will this allow you to make your own discoveries, it will inevitably put you in contact with enterprising expats with all kinds of ideas, opinions, and advice. If, however, you'd rather show up in Nicaragua with a more comprehensive listing of practicalities—or if you plan on traveling beyond the main regional centers—pick up a copy of *Moon Nicaragua*.

Many of the following restaurant listings do not have phone numbers or hours. And the restaurants that do have phone numbers often refuse to take reservations. Most restaurants open at 11 A.M. and close when the last customer leaves (usually around midnight), but if you find you are somewhere after midnight there is always the possibility of striking up a deal with a server to have the venue stay open a little longer.

GRANADA AND ENVIRONS
Accommodations

There are at least a dozen cheap and decent *hospedajes* in Granada (under US$10), some quite clean and sociable, especially **The Bearded Monkey** (across from the fire station, tel. 552-4028, thebeardedmonkey@yahoo .com) and **Hostel Oasis** (one block north, one east of the market, tel. 552-8005, www.nicaraguahostel.com); there are also plenty of class acts for a bit more cash. **Hospedaje Italiano** (half block west of Convento de

Guadalupe, tel. 552-7047, US$30) is spotless, well-run, and modern, and the rooms offer air-conditioning, a private bath, and TV. In a quiet but central neighborhood, **Casa San Francisco** (across from the Convento San Francisco, tel. 552-8235, www.csf hotel granada.com, US$45–60) is a charming U.S. expat-run colonial cluster of 13 beautifully decorated rooms. There is a small pool on the site and breakfast is included.

Remodeled in 2003, one of Granada's first luxury hotels **Hotel Alhambra** (on the west side of the park, tel. 552-4486, hotalam@tmx.com.ni, US$50) is built around a gorgeous landscaped patio and its location across from the park is the best in town. On the southeast corner of the central plaza, **La Gran Francia** (tel. 552-6000, www.lagranfrancia.com, US$85) is a careful blend of neoclassical and colonial elements in hardwoods, wrought iron, and porcelain—down to the last detail, such as the hand-painted sinks. There are 21 rooms, some with balconies, set around a courtyard and pool. The price includes breakfast.

Restaurants

One block north from the northeast plaza corner, **El Tercer Ojo** offers gorgonzola pasta, fine tapas and wines, and other delicacies in a gauzy atmosphere of candles, tiki torches, and soothing music. **Café Chavalos** (tel. 552-7118 or 852-0210, cafechavalos@yahoo.com, www.buildingnewhope.com, open Tues.–Fri. evenings) has delectable five-course meals prepared and served by Nicaraguan teens who have left a life on the street and are now taking control of their lives at this culinary college, restaurant, and sometimes Latin dance school. To get there follow Calle Calzada toward the lake and turn right at the Belles Artes building.

For Nicaraguan cuisine and lip-smacking steaks head over to **El Zaquan** (behind the main cathedral)—your nose should lead you to the meat-slathered, open-flame grill and dishes. Upscale and elegant, **El Arcángel** (on the southeast corner of the central plaza) has excellently prepared fusion cuisine, a blend of Latin American ingredients with international inspiration. It has a second-floor balcony bar as well.

Sights

Located just east of the park, the **Antiguo Convento San Francisco** (open daily 10 A.M.–5 P.M., admission US$2) features a dozen airy galleries set around landscaped courtyards that exhibit dioramas of the Chorotega and Nahuatl people, and includes a collection of 30 towering alter-ego statues collected a century ago from nearby Zapatera Island.

The plaza at the center of town, **Parque Colón,** is the epicenter of Granada's more interesting buildings, including its grand cathedral. Walk east along Calle la Calzada to reach the lakeshore.

On the park's east flank, in a colonial building, **Casa de los Leones** (open daily 10 A.M.–5 P.M., admission US$1.50) is an international cultural center that features art exhibits, craft classes, and the occasional concert.

A hike along the rim of **Volcán Mombacho** is not only enjoyable but will give you a bird's-eye view of the land around Granada.

For **shopping in Masaya** try the National Handicrafts Market, a short drive west of Granada, but also include time for a stroll to the hammock workshops and the viewpoint by the baseball stadium.

SAN JUAN DEL SUR AND THE SOUTHWEST
Accommodations

Small, warm, and friendly, **Rebecca's Inn** (25 meters west of the park, tel. 600-7512, martha_urcuyo@yahoo.es, US$18) is a great option with doubles; you get use of a kitchen.

Across the street from the beach, **Frederica's B&B** (tel. 568-2489, Rapido1@ibw.com.ni) has two lovely, fully equipped doubles for US$55. On the east side of town, 13-room bed-and-breakfast **Hotel Villa Isabella** (tel. 568-2568, jane101@aol.com, www.sanjuandelsur.org.ni/Isabella, US$65) is spotless and well run. It also offers four spacious condos for short- or long-term rental.

Find fully furnished adobe villas built into the hillside above San Juan at **Pelican Eyes Piedras y Olas** (tel. 568-2511, www.piedrasyolas.com, US$90–135). It has creative and gorgeous accommodations, a full range of services, and an infinity pool overlooking the ocean.

Make reservations at **Villa Paraíso** (tel. 563-4675, www.hotelvillaparaiso .com, US$20 d, US$55 suites) for La Isla de Ometepe's nicest accommodations on the breezy Santo Domingo waterfront.

Restaurants

A dozen identical Nicaraguan seafood joints line the beach in San Juan del Sur, and another dozen backpacker-targeted burger and sandwich shacks line the streets; take your pick. Here are a few of the more popular and/or refined options.

A longtime, reliable mainstay, **Pizzería Ristorante O Sole Mio** is run by an Italian expat and his wife. They serve authentic pizza and Italian dishes, imported wine, and seafood pastas.

Centrally located right off the southwest corner of the park, **Pizzería San Juan** features Don Maurizio's homemade pastas and pizzas, which are delicious, especially when smothered in lobster sauce.

In a class of its own, **Bar y Restaurante La Cascada** has tables set above the village and a prime view of the ocean and sunset from the Pelican Eyes Piedras y Olas hotel. The restaurant offers exquisite (and expensive) cuisine, including lamb, seafood risotto, and curries.

Sights

The best attractions in San Juan del Sur are natural ones—walking along the beach, watching the sun set, or fishing, sailing, and surfing. You can also try out **Da Flyin Frog Canopy Tour** (tel. 611-6214, tiguacal@ibw .com.ni, US$25 per person).

Punta Jesús María is a long, sandy peninsula beach on La Isla de Ometepe, just outside of Moyogalpa town.

MANAGUA
Accommodations

Most of the city's foreign-targeted budget accommodations (US$6–20) are located in Barrio Martha Quezada, a few square blocks near the Tica Bus terminal. On the other end of the spectrum, Managua's premium hotels (Crowne Plaza, Intercontinental, Princess, Holiday Inn) cater to business travelers and offer five-star service, airport shuttles, pools, dry cleaning, concierge, business center, top-notch restaurants, hundreds of rooms, and central locations; they can also cost over US$150 per night. Fortunately, Managua offers a surprisingly attractive array of practical midrange options.

Hotel Los Felipe (one block west of Tica Bus, tel. 222-6501) is the best of the budget hotels, with clean, safe, small doubles for US$20. Rooms have private baths, cable TV, and phones, and the shaded grounds include parking, Internet, and a small pool area; watch out for the naughty monkeys.

Hotel Europeo (75 meters west of Canal 2, tel. 268-4930 or 268-4933, www.hoteleuropeo.com.ni, US$40 d) has 11 clean, quiet, and nicely furnished rooms and includes continental breakfast, a small pool, laundry service, and cable TV.

The most convenient to the airport, **Best Western Las Mercedes** (across the street from the airport, tel. 233-2010, www.lasmercedes.com. ni, US$55 d) is a good place to decompress on the last night before your flight with a mixed bag of travelers and diplomats lounging by the pool and restaurant.

Tasteful, quiet, and gorgeous, **Hotel El Ritzo** (three blocks east and 25 meters south from Lacmiel, tel. 277-5616, www.hotelritzo.com, US$55) is one of only a few hotels worth considering within walking distance of the many restaurants and discos of the Carretera Masaya area.

Hotel Los Robles (across from Restaurante La Marseillaise, tel. 267-3008, www.hotellosrobles.com, US$85 d) is a charming, professional hotel with a tropical feel, consisting of quiet rooms set around a garden courtyard. It has a gym, pool, wireless Internet, great breakfast buffet, and all amenities.

Restaurants

La Cocina de Doña Haydee (one block west of Casino Pharaoh) serves Nicaragua's best specialties in a clean, quiet atmosphere with upscale street food and Nica home cookin'.

You can find traditional, reasonably priced Mexican food at **La Hora del Taco** (Monte de los Olivos, tel. 277-5074). The fajitas are a favorite.

Behind Casino Pharaoh, **Ola Verde** (tel. 270-3048, www.olaverde .info) serves fresh juices, salads, soups, hummus, and baba ghanoush—a pleasant menu of light vegetarian and chicken fare. Ola Verde sometimes has events and cooking classes.

La Marseillaise (Calle Principal Los Robles, tel. 277-0224) is one of the best restaurants in town, serving classic French cuisine in a gorgeous building filled with sculptures and paintings. The menu features delicious meat and fish dishes and to-die-for desserts.

Sights

La Laguna de Tiscapa is a breezy spot overlooking a volcanic lagoon and the rest of the city. The statue of Sandino atop the crater lip is one of Managua's most recognizable features.

Visit the city center **Plaza de la Revolución,** where many of Managua's historical sights are located, including the old cathedral ruins and presidential palace.

Las Huellas de Acahualinca (in Acahualinca, accessible by taxi only, tel. 266-5774, open Mon.–Fri. 8 A.M.–5 P.M., admission US$1.50) is a modest museum at the northwest end of the city displaying the 6,000-year-old traces of civilization.

Located in the Palacio de Cultura, **El Museo Nacional de Nicaragua** (tel. 222-2905, open 9 A.M.–5 P.M., admission US$1.50) highlights natural history as well as pre-Columbian ceramics and statues from all over Nicaragua's territories.

Open sun-up to sun-down every day of the year, the most tourist-friendly of the markets in Managua, **Mercado Roberto Huembes** offers fruits, vegetables, meat, cheese, flowers, hammocks, cigars, clothes, shoes, and the best crafts section this side of Masaya.

LEÓN AND THE NORTH

The following listings include highlights from the cities of León, Estelí, and Matagalpa, and are presented in that order.

Accommodations

Hostal Casa Leonesa (three blocks north and half a block east from the cathedral, tel. 311-0551, www.lacasaleonesa.com, US$45–60 d) is classic León in a converted colonial home. It has nine gorgeous rooms around a small pool and garden, each with air-conditioning, TV, hot water, and phone service.

Hotel El Convento (tel. 311-7053, www.hotelelconvento.com.ni, US$87 d) is one of León's finest. With a beautiful centerpiece garden and long, cool corridors adorned with art and antiques, El Convento offers all the amenities you could want, plus business services, a ballroom, restaurant, and local tours for its guests. Its 31 rooms also include bathtubs.

Hotel Estelí (a few blocks west and south of the park, tel. 713-2902, US$10–15) has a dozen basic rooms on two stories in central Estelí, each with a private bath and TV. Group discounts and secure parking are also offered.

Hotel Los Arcos/Café Vuela Vuela (one block north of the cathedral, tel. 713-3830, US$30–60) is Estelí's most charming hotel, and all profits go toward development activities of the Spanish NGO that runs the hotel, including their schools, continuing-education programs, and street children.

Small, quiet, and comfortable **Hotel Fountain Blue (Fuente Azul)** (tel. 772-2733, US$20) is near Matagalpa's third main entrance. The 12-room hotel has private baths, hot water, TV, fans, Internet access, free continental breakfast, and guarded parking.

Restaurants

In León, the profits earned at **Puerto Café Benjamin Linder,** a restaurant, coffee shop, bar, Internet café, and craft store, help support a local group of disabled children. **Casa Vieja Cafetín** (one block north of León's Hotel El Convento entrance) is a romantic little restaurant with decent surf, turf, and bar food.

Estelí's option for cheap Cuban food and fine cigars is **Comedor Pinareño** (one block south of the park). If you're looking for a cup of coffee and pleasant atmosphere, head over to **La Casita,** a stream-side coffee shop just south of Estelí serving yogurt, home-baked bread, fresh cheese, granola, juices, and coffee drinks.

There are plenty of steak-friendly Nica joints in Matagalpa, but **La Vita e Bella** (tucked into an alley in the Colonia Lainez, tel. 772-5476) is a great restaurant for pastas, pizzas, and other dishes.

Sights

A must-see for any walking tour of León is **La Catedral de León,** the largest cathedral in Central America. Said to have the largest and best collection of international artwork in Nicaragua, with an emphasis on images of colonial America, **Centro de Arte Fundación Ortiz-Gurdián** (admission is free) is one León's better galleries.

Built in 1874, **La Catedral de San Pedro de Matagalpa** reflects the opulence of Matagalpa at the time when coffee began its reign as the region's king crop.

ATLANTIC COAST
Accommodations

A Bluefields institution, **Hotel South Atlantic II** (tel. 572-1022 or 822-2265, US$32–58) has rooms with private bath, air-conditioning, TV, and phone service. It also offers a bar, restaurant, and travel agent on the premises. **Hotel Bluefields Bay** (tel. 572-0120, kriol@ibw.com.ni, US$35) is an elegant waterside bed-and-breakfast at the north side of town.

Casa Blanca Hotelito y Restaurante (tel. 572-0508, US$10–30) is the best to place to stay in Pearl Lagoon. It is clean, has good food, and offers tour services.

An excellent beachfront hotel on Big Corn Island is **Centro Turístico Picnic Center** (tel. 575-5204, verhodgson@yahoo.com, US$40 d), with rooms featuring air-conditioning, TV, queen beds, and a private bath. There is a great bar and restaurant on premises, and a reggae-flavored party scene when there are lots of people around.

Located on the cliffs of the southeast, breezy side of Little Corn Island, **Casa Iguana** (www.casaiguana.net, US$35) has a dozen raised, wooden cabins clustered around a communal, hilltop lodge where guests gather to eat, drink, and listen to the waves.

Restaurants

There are two decent options for waterside dining, the nicest of which is found at the **Manglares Restaurant,** located beneath Hotel Bluefields Bay and extending over the water on its own dock. The best place in town overlooks the water from atop the biggest hill west of town. Take a cab to **Restaurante Loma Rancho** to enjoy the views from atop the hill, across the street from BICU (Bluefields Indian Caribbean University). Finally, **Chez Marcel** remains the most exquisite dining experience in Bluefields. Dine on fresh fish and lobster in air-conditioned splendor.

One of the best restaurants on Big Corn Island, **Seva's Dos Millas ("Two Miles"),** serves top-notch seafood and ice-cold beer. A Little Corn Island eatery, **Bridgett's First Stop Comedor,** is a good locally owned choice for home cooking.

Sights

In Bluefields, the red-roofed **Moravian Church** was the first of its kind on the Central American Atlantic coast. Built in 1848 with English and French design elements, the style is reminiscent of New Orleans in the 1800s. Bluefields's raucous **Palo de Mayo Festival** (May Day celebration) is unique in Central America and not to be missed if you're in the area during the month of May.

The most popular swimming beach on Big Corn Island is **Picnic Center Beach,** a long, golden crescent of soft sand and turquoise water.

The **Pearl Cays** are six kilometers (four miles) east of a small Miskito village called Set Net. Hire a boat in Pearl Lagoon and enjoy the ride through the lagoon channels into the open Caribbean to these remote and mostly undeveloped islands.

There's one dive shop on each of the Corn Islands to get you to the many local (relatively shallow) dives along the reefs. On Corn Island head over to **Dive Nautilus** (tel. 575-5077, www.nautilus-dive-nicaragua.com), and on Little Corn Island try **Dive Little Corn** (www.divelittlecorn.com).

DAILY LIFE

© JOSHUA BERMAN

MAKING THE MOVE

So you've decided to take the plunge and settle down in Nicaragua—*¡felicidades!* Your friends may think you're a bit strange and you may consider yourself a brave pioneer—and both these things may be true. But the fact is, according to the immigration figures in 2005, more than 13,000 foreign residents have set up shop before you. Take heart in this knowledge, especially when mired in the deepest morass of bureacratic despair while wading through the visa process. If they could do it (13,000!), so can you. Think of it as a test; only the most patient and persistent will be deemed worthy of living in Nicaragua.

While you could probably stick around on a tourist visa, not being official will hinder your lifestyle in ways that matter, like being able to open a bank account and subsequently acquire services for your home like cable TV and Internet, so it is worth your while to go through the bureaucratic hassles necessary to get your residency, open a bank account, and make yourself official. This chapter will help you get through this annoying but ultimately feasible process and open the door for the next steps, which will enable you to settle into Nicaragua.

© JOSHUA BERMAN

Immigration and Visas

The easiest way to begin is to simply enter Nicaragua on a plain vanilla tourist visa (you get a 90-day tourist visa upon entering Nicaragua unless you are from one of a few restricted countries) and deal with getting a longer-stay visa once you're in the country. In the meantime, if you're still making up your mind about permanency, you can renew your tourist visa and get another three months to think about it by leaving and re-entering the country at any official border crossing. One-month extensions are also available (but by no means certain) by applying at the Office of Immigration (La Dirección General de Migración y Extranjería) in Managua, paying a fee, and possibly having to provide documentation.

All requests for resident visas must also be made at the Office of Immigration (tel. 244-0741, open Mon.–Fri. 8:30 A.M.–noon and 2–4:30 P.M.), located in a barn-like structure with a bright red roof on the east side of Managua (taxi drivers use it as a point of reference, but it's also described as being across the street from "Catastro," the land registry building, or INETER, the Institute of Geographical Studies).

On your way into the building for the first time, make friends with the street vendors outside. You'll be eating many lunches at their little shops before it's all through, but your persistence and good-natured obstinacy will eventually win the day and earn you the paperwork you require to make Nicaragua your home. It's not that the civil servants who comprise Immigration want to prevent you from staying in Nicaragua, it's that they have been programmed to use their leverage to extract as much money from you as they can, and they do this from within a government bureaucracy that is inefficient and whose legislation is being actively scrutinized and revised.

TYPES OF RESIDENCY

There are two main types of residency visas; when obtained, they grant you officialdom in the form of your very own *cédula* (residency card): the permanent residence visa *(residente permanente)* and the investor's residence visa *(residente inversionista)*. They are nearly identical, with the exception of one additional requirement for investors, and both require a number of authorized and translated documents. In essence, to become a resident you have to prove you do not pose a significant health risk, that you won't become an economic burden on the state, and that you are not a criminal. Sounds easy, doesn't it? The logistics of proving these things turn out to be

DAILY LIFE

A FEW TIPS FOR THE VISA PROCESS

Start the immigration process back home by gathering up and photocopying all your important documents, some of which will take longer to find than you expect. For example, Randy discovered when going through the process that he did not have a birth certificate, but some sort of proxy emitted by the hospital; he had to request an official birth certificate from the county, which took several weeks to arrive. Once you have the documents necessary, call the Nicaraguan consulate nearest you and establish contact with someone who can tell you if they will authenticate and translate your documents for you. If one consulate tells you no, try another just to be sure.

Once you're in Nicaragua with your visa application and to-do checklist in hand, buy a single, organized notebook to carry around at all times. Be sure to record the first name, last name, and telephone number for every single person with whom you come in contact, along with the purpose, time, and date of your meeting. Nicaraguan bureaucracies are cumbersome but not bottomless, and everyone has a boss with whom you can request an audience if things don't go well.

That doesn't mean you should demand to speak to everyone's boss. Rather, the very act of a Nicaraguan bureaucrat giving you his or her name and phone number removes the cloak of anonymity that normally allows them to treat you poorly, give you short answers, and otherwise try to brush you off.

In addition to the person's information, keep detailed notes on your conversation. This lets you refer back to conversations you may have had with other officials and gives you the immensely satisfying ability to say, "Really? That's not what your *jefe*, Don Pablo, told me Thursday morning." Being organized and having that type of information at your fingertips strengthens your case as you battle officialdom. As you get information or are redirected to some other office to procure some other document, write the steps down clearly and then ask the person with whom you are talking to confirm them for you. Not only does it radically diminish the risk that you get sent on a wild goose chase, it serves as a record of what you have been instructed to do in case you have to deal with any apparent contradictions by different officials.

a little intricate, but by no means is being granted residency in Nicaragua so burdensome that few ever succeed. You will need to invest lots of time and effort, but you will eventually get through the system. One expat reports that having a reputable Nicaraguan business partner greatly streamlines your way through the system.

Permanent Residence Visa

This is the most common *cédula* for which foreigners apply; it permits you to remain in Nicaragua for extended periods of time and requires fewer bureaucratic burdens than the investor visa. Officially, once you have met all the bureaucratic requirements listed below and your application has been successfully accepted, you can expect to receive the documents within two weeks. In practice, it often takes longer than that. Some (but not all) expatriates are forced to apply initially for a one-year residency permit unless they are married to Nicaraguans. After three consecutive renewals of the residency they will grant you a permanent residency card. This is not always true, however—some expats have gotten permanent residency cards on their first try. This is one of the many areas of Nicaraguan law that is undergoing change even as this book goes to press.

Of all the documents you must provide, your birth certificate, criminal record, marriage license, and health certificate must also be authenticated and translated. There are two ways to do this and no clear consensus as to which is more straightforward. The government of Nicaragua specifically requests that you have your documents notarized and translated before moving to Nicaragua via the Nicaraguan consulate nearest you (the nearer, the better, as there is a very real chance you will have to appear in person at some point during the process). The second way is to have your paperwork notarized and translated at the your nation's embassy in Nicaragua. The U.S. Embassy offers this service for its citizens (US$30 for the first document and US$20 for every additional document) but claims it will not notarize a police report. The third, riskiest option is to submit your paperwork without the necessary notary seals and see if the documents are accepted; as this process depends so much on the person with whom you deal at Immigration, it just might work—but you didn't hear it from us.

Following is a complete list and description of all necessary documentation:

Request for Permanent Resident Form: You can purchase this at the Office of Immigration for C$3.

Passport Photos and Passport: You must provide two passport photos taken straight ahead (that is, not a three-quarters-view head shot or profile) and with a white background, available at any number of photo and office shops throughout the country; as a foreign resident, it's a good idea to have a stock of passport photos in your possession anyway, as much official business seems to require them (Nicaraguans typically even attach a photo to their résumé when applying for a job, particularly when the job requires applicants have a "good presentation"). You must also provide photocopies of every page of your passport with the exception of pages that have never been stamped at all. Photocopy the cover as well. Always carry your passport to any official meeting or inquiry.

Proof of Income/Funds: The idea is to prove you are able to sustain yourself economically without becoming a burden on the government of Nicaragua. Officially you are required to provide a formal letter written on company letterhead of the Nicaraguan company or corporation with whom you are employed, and that company must be registered in the Nicaraguan government's *Registro Mercantíl* (business registry). In practice, would-be foreign residents wind up proving they can sustain themselves in Nicaragua by revealing information about their checking and savings accounts as well as sources of income from retirement pension plans, 401(k) plans, or IRAs. To do so, make sure to have not just recent statements but three to four statements for each account (proving you didn't just shovel the funds into that account that month) in both original and photocopy. You'll show them the original and provide them the photocopy for their records (if you don't provide a photocopy they'll take your original). In the odd case that it really is a Nicaraguan company that is providing your source of funds, provide a notarized copy of its legal registration in the *Registro Mercantíl.*

Proof of Dependency on Other Person (if applicable): If your primary funding source is another person, which is to say someone else declares you as a dependent, or your primary source of income is alimony payments, you must provide the above (savings statements, proof of funds) for that person as well as a letter signed, translated, and notarized by a Nicaraguan notary stating your dependency and the economic agreement that binds you to that person (e.g., alimony).

Certified Criminal Record from Your Country of Origin: You request this from your local police department. If you've moved around a lot, you need a record from every country in which you've resided for the past five years (if you've just traveled to a country but not resided there it doesn't count). You request that letter from your police department, then present it to the Nicaraguan consulate so the staff can authenticate it. They return it to you with a stamp indicating they recognize the letter as a valid document, not a forgery. The embassy may require you have the document translated. If so, there will likely be an official translator in house to do the work for you, for which you can expect to be charged.

Birth Certificate: This means your original birth certificate with a raised seal, as well as a photocopy for their records. Again, if you don't provide the photocopy they will keep your original. If you have children, provide a birth certificate for each of them as well as their corresponding photocopies. These birth certificates must be authenticated by the Nicaraguan consulate in your home country and translated if the consulate requests it.

Marriage License: If you are married to a non-Nicaraguan citizen you need only present your marriage license to the Nicaraguan consulate in your home country to be authenticated (and translated if requested). If you are married to a Nicaraguan you must provide the Nicaraguan marriage license and a copy of that person's *cédula*. Paradoxically, being married to a Nicaraguan requires more paperwork but encourages Immigration to look upon your case more favorably, as there is less perceived risk that you are going to disappear with bills unpaid and more certainty that you will be a productive member of Nicaraguan society. Emphasizing that point regularly throughout the process will smooth your way.

Certificate of Good Health: You need a letter from a native country doctor declaring you in good health and free from communicable diseases. The Nicaraguan government isn't too concerned with whether you have arthritis or a bad back; it is looking for AIDS, venereal disease, typhoid, tuberculosis, and such. Have your doctor mention these things specifically in the letter so there is no doubt whatsoever about the state of your physical health. This letter must be delivered to the Nicaraguan consulate nearest you to be authenticated, and translated, if necessary.

Carta de Baja: Obtained from the Ministry of Foreign Relations (Ministerio de Relaciones Exteriores, also called the *cancillería*), this is sort of a note of approval and essentially involves the *cancillería* checking to make sure you are not a persona non grata on any official government lists. The *cancillería* will request proof of your having paid the necessary deposit before they provide you the *carta de baja* (see the next item).

Cash Deposit: The deposit is mandatory and provides the government of Nicaragua with the necessary funds to deport you if for any reason they find it necessary. The deposit is currently US$2,500 and covers the price of a first-class airline ticket to anywhere in the United States (nice to know that if you are deported you will fly home in style), but expect that fee to rise at the whim of any director of immigration. You pay the fee into the "Immigration Special Account" (Fondo Especial de Migración) at the Banco de la Producción—account number 10025611277779—and retain your receipt as proof of the deposit. You have no right to request this money be reimbursed unless you rescind your Nicaraguan residency, at which point you may ask for the money to be returned to you. It's possible but not easy to do this. You will not receive any interest on the deposit.

Other Fees: You must pay several additional document-processing fees to a special office within Immigration called SERTRAMI (Servicio de Tramites de Inmigración). These include C$200 for the processing of your residence card (your *cédula*) and a C$50 service fee. Try not to get upset about paying a service charge plus a fee for the processing of that service charge: "It's how things work." And wait, there's one more fee, since the C$200 only covers the price of the card itself. A one-year (temporary) residency card involves a C$500 fee, payable at SERTRAMI. But most foreigners opt for the five-year residency card, which costs C$2,500.

Other Documents: At this point, things become less straightforward and more subject to the whims of the people with whom you are dealing at Inmigración. If you are a retiree living on a fixed income provided by your pension, you may or may not be required to provide your official IN-TURISMO Declaration. If you already operate a business in Nicaragua (which is unlikely if you are still living on a tourist visa), you are required to provide a copy of your Nicaraguan Commercial License, and if you are a student (which begs the question why you need permanent residency in Nicaragua), you will be required to provide proof of your registration with a university.

Investor's Visa

The investor's visa bears the same requirements as above, and some others. The most onerous one is a certificate from the Ministry of Development, Industry, and Trade (MIFIC, Ministerio de Fomento Industria y Comercio) recognizing the business you intend to establish in Nicaragua. Business investments of less than US$30,000 are exempt from this requirement, but you will also likely be denied the investor's visa and be encouraged to apply for a permanent residence visa instead. Very few foreigners take advantage of the investor's visa, and you cannot consider the purchase of your home and or land in Nicaragua as an investment for the purposes of this visa: It is intended for industrial entrepreneurs and the like.

THE APPLICATION PROCESS

Believe it or not, there is truly a process with a beginning and an end to it; it's what happens between those two fixed points that gets muddy. One reason things seem confusing is that many steps happen simultaneously, like your dealings with MIFIC and Immigration (if you are an investor), and others happen sequentially, like the airline ticket deposit, which must occur before the Ministry of Foreign Relations will grant you your *carta de baja*. The second reason the process is more nebulous than it ought to be is that different bureaucrats will require different things of you, or worse, give you different answers to your questions.

Once in Nicaragua, begin the process by going to the Immigration building and requesting a form for the appropriate resident visa. The form is important, but more important is the opportunity to ask questions of the person who gives it to you—and for a printed list of all the steps required (they have these, so make sure you get one!). Look it over and make sure the next steps are clear to you before leaving the building. At that point you can begin with the rest of the steps, like visiting the Ministerio de Relaciones Exteriores, placing the deposit in the Banco de Producción, and requesting authentication/translation services from your embassy, if necessary. When you have gathered all the required documents, return to Immigration to have them processed. The earlier you get to the office, the better luck you will have (a good mantra for Nicaraguan bureaucracies in general). You may be sent back with additional requests for documents once or twice, but don't be discouraged, just keep pushing forward!

Hiring a Lawyer

Looking at the mountains of paperwork that lies between you and official residency, it is tempting to retain the professional services of an attorney, and indeed, many Nicaraguan attorneys are willing to help you with your residency paperwork. This is a recommended avenue if your Spanish is not good enough to deal confidently with the sort of Spanish you find on official documentation.

However, if you've spent enough time in Nicaragua to feel comfortable with the language and speak Spanish well enough to represent yourself in person before immigration authorities, an attorney might be of limited use to you. Instead, consider taking along a Nicaraguan friend whenever you deal with Immigration. Again, the subtle message of your ability to fit into Nicaraguan society and the suggestion that you might "know people" will be helpful, but more importantly, the cultural interpretation your friend will provide during the process can be very beneficial. Should you decide to contract a Nicaraguan attorney you can expect to pay anywhere from US$250–500 (or more) for his or her services—your friend will probably only ask for dinner and a couple of Toñas.

Moving with Children

While there is no obvious impediment to moving to Nicaragua with children, very few families seem to do so, and for the time being, Nicaragua remains the playground of retirees, foreigners who have married Nicaraguans, development workers, and people looking for a simpler (and possibly cheaper) lifestyle. But don't let that stop you. Nicaraguans love children. They cherish them, adore them, dote on them, shine them up and show them off. It's refreshing, actually, to participate in a society where children are so highly valued, and this alone should prove that the idea of bringing your own children to Nicaragua should not be dismissed.

From a practical standpoint, the single biggest challenge to living in Nicaragua with children is the weak educational system, which means right away you'll have to find a school that meets your requirements for your children's education (see the *Language and Education* chapter). As for health issues, with the exception of infants, you will find your children are no more susceptible to concerns all expats face in Nicaragua, and may even develop a better immunity to the local bugs than you will. Teach your children how to deal with the hygiene issues Nicaragua requires, like not drinking tap water, being careful to wash one's hands frequently, not eating food that hasn't been recently cooked (or that they find on the ground), and so on, and they will be fine.

One family of missionary expats we met in the North arrived for an extended stay in Nicaragua with a two-year-old boy who had just begun speaking. When they moved to Nicaragua, their son immediately clammed up again and stopped saying even the simple phrases and words he had begun to use in the States. About two months later, he began speaking again—this time in Spanish! Before the end of the year he was communicating in both Spanish and English; he'd just needed a couple of months to figure it all out.

It should go without saying, but it's important to be sensitive to your older children's needs if you are making the move to Nicaragua during their adolescence. They might not be as excited about the "simpler lifestyle" of Nicaragua as you. Ensuring they learn to speak Spanish immediately will be a vital first step to their cultural assimilation as it will enable them to make Nicaraguan friends that will help ease their transition. During this time period, help them resist the urge to stay locked indoors watching American television and pining for life "back there." There are lots of adventures to be had in Nicaragua, from rafting to beach exploring to volcano hiking and more. Engaging in some fun activities with your children will help them learn to like their new home.

Moving with Pets

Due to extremely low priority placed on spaying and neutering pets, Nicaragua is overrun with many thousands of unwanted, maltreated stray dogs and cats looking for a loving home. A group of expats in Granada is attempting to address the problem, but there will be no shortage of fuzzy creatures to keep you company should you decide to adopt. If, however, you simply cannot live without your beloved Fido or Kitty, moving with a North American pet to Nicaragua is far easier than moving with a Nicaraguan pet back to the United States—provided your pet is a dog, cat, hamster, or bird. If your menagerie contains snakes, reptiles, or exotic creatures you will have a little more difficulty. And if you intend to take along your favorite horse or pony you will have more trouble still. Several companies (see the *Resources* chapter) offer transportation services for small mammals, birds, reptiles, and the like, but not horses.

Within one month of your departure date, visit a veterinarian and have your animal inspected and vaccinated, and make sure you have an up-to-date record of that animal's vaccinations over its whole life. If your animal has not already had a rabies shot, make sure to have it vaccinated, as rabies is still extremely prevalent in Nicaragua and your animal will be at risk. Next, have the veterinarian's letters notarized and then submit them to the nearest Nicaraguan consulate to be authenticated. There will be a charge for this service. Upon your arrival in Nicaragua customs agents will request to see the letter from the vet with its notary seal and the authentication seal or document that the Nicaraguan consulate provides you. You will be charged US$10 per animal. Bear in mind that airlines require you to have the veterinarian provide this letter within 10 days of your flight, which requires you to deal with the Nicaraguan consulate within that time frame. If that worries you, it should. Be prepared to visit one of the consulates in person to facilitate the process, if you need to.

Once in Nicaragua, expect a bit of a runaround. To date, Nicaragua does not impose a quarantine on imported mammals (provided they are arriving from the same continent—Europeans will have it different) but might impose quarantine on your bird with the mostly valid pretext that it needs to guard against avian flu. You may be able to talk your way out of this one, possibly with the help of a small-denomination greenback.

Take transport requirements into consideration when planning. For example, airlines will not typically agree to transport animals that weigh more than 70 pounds. Some bigger dogs run the risk of surpassing that limit. Likewise, most airlines have a physical limit on the size and shape of the kennel in which your animal is transported. Your alternatives are close to nil if your pet doesn't fit into a kennel of their dimensions, unless you are interested in driving it south and dealing with the combined regulatory requirements of the rest of the Central American isthmus and Mexico. And if you'd like take your horse, your challenges will be greater still. The expats who have talked about bringing their horse to Nicaragua—and actually done it—have driven, horse trailer, truck, and all, through Mexico and Central America to ensure they had complete control over the horse's environment. This is no casual undertaking.

CLEAR-EYED PRECAUTIONS: A REALIST'S GUIDE TO LIVING IN NICARAGUA

The cheap labor and land that attracted centuries of Spanish conquistadors and, in the 1850s, William Walker's mercenary thugs, still exist today. Thankfully, the invasions of today are peaceful ones. Now they are stimulated by a dramatic international economic imbalance that makes land in Central America's most beautiful country look like a great bargain. Nicaragua's fledgling democracy and favorable real estate prices are beginning to make noise with international real estate speculators and American retirees. At least land today is being paid for and bought, not forced and conquered. However, in a country as poor as Nicaragua, at times the end result is similar.

If the potential foreign resident is sincere in the desire to live with the Nicaraguans and not on top of them, to integrate as best as possible into Nicaraguan society, not create a parallel one, then Nicaragua can in fact be a paradise. The pace of life in Nicaragua is superb, the people are wonderful if you engage them, the food is excellent, and the scenery is second to none. It all depends on the potential investor's attitude, willingness, and ability to change and adapt, along with taking necessary, clear-eyed precautions in terms of land titles and geological concerns.

One of these is knowing how to confront the disastrous Nicaraguan legal system, one of the worst in the hemisphere. Grossly unfair court decisions are common in Latin America, but Nicaragua has a particularly bad reputation, and the court system does not necessarily favor those who just throw bribes and expensive lawyers at it. Contacts and political influence can often outweigh financial motives for judges. This can be very serious for a self-righteous foreign resident who speaks poor Spanish. Not to mention that nothing legal, property title or otherwise, is written in stone in Nicaragua. Anyone retiring or buying land would be wise to examine the property title with a Nicaraguan insider or title insurer.

Living in Nicaragua and not speaking at least passable Spanish is a bad idea. Nicaraguans probably have the lowest incidence of English proficiency in Central America, the exact opposite of southern neighbor

What to Take

Take everything you simply cannot live without and will not be able to acquire in Nicaragua, and nothing more. That requires two careful evaluations: what you simply cannot live without, and what you cannot acquire in Nicaragua. The first question is yours to answer and yours alone, but we can help you with the second.

You can find just about everything you'd need in Nicaragua provided you don't have exorbitant tastes: Imported goods are universally more expensive, sometimes up to 40 percent more so. Notably absent are general

Costa Rica. For important events a translator could be hired, but for the mundane day-to-day life chores like shopping, banking, fixing your car or house, getting a haircut, and sending a package, at least partial Spanish fluency is required.

There are other pertinent issues that your "expert investment tour guide" or enthused Realtor might conveniently overlook. Potential beach investors will not be likely to receive information about Nicaragua's intense oceanic seismic activity, which translates into more than 200 low-level tremors per month and 3-4 earthquakes per year off the Pacific coast of Nicaragua. Every 15 years on average this brings a destructive tidal wave to Nicaragua's Pacific coast (the last was in September of 1992). Few foreigners seem to take the time to go to the Nicaraguan National Geographic Survey (INETER) to examine volcano risk maps that include Granada, Las Isletas, the island of Ometepe, León, and many other places in Nicaragua's beautiful and ever-changing landscape. Perhaps the relatively low cost of land makes it is easier to overlook the fact that Nicaragua's stunning landscape is a direct result of its unstable geology – i.e., a rate of continental plate collision unmatched in the Americas. This constant movement is what has created Nicaragua's dramatic and beautiful relief of lakes and volcanoes, as well as frequent earthquakes, mudslides, and volcanic eruptions.

Nicaragua's tumultuous history of foreign invasions, manipulations, wars, and cynical politicians has miraculously failed to create a bitter or resentful populace. Nicaraguans are the most generous and humorous people in Central America. Nicaragua is a special case in Latin America. It would be wise to consider the beauty of Nicaragua's culture and people (as well as its land), rather than view Nicaragua as a golden opportunity to pounce on economic vulnerability and a people desperate for work. Following a Machiavellian impulse to capitalize on Nicaragua's poverty will only lead to more suffering in the future, and not just for the Nicaragua people.

(Contributed by Richard Leonardi, a photographer, writer, and investment consultant. Leonardi has lived in Managua for over 10 years and is author of the country guide Footprint Nicaragua; *his website is www .nicaraguaconsultant.com.)*

merchandise stores, common throughout the United States, where you can purchase housewares, inexpensive furniture, linens, bath supplies, and the like. You can certainly find all those goods in Nicaragua, but it will require a bit more legwork. Managua's overpriced malls cater to the Nicaraguan elite (the 10 percent of the population that owns 45 percent of the nation's wealth), and though you can find American specialties like Benetton and Gap, the price tags will put you in cardiac arrest. At Managua's new Galería Siman Santo Domingo, for example, you can even find brand names like Kenneth Cole and Gant! But once you are accustomed to getting around, you'll do better in the nation's open-air markets and smaller boutique shops, where you'll find better deals among the locally produced goods and goods imported from elsewhere in Latin America (and thus subject to fewer importation taxes).

Some examples: You can find fluffy towels and fine Egyptian cotton linens in Managua, but they will all be 40 percent more expensive than prices in America; or you can purchase not-so-fluffy towels and slightly scratchy linens elsewhere for prices that are reasonable even by American standards. You won't find fancy, factory-made wooden furniture sets, but you'll find skilled carpenters who can create furniture of your own design for reasonable prices. Appliances like blenders, toasters, and cappuccino makers are all available from Managua stores like La Curacao, but they are more expensive than back home.

Expats tend to take the following things from home: electronics, laptops and computer equipment, stereos, DVD players, etc., even if they simply bring one item at a time down in their luggage as they make trips back and forth. You may want to bring a fresh pair of your favorite footwear, as large sizes are difficult to find in Nicaragua, but don't worry at all about clothing, as you can get a custom-tailored wardrobe for reasonable prices once you're here. Also widely available are English-language books, mostly of the used-and-left-behind-by-backpackers variety, plus a few bookstores selling new, overpriced titles.

You should bring down any special medicines you take regularly, any toiletries you simply can not live without (although you'll find a pretty impressive variety of creams and shampoos throughout the country), and jewelry without which you simply wouldn't feel like yourself.

Another approach is to reevaluate what your "needs" are and simplify them. Once you've spent some time among Nicaraguan families and seen how much they are able to do with so few resources, you might reconsider some things you previously thought were indispensable. This is highly personal, but you might very well discover that in your new lifestyle in Central America you can live more simply than you'd expected.

That said, you can just as easily bring it *all* with you, particularly if you are a retiree. One incentive the Nicaraguan government has implemented in an effort to attract retirees to Nicaragua is a one-time tax break that allows retirees to bring US$10,000 of personal possessions plus their vehicle with them to Nicaragua. You still have to incur the expense of actually shipping all that stuff, of course, but if you rent a container and ship your belongings all at once, you can take the opportunity to bring south your nice furniture, kitchenwares, garden tools, computer equipment, fine linens, your wardrobe, and whatever else you can think to pack in there (just to make sure you're not a vehicle importer playing fast and loose with the rules, you are prohibited from selling your vehicle for five years following your move).

Alternatively, you could easily get on the plane southbound with nothing more than the clothes on your back and set up a decent house in Nicaragua based simply on what you purchase in country. In fact, that is what most expats we know have done.

GETTING IT THERE

Once you decide to move all your stuff down to Nicaragua, you need to find a shipping company that will deal with the high seas for you. Bernuth Lines is one such company. Based out of Miami, they will send you a container on a truck, which you proceed to load at your leisure. In go your boxes, furniture, even your vehicle. When you've finished, they send the truck down to the port at Miami, load it onto a Nicaragua-bound ship, pick up your container on the other end, and route it to Managua for you to clear through customs and pick up.

The second part of the process is clearing your goods through customs in Managua. The same company will hold your hand through this, too, for an additional fee, or you can choose one of the dozens of *agencias aduaneras* (customs agencies) to do it for you: Check any Nicaraguan telephone book once you arrive to find them.

LANGUAGE AND EDUCATION

Being able to communicate effectively will make the difference between simply surviving in a foreign country and making it your home, and Nicaragua is not a country where you can get away with just speaking English and hoping people understand you. This chapter covers some strategies for learning Spanish in Nicaragua and even for making that challenge an opportunity to familiarize yourself with the country, and we suggest some tactics for making learning Spanish a life-long experience.

We'll also look at opportunities for potential expats traveling to Nicaragua with their children, who need to make their children's continuing education a priority in their decision of whether or not to make Nicaragua their next home. You'll be happy to know many expats do move to Nicaragua and enroll their children in school programs that meet—and sometimes exceed—their needs. While dealing with educational opportunities is more challenging in Nicaragua than in other Latin American countries, the challenge is certainly one you can overcome.

© JOSHUA BERMAN

Learning to Speak Spanish

If you've ever felt indignant toward an immigrant in your own country who has been living there for decades without bothering to learn English (or whatever the lingua franca), well, the *zapato* is on the other foot now, *amigo,* and if you're planning on moving to Nicaragua, you should also be planning to learn *español.* Period.

This is more than a matter of respect for Nicaraguan culture and appreciation for where you are. It is a practical necessity. English-speaking Nicaraguans are few and far between, even in Managua, and outside of the capital your Spanish skills are all that stand between you, adventure, and disaster. The Nicaraguan police force is universally monolingual—can you talk your way out of a ticket? Likely, your maid and gardener won't speak a word of English either—can you understand why they didn't show up yesterday? Can you explain to them how you expect them to do their jobs? Your neighbors don't speak English, and the better you can communicate with them—share your personality, tell jokes, enjoy their company—the more they will warm to you and help look after you and your family.

Of course, it is possible to squeak by on the survival Spanish you remember from high school or the phrases you find in the backs of guidebooks—and a number of expats do just that, even for years! But in addition to missing out on cultural layers and depths that are the essence and joy of living in Nicaragua, such individuals risk the scorn of fellow expats, foreign travelers, and Nicaraguans who will view their laziness as a sign of either dullness, arrogance, or both. Learning a language is more difficult for some people than it is for others, and everybody makes mistakes. The key is listening intently to those around you, then paying attention to every syllable of every word you speak, making constant tiny adjustments toward perfecting your pronunciation. Luckily, there are plenty of schools, skilled instructors, and resources to help with the process.

SPANISH-LANGUAGE SCHOOLS

Nicaragua boasts a strong and growing network of independent Spanish-language schools where you can engage in a few days, weeks, or months of language study. With few exceptions, most schools follow the same basic structure, which involves a combination of language instruction and cultural immersion activities. That means 2–4 hours of class in the morning, followed by community service activities or field trips in the afternoon.

Competition constantly forces major changes in the schools listed

BODY LANGUAGE

Limber up your wrist and stretch out those lips. You'll need 'em both if you want to communicate like a true native. Watch people interact on the buses, in the markets, and on the streets, and see if you can spot any of the following gestures in action – then try some out yourself.

Probably the single most practical gesture is a rapid side to side wagging of the index finger. It means "no," and increases in strength as you increase the intensity of the wagging and the amount of hand and arm you use in the motion. In some cases, a verbal "no" in the absence of the **Finger Wag** is disregarded as not serious enough. Use this one liberally with pushy vendors, beggars, and would-be Romeos.

To pull off the **Nicaraguan Wrist Snap,** simply join the tips of your thumb and middle finger and let your index finger dangle loosely. Then with a series of rapid wrist flicks, repeatedly let your index finger slap against the middle one, exactly as you would do with a round tin of tobacco dip. The resulting snapping noise serves to either emphasize whatever it is you're saying, refer to how hard you've been working, or, when combined with a nod and a smile, imply something like, "Damn that's good!"

You can ask "what?" (or "what do you want?") with a quick **Cheek Scrunch,** occasionally performed with a subtle upward chin tilt. Use the **Lip Point** rather than your finger to indicate something by puckering up as if for a kiss and aiming where you want. Or, if you are listening to a friend's dumb story, point to the speaker with your lips while looking at everyone else to imply, "this guy's crazy or drunk."

The gesture North Americans would normally use to shoo something away – the outstretched, waving, down-turned hand – means just the

below, though prices have remained constant for quite a few years now (meaning they may be due to go up). There have also been a few teacher mutinies, when instructors split off to form their own schools, which sometimes thrive and sometimes don't. This makes it difficult to recommend one school over another. Moreover, to a certain extent, your choice of school is as much a question of geographical preference as anything else. If possible, travel around a bit (perhaps during your fact-finding trip) and visit some of the schools personally before committing. By hanging around at lunchtime you can chat up the current students, ask the teachers about their credentials and personalities, and gauge the professionalism of the business. Ask students how they feel about the lesson plan, their teacher's ability to engage and challenge them, and whether the lessons seem rote or ineffective. When talking to students (or reading their comments on public websites and forums), keep in mind that education is a highly subjective experience, and one student's experience might vary wildly from another's simply on the basis of his or her personality versus the teacher's.

DAILY LIFE

© RANDALL WOOD

A sign of neither victory nor peace, flashing a *"dos"* means you vote for the Sandinistas.

opposite in Nicaragua, where the **Downward Wave** (occasionally combined with the whole arm for emphasis) means "Come here." This one is a favorite with drunks in the park who love to talk at foreigners for as long as they are tolerated. The North American "come here"; i.e., the upturned and beckoning index finger, is a vulgar, possibly offensive gesture. Speaking of vulgar, a closed fist atop a rigid forearm indicates the male sex organ, and an upturned, slightly cupped hand with the fingertips pressed together into a point is its female counterpart. Here's one more for the road: Make a fist, lock your elbow into the side of your body, and move your hand up and down; combined with a dramatic grimace, the **Plunger Pump** tells the whole world you have diarrhea.

Prices quoted below are subject to change, and note that at any school, the more weeks you commit to, the lower your weekly rate drops. Most schools provide airport pickups if requested. For contact information on specific schools, please see the *Resources* section.

Granada

Granada is a natural choice for many students who love the city's aesthetic as much as its central location on the tourist trail. Roger Ramírez's One-on-One Spanish Tutoring Academy has received rave reviews and a constant stream of students since its humble, one-room beginnings. One-on-One's classrooms are a bit cramped, but their eight full-time (mostly younger) teachers rotate every hour, so that students are exposed to different personalities and accents as they switch between grammar, conversation, and other topics. A week of 20 hours of instruction costs US$95, plus US$70 for room and board with a family. Custom, group, and cultural activities can also be arranged, as can shorter lessons, or class by the hour. Casa Xalteva

TALKING THE TALK:
TIPS FOR LEARNING SPANISH

First the obvious things: Sign up for a class, hire a tutor, do your homework, buy (and use!) all the books, CD-ROMS, interactive tapes, and videos you can lay your hands on. These are things you can do before you even come to Nicaragua. Of course, being immersed in a culture that doesn't speak your language is the best way to become fluent, and in Nicaragua, you have the additional benefit of being surrounded by energetic, friendly, and above all, patient teachers. Still, you won't simply absorb Spanish by being around it – if it were only that easy! It takes time, constant *listening*, and you must learn slowly – *poco a poco* – one word at a time, until they start flowing together in sentences.

One of the most important tips we can give is not to be shy: *¡No tengas pena, hombre!* Extroverts invariably have an easier time learning a language, because outgoing people, by nature, speak more. This means they make more mistakes, and by constantly correcting these errors, they are awarded with a steeper, quicker learning curve. On that note, be sure to let your Nicaraguan teachers, friends, employees, and host family members know that you want to be corrected. Many Nicas neglect to help you with your pronunciation or grammar because they think you'll be embarrassed or angry rather than grateful. This is a face-saving move on their part, but it will stall your efforts immeasurably. The phrase to use with them is, *"Por favor, corríjame cuando haga un error."*

Next, purchase a pocket-sized notebook and pen at the corner *librería*, and keep them accessible at all times. Record new words you hear while out and about, or while reading the newspaper, then look them up in a

offers a similar package, US$125/week, with a stress on volunteer activities; it's highly recommended by former students, has a quiet location, and is part of a small group home for boys that is supported by your tuition. The experienced teachers that used to work in the beautiful Palacio de Cultura on the central park now own and operate the Cocibolca Spanish School, which offers full packages from US$195 and also weekend classes.

Laguna de Apoyo

If you prefer to avoid the distractions of the city, the Proyecto Ecológico is the only Spanish school in Nicaragua in a purely natural setting—the lakeside lodge is in the crater of an ancient volcano. The spot is incredible, only an hour from Managua, less to Granada, yet still tucked away in its own green world. Lodging and food are excellent; students are placed in a one-on-one and/or group learning context (maximum four per teacher) for five hours per day, five days per week. One week costs US$190, including classes, activities,

dictionary or, better yet, have a Nicaraguan explain their meaning to you without using English (they'll be especially amused when you jot down jokes, popular sayings, and dirty words – of which there are plenty in Nicaragua!). Then compile those words and phrases in a larger notebook (or on large poster paper in your room), study them repeatedly, and you'll start to notice and understand them more often.

Accept the fact that at first, you'll be speaking like an infant, which will be immensely amusing to Nicaraguans around you; laughing along with them will create a warm camaraderie that will only increase as your follies flow toward fluency. As you learn a language from the bottom up – constantly finding new words and expressions to describe what you are seeing and feeling – you are, in effect, building a new personality, just like you did when you first learned to speak your native tongue. This is an exciting, liberating, and frustrating experience, and it is an enormous part of the wild culture shock ride.

By all means, take a break from your studies and the Spanish language sometimes! Total immersion is intense, and trying too hard will burn you out. But regulate these escapes: Avoid the lure of too much English-language television and the constant company of English-speaking expats, diversions that are extremely easy to find in spots like Granada and San Juan del Sur.

Before long you'll notice your efforts are paying off, and in the process, you'll be joining the ranks of expats with Spanish-language disaster stories, like the time Randy wished his Nicaraguan friends a "Happy New Anus!" on December 31 (there's a big difference between "*ano*" and "*año*"), or the time Joshua asked his Nica host mother where his penis was (he meant comb – *peine*, not *pene*).

and room and board in the lodge. The weekend program has Spanish classes Saturday and Sunday, with all meals included, and a room Saturday night.

San Juan del Sur

One of the best deals around and easy to recommend is Doña Rosa Silva's Spanish School, offering four hours of daily instruction, up to six days a week for US$100—plus US$60 for a homestay; several of her students had nothing but good things to say. Also get personal instruction from Luis Vicente Lira's Spanish Lessons School in the middle of town, US$65 a week for three hours of daily instruction.

There's one school in the Casa de Cultura, across from the beach (it may still be unethically using the old NSS name and logo), but it is under brand-new management and we have not heard anything about it. Down the block across from the bank (right on the beach!) is the San Juan del Sur Spanish School with all-inclusive packages for US$195/week; it has very experienced teachers.

NICARAGUAN SPANISH

Spanish is the official language of the republic (as stated in the constitution), though indigenous tongues are spoken widely in certain areas of the Atlantic coast. To be more specific, 96 percent of Nicaraguans speak Spanish as their first language, 3 percent speak tribal languages (Miskito, Mayangna, and Rama), and 1 percent speak mixed languages of African and Caribbean origin (Creole and Garífuna). To hear pure Miskito, travel to Puerto Cabezas or any village along the Río Coco; in some of these villages Spanish is completely unknown.

Back on the Pacific side of the country, *el Nicaragüense* is unique among dialects heard in other Spanish-speaking countries, and bears as little resemblance to proper Spanish Castilian as, say, a Texan drawl does to the British royals' speech. Nicaraguan Spanish is spoken rapidly and liquidly, the words flowing smoothly together and eating each other's tails. The ends of words, especially those ending in an "s," are often swallowed. Upcountry campesino Spanish is inevitably less intelligible to the untrained ear than its urban counterpart, but it is also wonderfully melodic, with a distinct cadence and rhythm that is celebrated in many of Carlos Mejía Godoy's popular folk songs. But apart from urban-rural differences, the Spanish spoken in Granada is essentially the same as that spoken in León and Managua, without much regional dialect difference.

Latin American Spanish School is a recent start-up headed by a half dozen entrepreneurial and professional Nicaraguan Spanish instructors with, on average, over eight years' experience teaching foreigners. They offer a basic 20-hour instruction and activity package for US$120, plus US$90/week for lodging with private bath and three meals a day.

León

Schools are in flux in León, with a few new ones being formed at press time and the oldest one being disbanded. Ask about Spanish schools in the Casa de Cultura, or check the bulletin board at the Vía Vía Hospedaje for private tutors and lessons. Also, Va Pues Tours recently began offering an intensive, full-immersion Spanish course: US$195 for 20 hours of one-on-one class (over five days), including room and board.

Estelí

Estelí's advantage over other schools is the deliciously cool climate and a number of natural excursions accessible as brief day trips from the city. Estelí has lots of experience hosting and teaching *internacionalistas,* and its schools have been around for over a decade. Escuela Horizonte Nica has one of the longest track records in town, and claims to "promote peace and social justice for those living in poverty, those struggling against class, race, and gender prejudices, and those fighting for political freedom." We know, you just wanna learn the language. The school donates part of its profits to local organizations and has an afternoon activity program that includes visits to local cooperatives and community development programs. One week of class, with 20 hours of intensive study, afternoon activities, and homestay with a family costs US$165, but the school offers discounts for groups.

The CENAC Spanish School also gets high marks and has been around since 1990. It offers 20 hours of class plus room and board for US$140 a week. The Spanish School Güegüense is located 250 meters east of the Shell Esquipulas. Its afternoon activities include trips to Jinotega, Quilalí, San Juan del Río Coco, and local Estelí attractions. Class and homestay cost US$120 per week.

Managua

Viva Spanish School, offering intensive classes (20 hours per week), caters to students of all ages and backgrounds—one week of instruction, including all materials, is US$125. It also offers evening classes for people who live and work in Managua (four hours per week). Modules of study are available for missionaries, medical students, and businesspeople, covering specialized vocabulary in each area. Other programs include advanced courses, tourist Spanish, a literature class, and a specially developed children's program that includes games, art, and other activities.

Private lessons, tutoring, and guide services are offered by a friendly bilingual Managuan, Raul Gavarrette, and you may be able to find similar services at Nicaragua Spanish Schools (NSS).

STAYING WITH A HOST FAMILY

If you are already set up and living in a place like Granada, Estelí, or San Juan del Sur, you'll probably choose to attend only the classroom and activity portions of your Spanish school's programs. But if you'd like to live with a Nica family, most schools are eager to arrange a host family (or "homestay") for you, as many maintain a network of families that specialize in this. The fees for this service are usually very reasonable, ranging US$60–90 for a room and three home-cooked meals a day. Homestays are a great introduction to Nicaragua. They offer the opportunity to scope out the neighborhood from a Nica point of view and to assess your commitment to living in the country long-term. You'll get a taste of daily life and the chance to practice chatting with your soon-to-be neighbors.

Many Nicaraguan families involved in these programs have received training in how to host foreign guests with strange habits and weak stomachs; others haven't. It's difficult to judge what kind of deal you are getting, but if possible, visit the home before committing—make sure you've got your own room with a door that locks, and that things are generally clean. Foreign women will feel more comfortable in a home with lots of sisters, aunts, and grandmothers rather than one dominated by drunk and loitering brothers and uncles, so clarify exactly who is responsible for you and who lives there (Nica homes are often overflowing with a confusing array of visiting family and friends, who are often hard to distinguish from the immediate family).

Education

One of the universally agreed-upon weak points for foreigners living in Nicaragua is lack of a broad range of secular, highly rated bilingual schools for your children. There are a few options, but they are limited, and they are all in Managua. Of course some would argue that the experience of living abroad during one's formative childhood and adolescence is in itself an educational opportunity far exceeding anything your children could gain back in the 'burbs. Others caution that placing your children in the sheltered and privileged environment of a private international school guarantees a degree in snobbery and arrogance (horror stories abound of rich Nica kids who treat their teachers like domestic servants and/or doormats). This must be where good parenting comes in—or one of the do-it-yourself homeschooling options (see *Homeschooling and Distance-Learning Programs*).

INTERNATIONAL SCHOOLS
In Managua

Expats living in Nicaragua invariably send their children to one of the handful of private, bilingual, international schools in the country, many of which have strongly religious foundations and all of which are located in Managua.

There are five big players in the international school scene: the American Nicaraguan School (a.k.a. the American School), the Colegio Alemán Nicaragüense (a.k.a. the German School), the French School, the Lincoln International Academy, and the Notre Dame School (for contact information, please see the *Resources* section). Their comparative popularity changes with school administrations, as many international teachers work on a two- or three-year

FROM *KINDER* TO *QUINTO*: NICARAGUAN SCHOOL TERMINOLOGY

Understanding the Spanish vocabulary used in the Nicaraguan education system is important because several misleading cognates might otherwise confuse you. When enrolling your child, you will come across these terms. Starting with your little ones, *"el kinder"* is kindergarten, and *"pre-escolar"* is preschool; simple enough. But when Nicas use the word *"escuela"* (school), they are referring only to elementary school, also called *"primaria."* This covers first grade (ages 6–7) to sixth grade (ages 12–13). *"Secundaria"* begins with *"primer año"* ("first year," ages 12–14) and goes to *"quinto año"* ("fifth year," ages 16–17), which corresponds roughly to freshman through senior year in a U.S. high school, which itself is referred to as *"colegio"* or *"instituto."* Anything beyond that is *"la universidad."*

tour, and retaining quality teachers depends heavily on how well the administration treats them. Some generalities apply (as follow), but do your own research once you hit the ground to ensure that the school you choose meets not just your needs but also your children's. In addition to taking a standard school-sponsored tour of the grounds, seek out other expat parents on your own and ask about all your concerns. Note that most of these schools offer preschool and primary school classes in addition to high school grades.

The American School is overall the most popular and modern institution, not to mention the best funded. But it is also the most expensive of the international schools at about US$350 per month for tuition. This school's popularity also makes it harder to get enrolled, as there are limited seats each year (about a thousand total students from 39 nationalities).

The College Nicaraguayen Victor Hugo (the French school) provides a rigorous French and Spanish language education. American families whose children attend the school generally speak positively of the school and only point out that the French system requires more memorization than the American system does.

The "trilingual" German School is as rigorous as the American School, perhaps more so, and is the second favorite of most Managuan expats we surveyed. It offers preschool, kindergarten, primary, and secondary education and at last check had 640 students.

The Lincoln Academy is an Opus Dei Catholic school, and its curriculum reflects its strong religious foundation. The Notre Dame School is smaller and less expensive than the American School and offers an international baccalaureate that is based on advanced placement (AP) classes plus a standardized overall final exam that tests students in all subject matters studied.

St. Augustine Preparatory School is a private, co-ed, Catholic bilingual school. Beginning in 2001 with preschool to fourth grade, the school planned on adding a grade per year, offering your children "a school environment that reflects concretely and faithfully the Gospel of Jesus Christ and the teachings of the Catholic Church."

Outside of Managua

There are no bilingual international schools outside of Managua, though there are a couple of private school options in Granada used by expats. Maria Auxiliadora, which has both primary and secondary schools, was recommended by several Granada expat parents for its academic and extracurricular programs, but be sure to ask around for other options and recommendations. Maria Auxiliadora, like other private Catholic schools scattered around Granada and Carazo, has an ESL (English as a Second Language) program, but it is basic, so your children will be receiving their instruction primarily in Spanish should you choose this route. This could be an excellent opportunity; speaking about this challenge, one expat mother commented: "Learning completely in Spanish hasn't been a problem at all, but it's important that parents don't show any apprehensiveness in front of their kids. If the kids have the expectation that it's all going to work out, then it does. Anxious, squeamish parents transmit their fears onto their children and then they never learn Spanish. As long as the kids are well supported, it all works out in the wash."

Private and public schools must, by law, follow the same curriculum in Nicaragua. Public schools, however, because of a serious lack of funding and teachers who are paid a pittance to perform one of the most important jobs in the country, lag decades behind other school systems—even by Latin American standards. Note that while the international schools run on the American/European calendar (i.e., classes begin in September), Nicaraguan schools run on the Latin American calendar (classes begin in January).

HOMESCHOOLING AND DISTANCE-LEARNING PROGRAMS

Our brave, shrinking new world means your child can study online and get the same certificate as his or her classmates back home; a number of U.S. and Canadian "correspondence schools" specialize in this, and there are even accredited, home-based teachers who make a living offering their instruction online. If your move to Nicaragua is short-term (a couple of months to a couple of years), and you plan on putting your children back into school when they return to the United States, contact their current school or district to see if they can provide a curriculum or, at least, the educational standards used, so that your child remains up to speed. Individual schools and districts manage homeschoolers differently in terms of how much material and support they are willing to provide.

Alternatively, find a "distance-learning program" or "cyberschool." Do an Internet search on these terms and see what comes up, or begin with the web portals we've provided in the *Resources* section. You'll find thousands of resources—from complete packaged curricula provided by private schools (e.g., Calvert School and Laurel Springs) to "do it yourself" K–12 online programs, to all manner of guidebooks (the bible on the subject is *Home Learning Year by Year: How to Design a Homeschool Curriculum from Preschool through High School,* by Rebecca Rupp).

Parents who are already in academia themselves, or those who have the time, patience, and confidence, can teach their own children. Sometimes expats living abroad pitch in to form homeschooling cooperatives, in which they share in the education of each other's children. In fact, your very first move as a homeschooler should be to seek out like-minded parents in your community; chances are, in Nicaragua, you'll be pioneering such an effort, but it will be a lot less lonely an experience for your child.

UNIVERSITIES

One of only a few bilingual colleges in the country, Ave Maria College of the Americas is a Roman Catholic liberal arts school in San Marcos, Carazo, less than an hour from Managua. The setting is beautiful, the institution is well funded and modern, and standards for admission are high—as is tuition at nearly US$5,000 per semester for full-time students, plus another US$1,300 for room and board. Formerly administered by the University of Mobile (Alabama), the school was acquired in 1999 by Ave Maria of Michigan and offers a range of undergraduate and graduate degrees for about 450 students; scholarships are available, and, of course, there's "a strong commitment to moral values and the teachings of the Catholic Church."

Nicaragua's two biggest and oldest universities are the Universidad Autónoma Nacional de Nicaragua (UNAN) and the Universidad de Centroamerica (UCA). The former started in León before opening up a branch in Managua and then Estelí, while the latter is a Jesuit university with branches in every Central American capital. By American university standards both fall rather shy of the mark. If you find yourself in Managua and would like to take a course or two you are free to do so for about US$100 per semester, plus any number of bureaucratic fees and hassles.

Neither university offers English-language instruction because their clienteles are without exception young Nicas studying law, engineering, and business management, and many of those students are hoping to find scholarships *(becas)* to study elsewhere. Many Nicaraguan medical students receive decent training in Cuba, and others study in the United States or Mexico. The Managua branch of the UNAN has the strongest academic offering and the broadest course selection. However, realistically, for expats with university-age children, neither institution offers the education you'd probably like them to have. More than one female student has complained of their professors flirting with them between classes, and much of the coursework involves rote memorization rather than more practical problem-solving activities. There are many reasons to move to Central America to live, but the university system is not one of them.

OTHER STUDY OPPORTUNITIES

There are additional summer, semester, and extended internship academic and immersion opportunities in Nicaragua, several geared toward foreign high-school-aged teenagers. One is the "authentic full immersion high school experience" offered by the Nicaragua Summer Exchange Program of Spanish Through Leadership; it offers two four-week sessions in June and July that include homestays, academics, and activities in Granada. Cloud Forest Adventures offers a co-ed summer program for high school students, blending Spanish-language classes, ecological appreciation, and learning through outdoor adventure, community service, and cultural immersion (the three-week trip tuition of US$3,600 includes airfare). Additionally, some parents choose to simply enroll their children in one of the Spanish language schools listed above, which provides them with a more independent learning experience.

Other programs in Nicaragua include fieldwork at the remote La Suerte Biological Research Station on La Isla de Ometepe; semester programs like the one through School for International Training in Managua entitled "Revolution, Transformation, and Civil Society"; and alternative break trips like the university exchanges of Cultural Crossing in Bluefields.

Inevitably, learning-based trips begin to blend with those types of experiences offered by service organizations and pay-to-volunteer outfits; please see the *Volunteering* section of the *Employment* chapter and its associated listings in the *Resources* section.

HEALTH

The heat, humidity, and hygiene of a developing country in the tropics can lead to health concerns you never had to worry about back home. For better *and* worse, the vibrant richness of Nicaragua lacks the shiny white sterility many of us have come to expect from the 21st century. In general, there are more odors and organisms to deal with, but there are indeed ways to deal with them, and health-care facilities are not nearly as bad or archaic as you may think. In fact, most potential future residents of Central America list health concerns as their primary worry before arriving—but only a secondary worry once they've spent a few months there and realize they'll be all right. In the end, staying healthy in Nicaragua means being prepared and making smart choices.

Before you go, pick up Dirk G. Schroeder's *Staying Healthy in Asia, Africa, and Latin America,* an excellent resource and concise guide to preventative medicine in the developing world and small enough to fit in

© RANDALL WOOD

your pocket. Also be sure to consult the "Mexico and Central America" page of the United States Centers for Disease Control (CDC) website for up-to-date health recommendations and advice, or call its International Travelers Hotline (see *Health* in the *Resources* chapter). You can also contact the Nicaraguan Embassy in your country for more specific or up-to-date information, though embassies tend to err on the side of caution, so take their warnings with a grain of common sense.

Preventative Measures

Chief among the choices you make is what you decide to put in your mouth. Expect your digestive system to take some time getting accustomed to the new food and microorganisms in the Nicaraguan diet. During this time (and after), use common sense: Wash your hands with soap often. Eat food that is well cooked and hot when served. Avoid dairy products if you're not sure whether they are pasteurized; be wary of uncooked foods, including ceviche and salads. Know that pork carries the extra danger of trichinosis, not to mention that most country pigs are raised on a disgusting diet of garbage. Also, flies are notorious transmitters of food-borne illness; prevent flies from landing on your food, glass, or table setting. You'll notice Nicaraguans are meticulous about this, and you should be too.

INSURANCE

Whether visiting Nicaragua for two weeks or two years, you'll want some type of traveler or expatriate health insurance that carries medical evacuation or air ambulance coverage—not just lost luggage or canceled flight coverage (although many expat medical plans include these items as well). Nicaraguan medical care is wholly adequate for most basic treatment, but in the case of a serious accident, you'll want access to an advanced U.S. trauma center. Such plans are relatively inexpensive, especially when set up as purely catastrophic coverage. Chances are your current provider does not offer this type of coverage, but it's a good idea to ask your insurers if they know of any expatriate plan providers. Highly recommended is International Medical Group, which offers a range of short- and long-term expat plans. Because of the relatively low cost of medical care and pharmaceuticals, it is much cheaper and easier to pay out-of-pocket for routine treatment and medicine than it is to pay a higher premium.

VACCINATIONS

A certificate of vaccination against yellow fever for all travelers over one year of age and arriving from affected areas is *required*. Tetanus, typhoid, diphtheria, measles, mumps, rubella, and polio vaccines are recommended. Protection against hepatitis A and B is also suggested. Confirm these recommendations with your neighborhood travel specialist doctor.

Types of Health Care

PUBLIC VS. PRIVATE CARE

Says one Nicaraguan expat, "My basic recommendation for health care in Nicaragua is to never require it. There are just too many horror stories. Patient, heal thyself." Actually, the Nicaraguan public health system is decent for minor injuries, cuts, bruises, and gastrointestinal distress (parasites, diarrhea, and the like). In fact, once, when Randy visited the health clinic in Condega, Estelí, for stomach trouble he was surprised to be treated for free ("the government covers it," the doctor told him with a smile). But foreigners don't tend to use the public health-care system for much more than the basics, and certainly not for anything that involves surgery. Nicaragua's public hospitals, like most public health facilities in the developing world, are underfunded, understaffed, and lack modern equipment. They can deal with your broken arm but might not do so in a way that satisfies you completely or gives you the peace of mind that your break will set properly. (One Nicaraguan friend shared a hospital room with a teenager who'd broken a hip. They'd wrapped up both legs in a plaster cast with a solid rod that kept his legs apart as though he were sitting in a chair with his legs spread, then reclined him so both bent legs were up in the air. And that's the way he stayed for the next several weeks.)

HOSPITALS AND CLINICS

There are several private, modern hospitals in and around Managua. The two newest are the Hospital Vivian Pellas, a US$23 million facility seven kilometers (four miles) south of Managua founded by the nation's wealthiest family, and the Hospital de Managua in town. Both of them can take care of all kinds of routine medical needs for a fraction of the cost you are used to back home. Several other older and less-well-staffed hospitals remain in Managua, but none is as modern or as well-equipped as these two. Outside of Managua it's not as easy, so expect anything more serious than a broken arm to require a trip to the capital. Though there

DISABLED ACCESS

Few resources are available for wheelchair-friendly buildings and bathrooms, and things are not made easier by ruined sidewalks, rutted dirt roads, aggressive crowds, and open manholes. While Nicaraguans agree the disabled (who they call *descapacitados*) have equal rights, not much attempt is made to accommodate them. The foreign traveler with limited mobility will certainly struggle but will no doubt find compassion and ways to get by.

are many qualified medical professionals in Nicaragua who studied abroad in Mexico, Cuba, or the United States, there are also practicing doctors and medical staff that have less-than-adequate credentials. Use your best judgment. Public hospital doctors are underpaid and overworked. In all cases, hospitals and medical facilities typically expect immediate payment for services rendered, but their rates are ridiculously cheaper than back home, even for more serious procedures (appendectomy: US$800). Larger facilities accept credit cards and everyone else demands cash. Most cities also have private clinics that are more than happy to treat foreigners and well-off Nicas. Ask local expats or fancy hotels for recommendations.

Government-run health clinics, called *centros de salud,* exist in most towns throughout the country, usually near the central plaza. They are free—even to you—but often poorly supplied and inadequately staffed.

DENTISTS

Dental services are available in most towns, but take a look around at all the Nicaraguan gold teeth and gaps in the smiles to realize dentists may not always use the techniques or the materials you'd like. There are definitely numerous modern and well-trained options, however. In Managua, whether you need an emergency root canal or just a cleaning and checkup, we can vouch for the bilingual, professional services of Dr. Esteban Bendaña McEwan.

MEDICAL RECORDS

Think of Nicaragua's medical system as a cash-for-services industry, and it will become clear that doctors do not have any pretense of developing long-term care-giver relationships with you, and that you should therefore take it upon yourself to keep and manage your own medical records and the details of your medical history. Doing so will maximize the benefits doctors can provide to you when you need them. Start with a set of dental X-rays, a list of all your allergies, and a record of your shots. Translate the documents if you can, or pay someone to translate them on your behalf once you're settled into Nicaragua.

Pharmacies and Prescriptions

Pharmacies are plentiful throughout Nicaragua, existing in every city and town, often, as in Granada, clustered together on the same couple of blocks that include clinics and pathology labs. Many generic brands of modern medicines, produced in Mexico or El Salvador, are sold in Nicaragua. Because of a struggling economy and plenty of competition, some pharmacies may sell you medicine without a prescription, but it is always smart to play by the rules and either bring refill orders from home or see a doctor in Nicaragua.

BIRTH CONTROL

Condoms are cheap and easy to find. Any corner pharmacy will have them, even in small towns of just a few thousand people. A three-pack of prophylactics costs under US$2. Female travelers taking contraceptives should know the chemical name for what they use. Birth control pills (*pastillas anticonceptivas*) are easily obtained, even without prescription, in pharmacies in Managua and in larger cities like León, Granada, and Estelí. Other forms of birth control and sexual protection devices such as IUDs, dental dams, and diaphragms are neither used nor sold.

EYE CARE

Managua burgeons with eye clinics, optometrists, and well-stocked shelves of eyeglasses, and you can fill prescriptions for contact lenses as well. In all cases, things are more expensive than they were back home, so if you can bring an adequate supply for yourself you will be ahead of the game. Three pairs of contact lenses can cost US$80 in Managua, and a pair of glasses can easily cost several hundred dollars unless you choose a not-so-stylish frame. At any of these optometrists you can pick up saline solution and chemicals for your contact lenses, as well as at many pharmacies throughout the nation. Again, expect a 50 percent markup on everything.

Health Hazards

Health concerns in Nicaragua—and in most of the developing world, for that matter—fall into three broad categories: insects and animals, transmittable diseases, and environmental factors. In some cases they overlap, as in the case of malaria, which is transmitted by mosquito. Most problems are preventable if you learn how to take action and be aware of what makes living in the developing world different from living in the hyper-sanitary world of North America.

INSECTS AND ANIMALS

Welcome to the tropics, *amigo!* Invertebrates have been thriving here since way before the first human settlers, and they'll be here long after we're gone. What's more, to allow for air flow, most Nicaraguan architecture does not incorporate the idea of hermetically sealing out the environment. Nobody bats an eye at the various geckos, ant trails, thumb-size cockroaches, and other creepy-crawlies who commonly drop in to your home (sometimes quite literally) for a visit. Most are harmless, but watch out for the following.

Mosquitoes

Called *zancudos* by Nicaraguans, mosquitoes are most active during the rainy season (June–November) and in areas near stagnant water, like marshes, puddles, or rice fields. They are much more common in the lower, flatter regions of Nicaragua than they are in mountains, though even in the highlands, old tires, cans, and roadside puddles provide the necessary breeding habitat. The mosquito that carries malaria bites during the night and evening hours, and the dengue fever courier is active during the day, from dawn to dusk. They are both relatively simple to combat, and ensuring you don't get bitten is the best prophylaxis against disease—and carries far fewer side effects than malaria pills.

First and foremost, limit the amount of skin you expose—long sleeves, pants, and socks will do more to prevent bites than the strongest chemical repellent. Choose lodging accommodations with good screens, and if this is not possible, use a fan to blow airborne insects away from your body as you sleep. Avoid being outside or unprotected in the hour before sunset when mosquito activity is heaviest, and use a *mosquitero* (mosquito net) tucked underneath your mattress when you sleep. Hanging-type mosquito nets are available in Nicaragua, or you can purchase *tela de mosquitero* anywhere they sell fabric and have a mosquito net made by a seamstress.

SUN EXPOSURE

Nicaragua is located 12 degrees of latitude north of the equator, so the sun's rays strike the Earth's surface at a more direct angle than in northern countries. The result is that you will burn faster and sweat up to twice as much as you are used to. This means drinking at least twice as much water to replace the lost fluids. Try to imitate the locals, who do their best to stay out of the sun between 10 A.M. and 2 P.M. It's a great time to take a nap anyway. Use sunscreen of at least SPF 30, and wear a hat and pants. If you still manage to overdo it, treat sunburns with aloe gel or, better yet, find a fresh *sábila* (aloe) plant to break open and rub over your skin.

© RANDALL WOOD

Take it easy when it's hot outside.

Also, many pulperías sell *espirales* (mosquito coils), which burn slowly, releasing a mosquito-repelling smoke; they're cheap and convenient but full of chemicals, so don't breathe in too much smoke.

Spiders, Scorpions, and Snakes

Arachnophobes, beware! The spiders of Nicaragua are dark, hairy, and occasionally capable of devouring small birds. Don't worry, though; spiders do not aggressively seek out people, and do way more good than harm by eating things like Chagas bugs. If you'd rather the spiders didn't share your personal space, shake out your bedclothes before going to sleep and check your shoes before putting your feet in them.

Scorpions, or *alacránes,* are common in Nicaragua, especially in dark corners, near beaches, and in piles of wood. Nicaraguan scorpions look nasty—black and big—but their sting is no more harmful than that of a bee and is described by some as what a cigarette burn feels like. Your lips and tongue may feel a little numb, but the venom is nothing compared to that of their smaller, translucent cousins in Mexico. For people who are prone to anaphylactic shock, it can be a more serious or life-threatening experience. Be aware: In Nicaragua the Spanish word *escorpión* usually refers not to scorpions but to the harmless little gecko lizards (also called *perros zompopos,* "ant dogs") that scurry around walls devouring insects. And in spite of what your campesino friends might insist, those little geckos are neither malevolent nor deadly and would never, as you will often hear, intentionally try to kill you by urinating on you.

There are 15 species of poisonous snakes in Nicaragua, but your chance of seeing one is extremely rare, unless you're going deep into the bush. In that case, walk softly and carry a big machete.

Chagas Bugs

The Chagas bug *(Trypanosoma cruzi)* is a large, recognizable insect, also called the kissing bug, assassin bug, and cone-nose. In Spanish it's known as *chinche,* but this word is also used to describe many others of a whole class of beetlelike creatures. The Chagas bug bites its victim (usually on the face, close to the lips), sucks its fill of blood, and, for the coup de grâce, defecates on the newly created wound. Chagas bugs are present in Nicaragua, found mostly in poor campesino structures of crumbling adobe. Besides the downright insult of being bitten, sucked, and pooped on, the Chagas bug's biggest menace is the disease it carries, which manifests itself in 2 percent of its victims. The first symptoms include swollen glands and a fever that appear 1–2 weeks after the bite. The disease then goes into a 5- to 30-year remission phase. If and when it reappears, Chagas' disease causes the lining of the heart to swell, sometimes resulting in death. Unfortunately there is no cure for Chagas' disease. The best way to avoid being bitten by Chagas bugs is to sleep under a mosquito net, particularly when staying in old adobe buildings.

TRANSMITTABLE DISEASES
Diarrhea and Dysentery

Everyone's body reacts differently to the changes in diet, schedule, and stress that go along with traveling, and many visitors to Nicaragua stay entirely regular throughout their trip. Some don't. Diarrhea is one symptom of amoebic (parasitic) and bacillic (bacterial) dysentery, both caused by some form of fecal-oral contamination. Often accompanied by nausea, vomiting, and a mild fever, dysentery is easily confused with other diseases, so don't try to self-diagnose. Stool sample examinations *(examenes de heces)* can be performed at most clinics and hospitals and are your first step to getting better (cost is US$2–8). Bacillic dysentery is treatable with antibiotics; amoebic is treated with one of a variety of drugs that kill off all the flora in your intestinal tract. Of these, Flagyl is the best known, but other non-FDA approved treatments like Tinedazol are commonly available, cheap, and effective. Do not drink alcohol with these drugs, but do eat something like yogurt or acidophilus pills to refoliate your tummy.

Generally, simple cases of diarrhea in the absence of other symptoms are nothing more serious than "traveler's diarrhea." If you do get it, your best bet is to let it pass naturally. Diarrhea is your body's way of flushing out the bad stuff, so constipating medicines like Imodium-AD are not recommended, as they keep the bacteria (or whatever is causing your intestinal distress) within your system. Most importantly, drink water! Not replacing the fluids and electrolytes you are losing will make you feel much worse than you need to. If the diarrhea persists for more than 48 hours, is bloody, or is accompanied by a fever, see a health professional immediately.

Malaria

Though the risk of malaria is higher in rural areas, especially those alongside rivers or marshes, infected mosquitoes breed anywhere stagnant pools of water are found, including urban settings. Weekly prophylaxis of chloroquine or an equivalent is recommended, and the CDC specifically recommends that travelers to Nicaragua use Aralen brand pills (500 mg for adults). Begin taking the pills two weeks before you arrive and continue taking them four weeks after leaving the country. A small percentage of people have negative reactions to chloroquine, including nightmares, rashes, or hair loss. Alternative treatments are available, but the best method of all is to not get bitten (see the *Mosquitoes* section).

Malaria works by setting up shop in your liver and blasting you with attacks of fever, headaches, chills, and fatigue. The onslaughts occur on a 24-hour-sick, 24-hour-better cycle. If you observe this cycle, seek medical attention. If your blood tests positive for malaria, you'll most likely be prescribed a huge dose of chloroquine that will kill the bug.

Dengue Fever

Dengue, or "bone-breaking," fever is occasionally present in parts of Nicaragua and is a traveler's nightmare. The symptoms may include any or all of the following: sudden high fever, severe headache (think nails in the back of your eyes), muscle and back pain, nausea or vomiting, and a full-body skin rash, which may appear 3–4 days after the onset of the fever. Although the initial pain and fever may only last a few days, you may be out of commission for up to several weeks, possibly bedridden, depressed, and too weak to move. There is no vaccine, but dengue's effects can be successfully minimized with plenty of rest, Tylenol (for the fever and aches), and as much water and *suero oral* (rehydration salts) as you can stomach. Dengue itself is undetectable in a blood test, but a low platelet *(plaquetas)* count indicates its presence. If you believe you have dengue, get a blood test as soon as possible to make sure it's not the rare hemorrhagic variety, which can be fatal if untreated.

AIDS

Although large numbers of HIV infections have not yet appeared in Nicaragua, especially compared to other Central American countries, health organizations claim that geography, as well as cultural, political, and social factors, will soon contribute to an AIDS explosion in Nicaragua. Currently there are about 1,500 HIV-positive cases registered with MINSA (the Government Health Ministry), but one World Bank official estimates actual cases at 8,000. Exacerbating the spread of AIDS (in Spanish, "La SIDA") is the promiscuous behavior of many married males, an active sex-worker trade, less than ideal condom-using habits, and growing drug trouble. AIDS is most prevalent in urban populations, mainly Managua and Chinandega, and is primarily transmitted sexually, not through needles or contaminated blood.

That said, blood transfusions are not recommended. Travelers should avoid sexual contact with persons whose HIV status is unknown. If you intend to be sexually active, use a fresh latex condom for every sexual act and every orifice. Condoms are inexpensive and readily available in just about any local pharmacy. In Spanish, a condom is called *condón,* or *preservativo.*

Other Transmittable Diseases

Cholera is present in Nicaragua, with occasional outbreaks, especially in rural areas with contaminated water supplies. Vaccines are not required because they offer incomplete protection. You are better off watching what you put in your mouth. In case you contract cholera (the symptoms are profuse diarrhea the color of rice water accompanied by sharp intestinal cramps, vomiting, and body weakness), see a doctor immediately and drink your *suero*. Cholera kills—by dehydrating you.

Leptospirosis is caused by a bacteria found in water contaminated with the urine of infected animals, especially rodents. Symptoms include high fever and headache, chills, muscle aches, vomiting, and possibly jaundice. Humans become infected through contact with infected food, water, or soil. It is not known to spread from person to person and can be treated with antibiotics in its early stages.

Hepatitis B also lurks in Nicaragua. Avoid contact with bodily fluids or bodily waste. Get vaccinated if you anticipate close contact with the local population or plan to reside in Nicaragua for an extended period of time.

Most towns in Nicaragua, even rural ones, conduct a yearly rabies vaccination campaign for dogs, but you should still be careful. Get a rabies vaccination if you intend to spend a long time in Nicaragua. Should you be bitten, immediately cleanse the wound with lots of soap and get prompt medical attention.

Tuberculosis is spread by sneezing or coughing, and the infected person may not know he or she is a carrier. If you are planning to spend more than four weeks in Nicaragua (or plan on spending time in a Nicaraguan jail), consider having a tuberculin skin test performed before and after visiting. Tuberculosis is a serious and possibly fatal disease but can be treated with several medications.

ENVIRONMENTAL FACTORS
Air Quality

Windswept and agricultural Nicaragua is fortunate not to have the widespread air pollution problems prevalent in other developing (and developed) countries, though when farmers burn their fields during the dry season, the atmosphere can get that, um, not-so-fresh feeling. Of more concern are micro-environment air issues, such as the burning pile of plastic and rubber garbage outside your window—and we won't even get into noise pollution. Also, be aware that some agricultural areas (especially the Sébaco Valley and Chinandega) are subject to aerial bombardments of pesticides, so watch out for small, low-flying aircraft.

Solid Waste

This is certainly one of Nicaraguan's biggest environmental challenges. In addition to large-scale waste disposal and recycling shortfalls, expect an enormous amount of roadside trash, filth, and open gray-water sewage canals. Creeks and rivers that flow through any city are often foul-smelling cesspits that only get flushed in the rainy season.

Water Quality

While most Nicaraguan municipal water systems are adequately treated and probably safe, purified, bottled water is widely available. If you'd rather not contribute to the growing solid waste problem in Nicaragua, bring a single reusable plastic water bottle, which you can refill from the five-gallon purified water dispensers found in most hotel lobbies and restaurants. If you're here for the long term, you'll want one of those five-gallon jugs of your own, or consider a purifier for your tap. You'll pay a small deposit for each jug, and also must buy some kind of dispenser, but you'll save loads of money in the long run compared to buying liter bottles (and, of course, be doing the environment a big favor).

If you'll be spending time in rural Nicaragua, consider a small water filter for camping. Alternately, six drops of liquid iodine (or three of bleach) will kill everything that needs to be killed in a liter of water, good if you're in a pinch but not something you'll find yourself practicing on a daily basis.

Standard precautions also include avoiding ice cubes unless you're confident they were made with boiled or purified water. Canned and bottled drinks without ice, including beer, are safe, but should never be used as a substitute for water when trying to stay hydrated.

Smoking

Nowhere is smoking forbidden in Nicaragua, though it's not customary for people to smoke in public buildings, which seems to be more of a customary courtesy than a law. Nicaragua is by no means as smoky as some countries (like Indonesia, or Italy before 2005), but if smoke bothers you know that you are unlikely to find restaurants where smoking is prohibited, or even restaurants that distinguish between smoking and nonsmoking sections. On the other hand, if you are a smoker, you will find a handy selection of local-tobacco, cheap cigarettes for your consumption. Seasoned expats claim refraining from smoking makes their immune systems more resilient to dehydration and stomach troubles.

Safety and Crime

Believe it or not, Nicaragua is, for the moment, considered one of the safest countries in all of Central America. The main reason is that Nicaragua has been more-or-less successful at preventing the gang violence that has plagued its northern neighbors Honduras, El Salvador, and Guatemala. Petty crimes are your biggest concern, and inevitably, as the number of foreign visitors rises, they are becoming increasingly familiar in the dark corners (or big crowds) of popular tourist areas.

Bigger cities, like Estelí and Chinandega, have their shady neighborhoods to avoid, and, because of its size and sprawl, Managua is the most dangerous of Nicaraguan cities. Still, it's a pretty simple task to stay out of the unsafe barrios. Worsening poverty, desperation, and unemployment in the 1990s have led to a surge in gang membership and violence in the poorer neighborhoods, and drug use—including crack—is also on the rise. Still, by not entering unknown areas, not walking at night, and sticking with other people, you can reduce the chances of anything bad happening.

In general, the countryside of Nicaragua is peaceful and safe. Until a few years ago, the one exception was El Triangulo Minero, a mountainous northeastern region around the mining towns of La Rosita, Bonanza, and Siuna. The area was home to a loose band of armed ex-soldiers infatuated with the bandit lifestyle and calling themselves "FUAC" (Frente Unido Andrés Castro). Today, however, most of their members and leaders have been hunted down by the army or have given up the chase and gone back to farming and ranching.

For up-to-date information, check the latest U.S. State Department reports or the website of your embassy, though keep in mind that these institutions err on the side of caution.

Crime Prevention

Common sense should prevail. Avoid traveling alone at night or while intoxicated, and pay the extra dollar or two for a cab instead of walking. Women should not take cabs when the driver has a friend riding up front.

Pickpocketing (or hat/watch/bag snatching) occurs occasionally in crowded places or buses, but again, this is a situation that can usually be avoided by reducing your desirability as a target and paying attention. Try to avoid urban buses in Managua and, whenever possible (but especially when visiting the markets) avoid wearing flashy jewelry, watches, or

WOMEN'S CONCERNS

In Nicaragua, as in all of Latin America, women are both adored and harassed to their wits' end. Catcalls and whistles are as common as palm trees, often accompanied by an *"Adios, amorrrr,"* or a sleazy, *"Tss-tss!"* The perpetrators range from barely mustachioed *machistas*-in-training to washed-up old lechers, and include men of all ages in between. It will either comfort or offend you to know that Nicaraguan women are forced to endure the same treatment every day, and noting how they react will help you figure out how to deal. Most Nicaraguan women ignore the comments and blown kisses entirely, while some act flattered and smile confidently as they walk by. Acknowledging the comment further is probably ill-advised, as it will only feed the fire.

Physical harassment, assault, and rape are much less common in Nicaragua than elsewhere in Central America, but certainly not unheard of, especially when alcohol is involved. Take the same precautions you would anywhere else to avoid dangerous situations.

As for feminine hygiene products, tampons can be difficult to find, as almost all Nicaraguan women use pads *(toallas sanitarias)*. Most pharmacies and *pulperías* carry pads, usually referred to by the brand name "Kotex" regardless of the actual brand. Nicaraguan women favor pads over tampons due to custom as well as social stigma, as tampons are sometimes associated with sexually active or aggressive women.

sunglasses. Keep your cash divided up and hidden in a money belt, sock, bra, or underwear.

When you settle into Nicaragua make it a priority to give your embassy a call and register with the staff as an expat. That allows them to keep track of you in case of emergencies, provide warnings when appropriate, and just be helpful when necessary (they can also help you participate in elections back home, if you desire). Many embassies use a warden system for communicating with their citizenry; when you register with the embassy they will tell you who your local warden is and you will be encouraged to make contact with that person and then use him or her as your main point of contact in case of incidents—including theft or break-ins—and emergencies, including natural disasters.

Illegal Drugs

Regrettably, Nicaragua is part of the underground highway that transports cocaine and other illegal drugs from South America to North America; as such, it is under a lot of pressure from the United States to crack down on trafficking. Drug-related crime is rapidly increasing on the Atlantic coast, particularly in Bluefields and Puerto Cabezas. It goes without saying that all foreign travelers in Nicaragua are subject to local possession laws, which include stiff fines and prison sentences of up to 30 years. Canine and bag searches at airports, docks along the Atlantic coast, and at the Honduran and Costa Rican border crossings are the norm, not the exception.

Marijuana *(cannabis sativa)* is an herb that grows naturally and quite well in the soils and climate of Nicaragua, and is known as *"la mota"* or *"el monte."* Marijuana prohibition is alive and well in Nicaragua, despite regular (though discreet) use of the plant throughout the population, especially among Nica surfer and musician crowds. The anti-ganja policy allows harsh penalties for possession of even tiny quantities of cannabis, for both nationals and tourists alike. Know also that if anyone offers you some *mota* or *coca* (cocaine) it may be a simple invitation to get high, or it may be that a hustler or stool pigeon is about to rip you off and/or get you arrested. Use the same common sense you would anywhere else in the world.

Prostitution

Though illegal, *puterías* (houses of prostitution), thinly disguised as "beauty salons" or "massage parlors," operate with virtual impunity, and most Managua strip clubs have a bank of rooms behind the stage, some with an actual cashier stationed at the door. Then there are the commercial sex workers on Carretera Masaya, and the nation's numerous auto-hotels, which rent rooms by the hour. The situation is nowhere near as developed as the sex tourism industries in places like Thailand and Costa Rica, but it is undeniable that foreigners have contributed in no small way to Nicaragua's sex economy. Travelers considering indulging should think seriously about the social impacts that result from perpetuating this institution, and should start by reading the *AIDS* section above.

Police

With few exceptions, in Nicaragua the police force is essentially your friend. While police corruption does exist—Nicaraguan policemen earn a pitiful US$55–60 per month, almost a subsistence salary—the Nicaraguan police force is notably more honest and helpful than are the forces of other Central American nations. They are, however, rather unequipped. Expect them to help you to the best of their limited ability.

Theft

If you are the victim of a crime, report it to the local police department immediately (dial 118). Remember, if you've insured any of your possessions,

DAILY LIFE

© RANDALL WOOD

The Nicaraguan police force is on your side.

you won't be reimbursed without a copy of the official police report. Nicaraguan police have good intentions but few resources, lacking even gasoline for the few patrol cars or motorcycles they have—don't be surprised if you are asked to help fill up a vehicle with gas. This is not uncommon. Travelers are often shocked to find that the police occasionally do recover stolen merchandise. In fact, one friend of ours got an official police escort to the Mercado Oriental in Managua, where they found much of his stolen property for sale already.

Emergencies

Important phone numbers: police, 118; firefighters, 115 and 120; and Red Cross, 128. These numbers are universal through the nation. But don't expect calling one of them to lead to an ambulance racing through the city streets to carry you away to the hospital. You are very much obligated to prepare for contingencies on your own. As you investigate neighborhoods and cities where you'd like to live, ask the other expats as well as the locals what they would do in case of an emergency. You'll find with few exceptions they would expect to have to find a way to get themselves to the hospital, which means a friend who can drive. Make sure your social network is ample enough to cover you in cases where you need help. Also know your insurance's medical evacuation policy and emergency plans—this usually involves a 24-hour number to call—and carry your policy number on you at all times.

EMPLOYMENT

Nicaragua's status as one of the poorest countries in the hemisphere, where staggering unemployment levels are the norm, may give you pause when considering how you'll make a living there. But for skilled, patient, and creative individuals, there is considerable opportunity in Nicaragua's growing economy, especially in the fields of small business and nongovernmental organization (NGO) work where your commitment and knowledge can make a difference and help improve the situation.

When considering employment in Nicaragua, first be sure that by accepting a position, you are not taking a job away from a Nicaraguan who may need it more than you (e.g., he needs the salary to support his extended family and sick grandmother while you are just looking for a brief adventurous interlude). Usually this is not an issue, but it's an important thing to watch out for. There are far more young, educated Nicaraguans than you may realize and they should, in all fairness, have first dibs on the local job market (most Nicas, because of stringent visa

© JOSHUA BERMAN

requirements and other reasons, are unable to travel the world in search of employment).

That said, there is no understating the importance of the foreign entrepreneur who simultaneously creates employment for him- or herself and generates positions for Nicaraguans. For some, this may mean opening up a hotel, bar, or other service for the increasing number of foreign tourists in Nicaragua. For others it means setting up an import or export business; the U.S. Embassy reports a growing Nicaraguan market for foreign goods, including vehicles, auto parts, construction materials, computer and telecommunication equipment, and agricultural, food processing, and refrigeration equipment. Find a niche and make your mark.

The Job Search

Sectors where your managerial skills may be in demand include service industries like hotels, restaurants, and bars, which are experiencing significant corporate investment from all kinds of foreign chains and franchises, especially in and around Managua. Another important sector is education: Nicaragua is home to a handful of international schools, which sometimes hire accredited, experienced foreign teachers. Salaries are often commensurate to those back home, making this an entirely viable option, but acceptance standards are high. Or, teaching at a Nicaraguan school or university, on a Nicaraguan salary, may suit you if you have few material needs and enjoy seeing how the underprivileged get their education.

Working for your government's foreign mission in Nicaragua is another option, though often extremely competitive, and hiring is usually done through your native country's foreign service office. However, if you meet the right people in Managua and watch the classifieds, you may be able to find "local hire" positions; pay and benefits are minimal but enough to get by and, of course, a good foot in the door. In addition, your government's embassy or local aid office sometimes contracts work out to private firms, creating yet another possibility.

JOB-HUNTING TIPS

When in Nicaragua, make like Nicaraguans and dress the part (see *Customs and Etiquette* in the *People and Culture* chapter); this means clean, pressed clothes and a close-cropped appearance—unless of course, you're looking for a position on the Nicaraguan pro surf circuit, where shaggy is in and board shorts are more important than the boardroom. Otherwise, take your job hunt as seriously as you would back home. After you've gotten that shave and a haircut, make sure your résumé is in order and, if appropriate, have it translated into Spanish. Bring copies of any official paperwork, including Spanish-language proficiency, relevant awards, certifications, and diplomas. Many overseas employers will want to be assured of your "emotional maturity" so that they know you can handle the unique pressures of culture shock and living in the tropics. Reference letters attesting to your abilities may help with this, especially on impressive-looking letterhead stationery—the more stamps, seals, and signatures, the better.

WHERE TO LOOK

Like anywhere else, networking is the name of the game, so keep careful track of the people you meet and let it be known you're interested in being useful. Start by making friends in local expat circles, and by making good first impressions (foreigners who've been in town awhile are sure to have local contacts, but they'll be hesitant to share them with any old sloppy drunk, fresh off the flight from Houston). Popular restaurant, bar, and café hangouts sometimes have active bulletin boards where you can keep an eye out for Help Wanted signs and post your own Job Wanted message as well. This may sound old-fashioned, but foreign communities are still small enough throughout Nicaragua to make it totally viable.

Self-Employment

FREELANCING

Today's wired world is one where the independent writer, designer, stock analyst, trader, or web consultant can make a full-time living from anywhere in the world. Throughout Central America, it is increasingly common to see cybercafes-cum-offices filled with sun-tanned foreigners doing more than just checking their email. A two-week project that pays US$1,200 will get you nowhere fast in New York City, but in Nicaragua it can put you on easy street for three months or more, during which time you can generate even more work for yourself. The trick is not being distracted by all those people whooping it up around you every day—but how can you blame them? After all, they only get two weeks of vacation a year to visit paradise, while you're there year-round. Actually, it's easy enough to avoid the party scene, either by securing a fast Internet connection in your home or by choosing to live off the beaten path, in the countryside or in some little-visited northern city like Estelí or Matagalpa.

NOT FOR THE FAINT OF HEART: DOING BUSINESS IN NICARAGUA

We asked a number of expats, "What is the biggest challenge of running a business in Nicaragua?" in regard to the hotels, bars, tour companies, and development projects that they manage. These are a few of their responses:

"Succeeding. Maintaining patience. Not expecting things to go in a straight line."

"The disorganization of every institution in the country, public or private. You name it, they all screw up, a few try to screw you over. It would drive you nuts if it wasn't downright funny sometimes."

"Getting qualified personnel, getting started up (very stable market, but hard to enter from scratch), getting through the red tape, having lots and lots of patience, not coming on too strong and not getting carried away by innate Western ideas and procedures."

"Remembering what day it is! We love doing business in Nicaragua."

"Not being able to be in two places at once. Finding trustworthy help and being gruff or demanding when it may not come naturally. Also, asking opinions and not getting them: Often I will ask a worker if he prefers one task over another and he will just say 'whatever you say, boss,' when honestly I want to cater to his likes or dislikes. It almost seems like it is disrespectful to express your opinion to your *jefe*."

"Having to forget every rule that applies in the rest of the world and start new."

"Getting past the good intentions of companies or workers providing services to you and receiving a concrete answer on when the product will be delivered and when the job will get done. Also, receiving proposals from our providers who can be slow with a response and work on 'seeing is believing,' so after the business was up and running we were finally sent a proposal by certain providers who missed out on an opportunity."

"Red tape, bureaucracy, thieving and bribery, keeping records by hand, *in writing* (i.e., no computer records allowed), lack of a real tourism board, and ridiculous rules that seem to be made up as they go along."

"Logistics, connectivity, and adjusting to 'Nica time.'"

"The biggest challenge in running the project has been organization and communication. It is tough enough to merely get groups of people together in the same place and at the same time, let alone actually organize and make something happen. Patience and a good sense of humor have been key."

"We pay lots of taxes and the bureaucracy is frustrating."

"Finding quality workers whose skill level matches their desire level and accepting that it takes a week to do what you can do in one day in *gringolandia*."

"It is that if there is the slightest hiccup anywhere in the country (dramatic Nica politics, mudslides, plagues of rats, volcanic eruptions, student or worker strikes with burning tires and buses in the street, etc.), tourists don't come and locals stop spending money. Being in business here is not for the faint of heart. Luckily, I have a very strong ticker."

STARTING A BUSINESS

Starting a business in Nicaragua requires a basic sense of the market, an appetite for risk, and some sort of financial backing. More importantly, it requires the patience and ability to deal with bureaucracy, paperwork, and the unexpected. If you fit these requirements, the Nicaraguan economy is rife with opportunities to fill gaps left unmet by current marketplace participants. So instead of complaining that there's no video store in town, set your mind to developing a small business and prepare to set up shop. Sorry you can't find sourdough bread, a decent cappuccino, or footwear any bigger than an American size 8? You have the opportunity to do something about it.

Red Tape

In most cases, you'll begin by registering your business with Nicaragua's Ministry of Development, Industry, and Commerce (Ministerio de Fomento Industria y Comercio, or MIFIC) as a corporation, or "Sociedad Anónima" ("S.A." will follow your business name, just like "Inc." in English). Be prepared for lots of paperwork and ridiculous registration and notary fees, despite the fact that MIFIC has made considerable efforts to streamline the process. ProNicaragua, a private-public organization set up in 2002 to assist foreign investors, reports the total costs for registering a corporation at about US$2,300 and the required time at 2–3 weeks. This is a huge improvement for a process that used to take six months or more.

One of the reasons for the improvement is the relatively recent Ventanilla Unica de Inversiones, which MIFIC translates into English as your "one-stop shop" for business registration. The Ventanilla Unica is located within the MIFIC office in Managua, where representatives from all the players in the process are on hand to take your money—er, help you through the process. They include: MIFIC, the Supreme Court (Corte Suprema de Justicia), the Office of the Mayor of Managua (Alcaldía de Managua), and the Directorate General of Taxes (Dirección General de Ingresos). Aside from the convenience of not having to race around Managua to all these different offices, the goal is greater coordination between the agencies involved, but this is still being ironed out, as are a few other details. MIFIC reports it is looking into online registration of businesses, but we'll believe this when we see it. In the meantime, you can download a 15-page PDF file entitled *Guia Para Inicio de Operaciones,* a getting-started guide that is rife with long checklists and flow charts describing what lies ahead.

Investment Incentive Law 306

In an effort to step up foreign investment, the Nicaraguan government passed Investment Incentive Law 306, excluding some new tourism-related businesses from income and real estate taxes for up to 10 years and allowing duty-free import of material for your business. The law takes the form of a 38-page decree, originally passed in 1999 and amended in 2003, and is primarily targeted at big-time investments of more than US$50,000, although in 2005 the requirements for hotels and restaurants were eased significantly. A number of expats with whom we spoke decided not to apply for 306 because of concerns about paperwork and bureaucracy (or because their investment was too small to qualify), but those who have gone through the process of applying have reported they are quite happy with the benefits they received through the program.

"Tourist activities" covered by Law 306 include the hotel industry; private property investment in protected areas (national parks and historic towns); travel agencies and tour operators; airline services; food, drinks, and entertainment businesses; infrastructure improvement (roads, telecommunications, docks, etc.); Nicaraguan handicrafts production; vehicle rental (boat service or car rental); and last but not least, motion picture production (provided that the Nicaraguan government deems the movie you are filming will attract tourists).

For the full text of Law 306, and to begin the necessary application process, contact the Head of Investment (Responsable de Inversiones) at INTUR in Managua, or obtain the snappy brochure and English translation of the law from ProNicaragua.

Workers' Rights and Labor Laws

Before accepting a job or hiring an employee, take the time to research current Nicaraguan labor laws. The Labor Code that was written into the 1987 constitution was last updated in 1996.

Labor law stipulates an 8-hour workday and sets a legal workweek maximum of 48 hours, with one day of rest. The Labor Code also mandates quite generous medical (including maternity) leave and vacation provisions, and upon termination, the employer must pay a month's salary for each year worked, up to five months' salary. Also, at year-end, employers must pay a bonus of an extra month's salary.

The fact that labor laws are lightly enforced in Nicaragua and that workers are often completely uneducated about their rights should be seen as an opportunity for foreign employers to set a positive example in the way they treat their workers—not as the chance for further abuse.

MINIMUM WAGE

The last minimum wage increase took effect in 1997, voted into place by the National Assembly. The actual amount varies from sector to sector, with construction workers guaranteed the highest salary (about US$100 per month), apparel manufacturers receiving about half that, and agricultural workers receiving the lowest rate (less than US$40 per month). However, like other labor laws, minimum wage is rarely enforced throughout Nicaragua, especially with jobs that require extended hours, like live-in maids, security guards, and agricultural workers.

Working for a Nonprofit

One meaningful—and challenging—way to keep busy is by volunteering for or, occasionally, finding a paid position with an international aid outfit of a local NGO (nongovernmental organization—in Spanish *ONG*, pronounced *"oh-enney-hey"*). Making such a commitment guarantees that you'll have more direct and meaningful contact with Nicaraguans than, say, sitting in a tourist bar all day. Some basic Spanish is required, and usually there's a minimum time commitment of at least several weeks.

VOLUNTEERING

If you're willing to work for free, there are enough volunteer opportunities in Nicaragua to fill a lifetime. We've provided a number of established volunteer opportunities in the *Resources* section, but for the independent foreigner with an open mind, technical skills, conversational Spanish, and lots of patience, setting up your own volunteer experience is sometimes a possibility. Some organizations will gladly accept your help, usually for a minimum of two weeks, and a few may be able to offer room and board (though if staying with a family, you should always offer to pay for expenses). Be very clear (with yourself and with the NGO) about what it is you are actually offering. Volunteers with no technical knowledge, poor language skills, and lack of cultural sensitivity are often more hindrance than help to an underfunded, overworked grassroots organization; your disruption of an ongoing project and established routine may not be the worth the warm-fuzzy feelings and photo-ops you stand to gain from the experience. If setting up something on your own, be sensitive to the NGO's

HELPING OUT: HAZARDS AND HIGH POINTS

When faced with the vivid, shocking images of poverty that are as much a part of the Nicaraguan landscape as lakes and volcanoes, foreigners unaccustomed to such realities often experience a knee-jerk response of immediately wanting to *give*. This healthy, human reaction is unquestionably a good thing, but when done in a purely material and impulsive way, it can have quite unintended consequences. The creation of dependency and paternalistic inequality are chief among these, and can occur on any number of levels, from the individual (showering cash, clothes, and candy on every underprivileged person you meet) to the international (dumping billions of dollars of aid on every poor government with no accountability).

Though cold, hard cash is always needed, there are other vitally important things to give as well. They include your time, attention, skills, knowledge, and, most importantly, your compassion. You can, for example, toss a few coins to a ragged child, providing him with an income for another jar of glue to get stoned on, plus a ready incentive to stay on the streets; or you can spend two hours a day for a couple of weeks playing games with the same child by volunteering at a center set up for that purpose, where children are given food and classes in a safe, drug-free space. Likewise, you can descend on a poverty-stricken village and, unasked, build a whole street of new homes, or you can take the time to make friends in the same community, listen carefully to their needs, and realize that they are wholly content with their accommodations but what

long-term vision, and be aware of any religious or political affiliations it may be pushing on the side.

It is a much better idea, especially if your experience volunteering overseas is limited, to sign up with an organization that has an established program for placing foreign volunteers. Many Spanish language schools incorporate community service and homestays into their curriculum. There are also numerous volunteer programs in Granada, San Juan del Sur, and other parts of Nicaragua where you can get your feet wet in the NGO world, work on your Spanish, and learn more about other opportunities. Most importantly, you'll meet other expats, each with their own stories of how they got involved in community development work, usually involving some unplanned, opportunity-based chain of events with a steep learning curve of trial and error as well—giving you the opportunity to learn from their mistakes.

Pay-to-Volunteer Program

Another option is to sign up with an organization that specializes in placing both short- and long-term volunteers in Nicaraguan communities,

they really need are small-loan opportunities, so that they can start their own businesses.

Sustainable solutions take time. A long time. Even Peace Corps Volunteers with two full years at their disposal have trouble making lasting, tangible changes. An expat who settles down for a while, who becomes an active member of his or her new community, has an extraordinary opportunity to help. Many expats have done just this, and tapping into their existing projects, networks of like-minded friends, and the *confianza,* or trust, that they have built in their communities will give you a huge head start. So will linking up with compassionate, energetic Nicaraguans who have devoted their lives to social justice and community development work.

Of course, donating money and material goods is extremely important and we do not mean that you shouldn't help out in this way; just be sure that you are giving to a project with long-term visions whose ultimate aim is for its recipients to take control and help themselves.

One final set of caveats: If you would like to donate clothing, be sure that it is appropriate to Nicaragua's tropical climate and that the condition of the items is something you yourself would accept (i.e., no missing buttons or zippers, no rips or tears). If you would like to give school supplies, you'll accomplish far more good by purchasing them in Nicaragua at a family-run corner store than you will by lining the corporate coffers of some mega-box-store back home. Finally, if you'd like to donate books, be sure they are in Spanish.

finding them housing and work projects, and providing basic medical and administrative support to volunteers. For many of these organizations, you'll actually pay a tuition to cover the overhead costs, which is often not much more than the expense of doing it on your own. For your money, you'll often get pre-trip orientation materials, some language and technical training, arranged and safe accommodations, and clear expectations of the project. Some work exclusively with university students in the form of alternative breaks or semester programs; others are geared toward graduates and adults; still others toward skilled professionals. Always contact former participants as part of your research before committing to such an organization, and make sure your work project and living conditions are well defined.

Peace Brigades

Short-term service trips, points out Phoebe Haupt, a longtime trip leader on the Nicaraguan Atlantic coast, are perhaps more useful in opening the eyes of the participant to the realities of the developing world than in getting much work done. Given the short time frame of service trips, it's hard to get to know the dynamics of the community in which you're working, and working with the already-empowered tends to reinforce them. Nevertheless, joining a short-term service trip is a great way to experience a place like Nicaragua at very little impact to your life back home. If you are intent on heading to Nicaragua to make a difference, start out with something a little longer term than a short-term service trip.

"Learning tourism" often consists of some hybrid of organized educational and pay-to-volunteer trips (some with a recreation element thrown in for good measure). Numerous nonprofit solidarity organizations (most based in the United States and Canada) offer short-term educational tours throughout Nicaragua. Most explore a specific topic, such as fair trade coffee production, women's empowerment, labor rights, or environmental issues. There are also construction/housing projects, handicraft production, and potable water projects. Signing up for these kinds of trips may cost more than traveling and volunteering independently, but the unique experience and access is often well worth the money. Consider this option either as a one-of-a-kind introduction to Nicaragua or, after you've lived there awhile, as a way to explore a side of the country that you simply won't find on a standard activity-based tour. Such trips are offered by universities, Sister City associations, church groups, labor rights and solidarity groups, and many other NGOs. We've listed a few of these groups in our *Resources* section, but the best overall resource is an organization called Transitions Abroad, which, in addition to its practical website, publishes a monthly magazine and numerous books on working, studying, and volunteering abroad.

The U.S. Peace Corps

A number of developed nations sponsor extremely intensive, relatively long-term, overseas volunteer opportunities for their citizens, including Canada and Britain's Volunteer Services Overseas (VSO) and Ireland's APSO. None, however, are as well established, as large, or as well funded as the United States Peace Corps, which maintains a strong presence in Nicaragua. The Peace Corps (El Cuerpo de Paz) is a U.S. government program created by John F. Kennedy in 1961. Its original goal was to improve the image of the United States in the third world (and thus decrease the temptation for the world's poor to turn to Communism) by sending mostly young, idealistic volunteers deep into the countryside of developing countries. Today, more than 165,000 Americans have served as Peace Corps Volunteers (PCVs) worldwide, and there are currently more than 7,000 volunteers serving in 90 countries around the world. If an applicant (U.S. citizens only) is of-

© JOSHUA BERMAN

Peace Corps volunteers are found in the country's most remote corners, where they live for two years.

fered an invitation to serve at the end of the Peace Corps' lengthy application process, he or she receives an intensive three-month training in the host country's language and culture, as well as in technical aspects of the particular assignment, followed by a two-year tour, during which a barebones living allowance is received.

The first Peace Corps Volunteers arrived in Nicaragua in 1969. PC-Nica took a hiatus during Sandinista control and was invited back in 1991. About 160 volunteers are currently serving in Nicaragua, situated in some of the most remote corners of the country, as well as nearly every major town and city (except Managua and the Atlantic coast because of safety concerns). PCVs work in one of five sectors: environment, agriculture, small business development, youth at risk, and community health.

WORKING FOR AN AID ORGANIZATION

While volunteering for a local NGO can be as simple as showing up at its door, finding work with an international relief organization is much more involved, even for unpaid positions. International organizations like Habitat for Humanity, Catholic Relief Service, International Rescue Committee, Lutheran World Service, CARE, United Nations programs, and many others have their own application procedures and time requirements. Those offering salaried positions usually require significant overseas experience and advanced degrees in fields such as international relations, public health, economics, or civil engineering.

FINANCES

You won't escape money matters by moving to Nicaragua. In fact, you'll find Nicaraguans are just as concerned about making and spending *"re-ales"* (pronounced *ray-AL-es,* slang for *dinero*) as anyone else in the world. Although many Northerners head south of the border because of the fabulously cheap and simple lifestyle they've heard about, most run up against reality rather quickly. That is to say, they find that a "cheap" cost of living depends entirely on their personal definition of what a "simple" lifestyle actually entails. Knowing what to expect in terms of basic living expenses like entertainment, fuel, rent, household help, and taxes will go a long way in preparing you to make a decision about moving to Nicaragua. So will a general discussion on Nicaragua's currency, banking system, and investment opportunities. Finally, you'll learn the most about the finances of living abroad by talking with expatriates who've been doing it for years; we've provided a few such voices, but feel free to conduct your own survey during your fact-finding trip to Nicaragua.

Cost of Living

No doubt about it, it's cheaper to live in Nicaragua than it is back home. Right? Maybe. Let's start with the lifestyle. Rural Nicaraguan farmers typically live on less than US$2 per day, consuming what they grow, pulling drinking water from the well, fermenting their own liquor, generally living off the land. Though there a few back-to-the-farm expats trying to do the same (particularly on La Isla de Ometepe), it's probably not the lifestyle you had in mind. On the other end of the spectrum, the top 2 percent of Nicaragua's elite can burn through a stack of US$100 bills more quickly than a Roaring Twenties Rockefeller. Somewhere in between are Nicaragua's small middle class and the bulk of its expat community. Sure you can live for less than you did back in Toronto, Paris, or Seattle, but ultimately, lifestyle is a personal choice, and how much it'll cost depends on how simple—or sumptuous—you choose to make it.

BASIC EXPENSES
Food

Fruits and vegetables produced in Nicaragua are inexpensive by any standards, but anything exotic or imported is not. What's "exotic?" Apples, for one, which come either from the United States or Chile, and can cost as much as US$1 each. Tough and chewy local beef is inexpensive, but not so South American steaks. You can get most imported and local food products with little trouble in Nicaraguan supermarkets, including breakfast cereals, spices, and dairy products, but will have a harder time locating treats like hummus, bagels, shiitake mushrooms, and lentils. Expect to pay about US$200 per month for the first person, and an additional US$100–150 per additional person for your grocery budget. That amount decreases quickly if you make a conscious effort to cook for yourself and eat local products, including basic grains and vegetables that might seem foreign at first, like *quiquisque, chayote,* and *nancite.* The best way to do this is to have a Nicaraguan maid cook your meals, which will incur a different cost (see *Household Help*).

Entertainment

A night out in Managua typically means racking up US$3 movie tickets, US$2 taxi rides, a few *discoteca* cover charges ($2–5), and whatever you consume on top of that (anywhere else in the country, you'll save a few bucks on taxis and entrance fees). If you drink alcohol, you'll find Nicaraguan

THE COST OF LIVING: A FEW DIFFERING VIEWS

We interviewed a variety of permanent expats living in Nicaragua who reported living comfortably for anywhere between US$400 and US$1,000 per month. Note that all interviewees below live either in Managua, Granada, Carazo, or the Pacific southwest; we have both lived in northern Nicaraguan villages for less than US$200 per month. Following are some of the responses we received to the question, "How do you feel about the cost of living – are you living cheaply compared to back home, or is it not such the great deal that people say it is?" As you can see, it's all relative.

"In Nicaragua, it is definitely bargain living, even though in Granada prices escalate periodically and are not quite as inexpensive as one would believe. Gas is more than in the U.S., electricity is high, phone service is high, car insurance is a bit lower, cable is a bargain."

"Much more expensive than planned. My house needs continual work due to shoddy building practices here."

"Very cheap compared to London."

"I'm living very well and it is inexpensive."

"It is not cheap to live here. Some things like bananas are cheap, but overall it is expensive."

"The cost of living is cheap. However, if you are working and earning a Western income, then it is *very* cheap. It can be more expensive if you have no kitchen or if you are here for only a short time."

"If you wish to live at a high U.S. standard with all imported products and service, the cost of living is high, but still lower than in the U.S. If you are willing to compromise on certain things, the cost of living is perhaps 35 percent cheaper."

"No, we don't live cheaply because we are running a business that costs us a lot of money. But it is possible to live very cheap if you are low-maintenance. Electricity and gas are expensive."

"I consider it expensive to live here. Imported goods are very expensive."

"Yes, it's cheaper, but I have less to spend due to a lower income."

"It's quite a lot less. It's not hype, in particular if you cook at home. I don't really budget, but honestly, it's about 20 percent of what I pay at home."

beer and liquor relatively inexpensive compared to back home. A cold beer might cost US$0.50 to US$1, and a bottle of excellent quality rum can be had for about US$5. It adds up, of course, especially if you can't do without imported fancies like Kentucky bourbon or Chilean merlot. A few specialty shops in Managua and Granada cater to such tastes, but like we said, it'll cost you.

Fuel

Gasoline and diesel fuel will be an expensive part of your monthly budget, especially since they translate into taxi and bus fares as well. Expect gasoline prices 150–200 percent higher than they are in the United States. Depending on how exclusively you rely on your gas-guzzling 4x4, you might be investing several hundred dollars in fuel expenses monthly. Using a diesel vehicle reduces that expense but not to the point where your monthly fuel expenses won't be a major line-item in your budget.

Rent

Rent varies depending on the city, the proximity to points of interest, the quality of the house or apartment, and demand in that region. That is to say, "location, location, location." In a small town with not much to do but talk to your neighbors and listen to the birds, you could conceivably rent a little place for US$50–100 per month. But you get what you pay for, which may include an outdoor latrine, improvised wiring, and plenty of six-legged roommates. Move to Granada and rents go up drastically: US$300–400 for a little place and up to US$700 or more for an ample colonial space.

Should you make Managua your home you must immediately decide if you want to live in one of the exclusive neighborhoods preferred by Western expatriates and Nicaragua's well-to-do, or if you'd be comfortable in one of Managua's nondescript middle-class residential neighborhoods. The first option gets you a modern and comfortable home in one of the safest neighborhoods in the city, green grass on your lawn, and quiet neighbors, but it can set you back well over US$1,000 per month if the house is "family sized," that is to say, the size of a place you'd expect to find in any American suburb. Embassy staff, development workers, and the well-to-do tend to wind up in safer but more expensive homes, and are happy to pay for the extra comfort that makes life in Managua bearable. If you decide to "go Nica," your price will drop to US$400–500 a month, but you might not be thrilled with your surroundings. This means noisy neighbors, blaring music at all hours, more staring and attention than you're probably happy with, and a greater degree of danger from pickpockets, casual muggings, and the like. A few apartment buildings offer even cheaper options, especially near the universities (we once rented a one-bedroom/kitchenette/one-bath apartment for US$250 in Reparto San Juan, where we worked on the first edition of *Moon Handbooks Nicaragua*).

Household Help

Nicaraguans and expatriates alike agree that having household help is not just a luxury, but somewhat of a necessity in a place where ordinary things take considerably more time and energy than they do back home. It's easy

ADDITIONAL EXPENSES

Nicaraguan law stipulates an eight-hour workday and sets a legal work-week maximum of 48 hours, with one day of rest. Nicaraguans often work a half day on Saturday. Nicaraguan tradition – and law – also mandates you pay an *aguinaldo* at Christmas to each of your staff. The *aguinaldo* is a 13th month of salary, which means in the month of December everybody earns a double salary with which they pay for gifts and holiday expenses. Don't forget to factor this additional annual expense into your budget.

The Labor Code also mandates quite generous medical (including maternity) leave and vacation provisions, and mandates quite clearly what you must pay to an employee that you discharge. It's tempting to complain about these additional expenses, but don't bother. Nicaragua is one of many Latin American countries with a long history of worker exploitation that dates back to Spain. Rather, thank the Sandinista revolution and subsequent administrations for finally doing something to protect an already vulnerable workforce. To understand the law, visit the Ley Laboral website (see the *Resources* section of this book), which answers in FAQ format most of your questions.

Should you decide to fire your household staff, Nicaraguan law provides protection to that person and requires you to follow certain rules. First, you must pay the earned portion of the *aguinaldo* and all vacation days earned but unused for that year, so for example if you fire someone in June who has worked since January, you would need to reimburse that employee of half of the *aguinaldo* (i.e., one-half month's salary) and any unused vacation days to date. If the person has worked for you for longer than one year you must first notify the Ministry of Labor and pay one month's salary for each full year worked (up to five years maximum). The Nicaraguan Labor Code stipulates that if you fire someone for no good cause you can be

to hire a maid for cooking and cleaning *(la empleada* or *la domestica)*, a gardener for groundskeeping and landscaping *(el jardinero),* a driver *(el chofer),* or a night watch-person *(el selador).* Talk to any Nicaraguan living in Miami or Texas and it's the first thing they'll complain about: "Back in Nicaragua I had two *domesticas,* one gardener..." You get the picture. While household help can be prohibitively expensive back home, it's reasonable in Nicaragua, though you can expect prices to rise as Nicaragua's economy strengthens and as additional expats compete for reliable maids and cooks. A good estimate of the expense is US$100 per staff-member per month. A good live-in maid/cook commands a salary of about US$35 per week and a gardener about US$25. Maids that don't live on the premises are paid a bit less but are reimbursed for transport.

Night watchmen, or *seladores,* charge about US$25 per week. You might consider not hiring a *selador* if your maid sleeps on the premises, but it's

brought to court and forced to pay an indemnity to that person. This has been known to happen in Nicaragua, and you'd better believe the courts are on the side of the Nicaraguan worker, not the wealthy expatriate.

Nicaraguan employees earn, in general, two weeks of vacation for every six months they work, but in practice, most household workers prefer to work through their vacation time in exchange for additional salary; you can negotiate this. Regardless of vacation time, Nicaraguan employees are not required to work through national holidays (of which there are several) and are to be reimbursed for those days.

Unlike back home, in practice Nicaraguans are happy to have employment and will negotiate with you over the details rather than resort to lawyers and the courts. But they will fight for their rights. Expats who have appeared before the courts of the Ministry of Labor report it is generally fair, but why let things get to that point?

It is in your best interest to maintain an open, formal, and professional dialogue with your help in regard to holidays, sick days, and vacation. Ask them if they intend to work on holidays and what they expect to be paid for that time; ask them if they intend to take vacation. Keep good records: Have your employees sign for every check they receive and keep a log of vacation and sick days taken. The Nicas say *"cuentas clara, amistad larga,"* ("clean accounts, long friendship") – take it to heart.

Lastly, try to be understanding of the needs of the people that work for you. Though grateful for the employment, most Nicaraguans are trying to balance their responsibilities to you with large families, sick children, and many more obligations you will never know about. Having respect for your staff and being flexible but setting down the rules clearly will lead to a healthy and productive relationship from which you will all benefit.

definitely worth the money to have a gentleman with a machete or shotgun doing laps around your premises, especially in Managua. In all cases, it's not the machete that deters crime, but the fact that your home is occupied 24 hours a day. Nicaragua isn't a country known for violent crime, but homeowners are particularly susceptible to casual robbery and break-ins, and foreigners doubly so since they are perceived as fabulously wealthy. The more trustworthy staff you have in your residence, the less likely you are to be a victim of casual breaking and entering. Even that won't completely prevent it. While living in an embassy-rented home in the affluent Las Colinas neighborhood in Managua, Randy once had every ripe avocado stolen from his tree, plus a bucket in which the thief carried them off, despite the maid and gardener who were having lunch inside.

You are expected to feed your staff the meals they eat while on your premises, and to pay medical expenses for your staff as well. Depending on how big-hearted you are, you can expect a litany of other little needs—"my daughter's school uniform," "a repair for my boots," "some drops for my son's pink-eye," etc. To a certain extent your relationship with your staff is yours to determine since Nicaraguan law dictates only the basics of what is and is not required of you. Some Nicaraguan household heads (and expats, too) abuse this relationship in the name of "not forcing prices upward," or just to make a public show of their wealth. For example, we've seen Nicaraguan wives bring their maids with them to wait in bank lines or, once, a family in an expensive Managua restaurant that brought their maid to watch the children while they ate. The maid did not eat—she'd probably eaten beans and rice back home. Nicaraguans generally do not eat with their staff but ask them to eat afterward, and not at the family table. Feel free to reject such rules and, of course, to help with the dishes. Randy made a point of allowing the staff to eat whatever the cook had prepared for him, something that would probably seem reasonable to most foreigners but was rather astonishing to most of his Nicaraguan friends.

You are also expected to provide for your staff's medical expenses, even expenses incurred outside of working hours. Your largesse will quickly be abused if you are not careful, however, so inspect every prescription carefully and be wary of sudden hypochondriacs trying to take advantage of their good will. Conspiring doctors will sometimes write a prescription for three similar medicines when one will do.

Finding dependable household help, incidentally, is more difficult than you think. The labor pool is enormous, of course, but the pool of qualified staff who know and comprehend your crazy foreigner ways—from the cook that understands your silly insistence on cooking vegetables every day to the gardener who understands why you don't want a patch of swept dirt for your lawn, even if "that's the way we do things here"—is limited. Good staff are zealously passed from household to household; recommendation of friends and family is the first place to start when looking for household staff. In fact, without exception, every expat we interviewed said they found their household staff through trusted friends and colleagues.

BALANCING YOUR BUDGET

As you move to a less expensive country, ensuring you have enough money to get through the month isn't an overly onerous task. Remember that Nicaragua runs mostly on cash, foreign checks may take 3–4 weeks to clear, and opening a local bank account can be frustratingly slow, especially if you have no job. For the early weeks, count on ATMs or the cash you bring while you establish your bank account and get settled. Unlike in the United States, you can move into most rented houses with little more than a signature and the first month's rent. Not until people start abusing their landlords' trust, skipping town without paying the last month, etc., will Nicaraguan landlords start requiring security payments and months of rent paid in advance. Buying a place is a bit more complicated in legal terms but still requires cash paid up front, so don't count on finding any mortgagers. From that point, your expenses will be dictated by the lifestyle you want to lead. It will likely be a less expensive lifestyle than you lived back home—folks we spoke with reported total costs to be 20–75 percent what they were at home. Successful budgeting in Nicaragua means having enough cash on hand to cover daily or weekly expenses, but no more than you would risk losing to theft or burglary. Definitely split your cash up in a few money belts and other hiding places. Most expats agree you can live on about US$800 a month if your tastes aren't too fancy and you don't require much air-conditioning. Says one expat, "that even buys a little beer, too." Expats living more extravagant lifestyles—or just drinking more beer—budget around US$1,200 per month.

Banking and Currency

Nicaragua is still, by and large, a cash society. You can get by for weeks on end without needing either a credit card or a check. Heck, in some places, you can still barter. We know at least one Managuan medical doctor who has been paid for services rendered with chickens, eggs, and corn. From a traveler's perspective, that means being careful not to totally rely on credit cards and travelers checks (at least, when straying farther than Managua or Granada, where credit cards and ATMs are increasingly common). From the perspective of someone who wants to make Nicaragua their new home, it means being a little more creative with your accounting.

CURRENCY

Nicaraguan currency is the córdoba, named after Nicaragua's founding father, Francisco Hernández de Córdoba, and abbreviated throughout Nicaragua (and throughout this book) as C$. The córdoba is divided into 100 centavos (cents), but in practice, nearly everything is rounded off to the nearest cordoba, or to a multiple of 25 cents. The most popular decimal amounts have nicknames you should learn your first day in country: 50 cents is called *"cinco reales"* and 25 cents is called *"un chelín."* The córdoba is also colloquially called the *"peso,"* but sometimes the dollar is called the same—hopefully, you'll know by context which currency they're talking about. Finally, money in general is called *"plata"* (silver) or *"reales,"* as in the ever-popular phrase, *"no tengo reales"* ("I don't have any money"). It's not as confusing as it sounds, once you've had some practice.

Exchange Rate

In January 2006, the official exchange rate was just over 17 córdobas to the dollar, but the Central Bank of Nicaragua has established a sliding peg exchange rate, which means the exchange rate gets just a little bit worse every day. That doesn't mean much to expats thinking in dollars, for whom, to a certain extent, goods produced in Nicaragua get a little more affordable every day. But to Nicaraguans purchasing goods produced elsewhere, it means costs are constantly going up while salaries are not. Check the day's exchange rate at the Central Bank's website (www.bcn.gob.ni).

Because the córdoba's value changes from day to day, lots of prices are quoted in dollars, and you can expect just about anyone to take your dollars (banknotes, not coins) in payment. The disadvantage to paying for things in dollars is the on-the-fly calculation of the day's exchange rate that more often than not leaves you with a lousy deal, so get in the practice of working with—and thinking in—córdobas. U.S. dollars are the safest foreign currency to handle. Bancentro in Managua can exchange euros, but it doesn't offer a very good rate, and outside of the capital, it's dollars or nothing. Neighboring currencies like Honduran *lempira,* Costa Rican *colones,* and Guatemalan *quetzales* are useless in outside border posts, unless you need a bookmark for your novel. If you travel outside of Nicaragua, be careful to spend or change your remaining currency as you cross the border. The one minor exception is in the far lower reaches of the Río San Juan, where the farmers are far enough removed from Nicaragua and close enough to business centers in Costa Rica that they actually prefer *colones* over córdobas.

OPENING A BANK ACCOUNT

Opening a local bank account is relatively simple and requires little more than some cash and your *cédula* (residence permit). The only way you can open a bank account without a *cédula* is if you are an employee of your country's embassy, or if you are working for one of the large international companies operating in Nicaragua (Coca-Cola, for example). You may also be asked to provide evidence of good financial standing elsewhere (i.e., bank statements from some other bank) or two letters from clients of the bank

DAILY LIFE

© RANDALL WOOD

campesino credit union

with whom you'd like to open an account, vouching on your behalf. Having written proof of a local job may speed up the process.

Competition between banks is stiff, so shop around. Because of the characteristics of the Nicaraguan market, banks must offer higher interest rates (sometimes 4–6 percent higher) than they do in developed markets back home. Along with higher rates comes a higher degree of risk. The U.S. government uses Bancentro, because an American company owns a majority share. Bancentro is also one of the older and better established banks in Nicaragua, and is the only one that deals at all with European currency (the euro). Other reputable banks are BancoUno, BAC (owned by the powerful Pellas family), and BDF. At any Nicaraguan bank, you can open córdoba-denominated or dollar-denominated accounts. Foreigners, without exception, choose dollar-denominated accounts; most Nicaraguans also use dollar-denominated accounts if they have the capital to do so.

Opening up a checking account is equally easy, but because Nicaragua is a society that functions almost exclusively on cash, there is little need for any but business owners to open a checking account. Nicaraguan businesses pay their employees either by bank transfer (rarely) or by envelopes of cash (more common). Most expatriates maintain a bank account or two back home and bring a box of checks for their home account with them to Nicaragua. Having an American checking account can be useful, especially if you are paying credit card bills back home using checks, as American credit card companies will only accept checks that draw on American accounts. This is also the simpler option for the increasing number of people who rely on online banking.

CREDIT CARDS

Since the late 1990s, Credomatic has provided credit card services to Nicaragua, and as a result most midrange to high-end restaurants and hotels accept Visa, Mastercard, and, less frequently, Diner's Club and American

Express. Do not depend on your credit card, however. For starters, if it's bill-paying time and there's a power outage either where you are living or in Managua, the credit card system can be down for hours at a time. And many many places still don't deal with credit cards at all because they are unwilling to pay the Credomatic fees that keep them connected.

Which credit card to use? Many retailers outside of Nicaragua do not honor Nicaraguan credit cards, including popular online resources like Amazon.com or eBay. Nearly every expatriate we know maintains a foreign credit card and either has the bills sent to them in Nicaragua, has someone pay them at home, or pays online. This is a serious consideration, especially for those who like to shop online.

Keep in mind that when living in Nicaragua your credit card bills will reliably land in your mailbox on or after the date they were due, so it's important to keep an eye on your use of the card and send in estimated payments to your credit card company in advance of when they are due, or deal with a bank that facilitates electronic payments so you can check your statements online and deal with them before the creditors come knocking on your door.

Taxes

Although the authors of this book are neither attorneys nor accountants and ultimately you are responsible for ensuring that your particular tax obligations are met, we can at least give you a general lay of the land and explain what is expected.

Income Tax

Basically, if you earn income in Nicaragua through paid employment or a business you own, you are expected to pay taxes to the Nicaraguan government. You are also expected to pay taxes on any money whose sum is greater than US$5,000 if it is held in Nicaraguan bank accounts. Some expatriates open accounts in Panama or the Cayman Islands for that reason alone. When you open your business, you are required to register it with the local town government *(alcaldía)* as well as the national government, which will assign you a Registro Único de Contribuyente, or RUC, which is your tax identification number. You will then be expected to pay annual income taxes to the Dirección General de Ingresos (DGI), which are a modest 10–30 percent for most residents.

If Nicaraguan business owners aren't thrilled about paying taxes, it's because at least one porcine former minister of taxes has used public revenue to build himself luxurious beach houses. You as a foreign national cannot expect to get away from your obligations, however, as your accounts will be scrutinized more carefully than others', and unless you "marry up" in Nicaragua, you most likely don't have powerful family connections to help you out. Writes one expat, "I pay Nicaraguan taxes as I think as a foreigner you make yourself vulnerable if you don't."

Property Tax

Your property is also assessed a tax. Expect to pay 1 percent of the value of your property annually to the *alcaldía*. Small farms of fewer than 30 *manzanas* of land (approximately 12 hectares or 30 acres) are exempt from property taxes, but some zealous municipal officials try to force foreign nationals to pay it anyway, on the grounds that they're rich. Many foreigners try to sneak out of paying the tax—and do—but the government is getting more vigilant and gaining experience, and the fines for tax evasion are steep. Remember, they've got an airline ticket home with your name on it (at your expense, of course)!

Taxes Back Home

Living overseas does not exempt you from paying taxes on income earned back home. Your bank accounts, properties, and other assets will be assessed taxes the same as always, which you will be expected to pay your home government. Two things are worth calling out: First, you can probably declare an exemption on income earned from paid employment or entrepreneurial income in Nicaragua, as you are presumably paying taxes to Nicaragua for that amount and should not have to pay your home government as well. Second, American government workers must declare and pay taxes on their government income, regardless of earning it in an overseas location, but nongovernment workers and employees of international organizations like multilateral donor agencies (the World Bank et al.) can earn their salaries without paying taxes.

Sales Tax (IGV)

Nicaragua's sales tax is a stunning 15 percent, the highest in Central America. Sales tax in Nicaragua is called IGV *(impuesto general de valor)* and is supposed to be added to everything you buy or sell in Nicaragua. In practice however, IGV is only added in bigger stores, restaurants, and bars. Small businesses, open markets, and about 60 percent of Nicaraguan businesses don't collect, pay, or care a hoot about taxes, and the DGI's laudable slogan *"si pagamos todos, pagamos menos"* (if we all pay, we each pay less) hasn't done much to change this. Embassy staff are not required to pay IGV, but in practice this policy is a hassle. Foreign embassy staff must pay taxes assessed at the point of sale and then submit their receipts in batches to the DGI to process a refund. The lines, bureaucratic hassle, and small ticket dollar values of the whole process are impediment enough that many foreign embassy staff either don't bother with it or assign the unwelcome task to an embassy employee.

Investing

Few foreigners invest outside of the real estate market in Nicaragua, but for those investors with a high tolerance for risk, there are a few opportunities to purchase equity shares and government debt. A privately run stock market known as Bolsa de Valores de Nicaragua began operating on January 31, 1994, under a legal framework founded in 1990. Its primary advantages are tax breaks on any earnings from the sale of stocks and a complete lack of capital restrictions that would prevent you from removing your earnings from the Nicaraguan economy. The legislation that provides the legal framework for the stock market is still inchoate, but government determination to strengthen this aspect of Nicaragua's capital markets means this sector will almost certainly strengthen in the future.

In the early days, the bulk of transactions in Nicaragua's stock market were in property indemnification bonds. Greater in volume and in potential than Nicaragua's nascent stock market is its growing bond market. Several large Nicaraguan industries regularly issue bonds, including Casa Pellas, Nicaragua Sugar Estates, Credomatic, and Café Soluble, as does the Nicaraguan Central Bank. The bonds are traded through a handful of agents, including LAFISE, Invercasa, and Invercentro.

Purchasing government debt is easy, as the Nicaraguan government regularly issues short-term debt instruments that pay interest over 3–5 year periods at rates marginally higher than bank rates—like 15-year bonds that pay up to 10 percent, for example. The risk in these instruments is relatively diminished by the fact that Nicaragua is bound by a host of agreements with international lenders that restrain its ability to default—but that's no guarantee, and more than one multilateral lender has threatened to suspend Nicaragua's programs from time to time to enforce compliance with financial obligations. Private companies tend to issue short-term repurchase orders ("repos"). There are other debt instruments floating around the market. If you are interested in knowing more about BPIs (Bond of Compensation Payments), CBTs (Compensation Tributary Benefits), or Certiagros, you should get in touch with one of the agencies mentioned in the *Resources* section.

Equity shares in private sector companies are far riskier, prone to less government oversight, and not very common in the first place. Still, start with a conversation with your local banker, or visit the LAFISE group in its big green building on Carretera Masaya, a new and powerful participant in the Central American banking sector. Founded in 1990 by a Nicaraguan entrepreneur, LAFISE (Latin American Financial Services) employs several hundred people and does over US$2 billion in financial transactions per year. For starters, ask about the CASEIF product—a composite of small enterprises across Central America (not just Nicaragua). The market research team can just as easily help you determine what opportunities are available and help direct you to funds that meet your needs and expectations. Another big player in the Nicaraguan stock market is Invernic, a fairly new and modern stock brokerage.

One sector they will almost certainly mention to you is the slowly opening market of privatized public utilities. Privatized public utilities is a hot topic both within the academic world of economics and around the table with a bottle of rum. We won't get into the polemic here, but suffice it to say that if you accept the premise, recently privatized utilities, including ENITEL (the phone company), are one sector to which you might pay attention. Sound exciting? Keep it in perspective: You're in Nicaragua. High payoffs are commensurate with high risks, and only you know how much you're willing to put on the line.

COMMUNICATIONS

Unless you're trekking deep into the Bosawás forest reserve or plan on paddling far down the Río San Juan, staying connected with the world will not differ much from what you're used to. In this regard, Nicaragua has come a long way since the 1980s, when a phone call meant a dangerous trip into town and a long wait in line for a crackly connection.

Today, you can relatively easily install phone service in your own house, hook up to the Internet, and carry around a cell phone. So don't think moving to Nicaragua means losing touch with your friends and family back home. In fact, with an Internet café in just about every medium-sized town, travelers passing through Nicaragua find they can stay as connected as they wish. And for long-term expats it's easier still. Getting in touch, Nica style, requires getting to know a couple of tricks, and getting your home connected to the telephone and Internet requires some patience.

© RANDALL WOOD

Telephone Service

PUBLIC PHONES

The national phone company, Empresa Nicaragüense de Telecomunicaciones (ENITEL), was completely privatized in 2003. Every major city has an ENITEL office for making calls, as do most small towns. In many villages without an ENITEL office, you'll find a local family renting out their private phone or one contracted through ENITEL. Even in large cities, ENITEL offices are not staffed 24 hours a day; rather they operate on some variant of 8 A.M.–5 P.M. and limited hours on the weekends. That's not to say you can't place calls outside of those hours from your own phone, just that you can't rely on the phone office to attend you if you don't have a fixed line in your home. To place a call from an ENITEL office, go to the front desk and tell the operator where you'd like to call. The operator will place the call for you and, if it goes through, will then send you to one of several private booths to receive it. When you complete the call, go back up to the front desk to pay.

Alternatively, look around for relatively new ENITEL and Publitel pay phones, each requiring a different kind of prepaid card; there are also many Bell South coin-operated phones in corner stores, but these are usually more expensive. The store in front of which the pay phone was planted is a likely place to buy a phone card; otherwise purchase them in advance from the ENITEL office.

FAXES AND TELEGRAMS

Most ENITEL offices have fax machines as well. A two-page international fax may cost you US$4–5 to send, a local fax about US$1. Also check in copy shops, Internet providers, and post offices . Many Correos de Nicaragua (post offices) also offer both fax and telegram service. Yes, telegrams. To send a telegram to your compatriot in another Nicaraguan town, you must dictate it to the postal clerk, who will charge you a by-the-word rate and will then key it in or read it to the clerk in that recipient's town. Not surprisingly, if you try to send an English-language telegram the results will be disappointing.

INTERNATIONAL CALLS

To make expensive, old-fashioned direct calls overseas, step up to the nearest ENITEL desk and give them the number. You'll need to know your country code: Canada and the United States are 1, Germany is 49, Spain 34, France 33, and Great Britain and Ireland 44. A complete listing of country codes is in the front of the phone book.

DAILY LIFE

It's probably cheaper to use your calling card account from back home; tell the operator to connect you with the international bilingual operator for your company, or dial directly: AT&T, tel. 1/800-0164; MCI, 1/800-0166; Sprint, 1/800-0171. Once you connect with the international operator, tell them your card's 800 number, then enter your card number and place your call as you normally would. In many larger cities the ENITEL offices will have specially marked booths with direct hookups to international companies like MCI or AT&T, circumventing the need to use an operator, but possibly adding hidden charges.

© RANDALL WOOD

Cell phones are slowly replacing these trusty old friends.

Internet Calling

By far the cheapest and, increasingly, easiest way to phone home, web-based dialing is all the rage, especially in tourist sites with fast connections, like Granada, where competition drives rates to as low as US$6 per hour to call the United States, Canada, or Europe. This phenomenon is sure to expand and the prices sure to fluctuate; always ask at the most modern Internet place in town about *llamadas internacionales.* Do-it-yourself Internet dialing programs like skype.com and voip.com are even cheaper than the booths in Internet cafés (skype is actually free if calling another skype-equipped computer anywhere in the world!) but may be blocked by the shop owners, who don't profit from you dialing directly. However, this is by far the best way to call abroad from your own high-speed connection in your apartment or house—or even from your WiFi-connected laptop, as long as you have a microphone and headset.

LAND LINES

Obtaining a land line—either for making calls or connecting to the Internet—is not the year-long affair it used to be, but it's still going to take some patience. Your first step is to request a land line from the local ENITEL

DAILY LIFE

MAKING THE CALL: NICA TELEPHONE NUMBERS

Nicaragua totally revamped the nation's phone number system in 2005, changing most of the country's regional exchange codes, so be sure you have the newer version of whatever number you're trying to call. Your best bet is to find the latest annual copy of La Guía Telefónica (the phone book), which has excellent and up-to-date information on placing your call, finding international country codes, etc. It's also an unexpectedly decent resource for certain basic tourism information, including hotel listings, government offices, and important festival dates; pick up a free copy in Managua, at the Publicar office next to the Plaza España La Colonia supermarket, or at a local ENITEL office.

When making **calls within Nicaragua,** prefix your number with a 0 when dialing out of your municipality or to any cell phone. Cell numbers begin with 88, 86, and 77, and they cost extra to call. Satellite phones are wickedly expensive to call, begin with 892, and do not require a 0 beforehand.

When **calling Nicaragua from overseas** you need to use Nicaragua's country code which is 505. First dial the international code, then 505 plus the number. For example, from the United States, dial 011-505-XXX-YYYY.

Here are a few important numbers to jot down:

- Information: 113

- ENITEL customer service: 121

- Long-distance/collect-call operators: 110 and 116

- Police: 118

- Firefighters: 115 and 120

- Red Cross: 128

office. The cost of running a land line from the network to your residence typically costs just under US$200 and can take up to three months from the time you solicit it, though response times are dropping dramatically since ENITEL was privatized. In fact, if you live in certain parts of Granada, San Juan del Sur, or Managua, you can get connected within a week. You will need to provide lots of paperwork, and what they ask you for depends on who you speak to, how well you speak Spanish, and, apparently, the phase of the moon. That is to say, customer experience on this subject varies. At a minimum you will be asked to provide your passport, cédula, a copy of your lease (if you're leasing) or the title on your property. You are also requested to provide the name of a fiador, someone in good standing with ENITEL who will vouch for you as a potential good client of the company. But you might be asked to show three months' worth of utility bills to prove you truly do live where you say you do. If you're unlucky, the clerk might capriciously request something like a letter from your embassy. Sometimes you can talk your way out of the more onerous requests, but the fact is, ENITEL is unwilling to invest the time and equipment necessary to connect your new house to the telephone system if they are not sure you are a good business risk, and in this case, being a foreigner with money is not enough to provide the assurance that you won't just disappear after a month or two. Expats report that getting a land line can take six months and recommend buying or renting a place that already has the line installed. Better real estate agents will help you hire a lawyer to deal with these things on your behalf.

An excellent alternative is to request a *planta fija,* essentially a phone that looks like a land line but works using cellular technology. Both ENITEL and Movistar offer this service. It is a particularly useful way of circumventing the challenge of connecting a remote or coastal home with phone service. The service results in a higher phone bill—particularly for calls to the United States—but most expats are able to keep it below US$100 per month. The *planta fija* works the way a regular cell phone does—with prepaid cards or monthly dollar-amount plans.

Expect to pay less for phone calls at night. You will have an easier time making connections at night as well, as Nicaragua's still-growing physical network has a limited capacity and frequently saturates during peak calling hours. A five-minute local call costs about US$0.75 (C$10). International call rates vary depending on who your international carrier is, but you can expect a 10-minute call to the United States to cost about US$8 and to Europe US$12.

CELL PHONES

This market has boomed since the late 1990s and you now have several options, not to mention enough competition to keep all the players striving to improve their services. And while the expats with whom we spoke differed on their cellular company, they all agreed on one thing: It is expensive to own and use a cell phone in Nicaragua; most pay at least US$50 per month, sometimes more. On the other hand, every teenager in town has a cell phone protruding from his or her pocket, so it can't be *that* bad. Most everyone uses either Movistar or ENITEL services, but Sprint PCS also participates in this market. All of these companies offer dollar-amount limited plans (e.g., US$20 a month for a fixed number of minutes) but also offer prepaid calling cards. You can buy the cards in most pharmacies and small convenience stores, scratch off the code on the back of the card, and use it to add additional minutes to your phone. Expats claim Movistar (formerly Bell South) has greater coverage, even out at sea, while

ENITEL is only strong near major cities and Sprint PCS is spotty altogether. But whichever company you go with, you'll need to either have their sim card installed in your cell phone or purchase a phone from the company. A surprisingly modern and diverse selection of stylish phones is available for purchase. Nicaraguan cell networks are GSM, by the way, not GPRS, so they transmit voice and SMS messages only, so leave your Blackberry or Treo at home.

Coverage throughout the Nicaraguan countryside's major population centers is decent, though there are pockets where no signal gets through, particularly in eastern Matagalpa and Jinotega. Expect good coverage along all the major highways that connect Managua with Granada, León, Chinandega, Estelí, and Ocotal, but no signal once you wander off the beaten path.

Postal Service

Correos de Nicaragua offers postal service between Nicaragua and the rest of the world, and sometimes additional services as well. Every municipality larger than about 3,000 people has a post office, even if it's a tiny one; in some cases they share space with ENITEL. If you're not sure, start searching around the center of town; the post office is usually no farther than a block or two away. Letters and postcards cost about US$0.50 to send to the United States or Canada; prices for destinations in Europe or Asia tend to be about US$0.75. How long your letters take to get there is hard to predict. In general, letters to the United States and Canada arrive in about a week and sometimes less; mail to Europe can take two weeks and mail to Asia can occasionally take over three.

Receiving Packages

It's hard to pin down the Nicaraguan mail service. Ideally, packages mailed to Nicaragua arrive within two weeks, but from time to time packages will take up to three or four months and arrive intact with no explanation whatsoever for their delay. Whose desk it sat on for all that time is anybody's guess. While some people have gone years without a missed package or letter, others have horror stories, indicating more a weakness in the institution than widespread incompetence. One of our friends noticed a package he was expecting with his favorite shirt had taken longer to arrive than expected, and went to the post office to complain about it, only to be attended by a clerk wearing the shirt (he opted to keep his complaints to himself rather than accuse the worker and risk receiving no more mail for the rest of his life). Another friend in Granada has not missed a package except for one time: "My daughter sent me a package of chocolates. I never received them. Many months later, a post office employee reminded me that when I received a box of chocolates again, please remember to give some to them."

Worst of all are packages containing items of declared value where customs gets involved. Heaven help you if somebody sends you a digital camera, film, laptop, or portable radio. Customs will take charge of your package, slowly and methodically "process" it, assess exorbitant fees, and generally get in your way. No longtime expatriate in Nicaragua ever requests friends or family back home to send these types of things, electing either to carry them down in their luggage from back-home shopping trips or have friends bring them.

Sending Packages

In a far more predictable process, packages take about two weeks to get to North America and from three to four to get to Europe and Asia. It helps to write the destination country in both Spanish and English to make perfectly clear where your package is headed. Packing up your goods is a bit harder than you remember it being back home: There are fewer loose cardboard boxes floating around and not an awful lot of brown paper and packing twine. Nor are there "parcel packing" services like you'd find in India or Asia. Your neighborhood *pulpería* is a good place to start in your search for boxes; expect to be asked for a couple of córdobas as compensation. Most *librerías* (bookstores) sell thick envelopes in different sizes. Some, but not all, have brown paper as well.

Postal Boxes

Securing your own post office box, or *apartado postal,* is recommended for long-term residents. Because mail carriers make mistakes, don't like to deliver when it rains, and are more interested in what you receive than they should be, a post office box helps ensure you receive your important mail. If you live in Managua, post boxes are close to a necessity. The annual fee, payable in six-month installments, is usually less than US$10 and worth every penny.

Nica-Boxes and Courier Services

Most expats we know, particularly those who receive large amounts of mail and/or run a business that requires a trustworthy and reliable physical address, have what is known as a Nica-Box, supplied by a company called Trans-Express. A Nica-Box is essentially a Miami-based post office box. Mail is collected in Miami and delivered to Nicaragua by cargo plane, and the Trans-Express staff deal with customs and taxes on your behalf, charging you when you pick up your packages and mail. Nica-Boxes incur an annual payment but are worth it because your clients and friends can post their letters with the postage required for Miami, not Nicaragua, and the added reliability of the service is invaluable. In addition to a variety of monthly plans and a by-the-package payment program, Trans-Express also offers customs-processing services for your packages.

Since the late 1990s, the overnight couriers like FedEx and DHL have been operating in Managua, charging prices equivalent to those in the United States and elsewhere. These are an efficient but pricier way of sending and receiving packages.

Internet

ON THE ROAD

Internet shops first began appearing in larger Nicaraguan cities like Managua and Granada around 1998 and are found just about everywhere now. Cyber-cafes *(los ciber)* are as common as *pulperías* these days, typically charging about US$1–2 per hour, billable in 15-minute increments. Better places serve coffee, beer, and snacks to sustain you through those long hours of emailing. Note that in some out-of-the-way places your Internet cafés are run over wimpy dial-up links, but in larger towns like Granada or San Juan del Sur, broadband is the norm.

© JOSHUA BERMAN

Internet cafés are everywhere.

Traveling with your own laptop and attempting to plug in to local cyber-cafes' broadband connections is no longer the mystery it once was to shopkeepers. Especially in newer, more central cyber-cafes, this can be quite easy. It can also still cause quite a bit of confusion, so be prepared. WiFi hot spots are few and far between in Nicaragua but expect that to change *pronto*. At present, the only hot spots we're aware of are in the bar-restaurants of Pelican Eyes Piedras y Olas (San Juan del Sur) and Norome Resort (Laguna de Apoyo), which may be two of the most scenic connections on the continent. Also check with the fancier Managua hotels.

INTERNET IN YOUR HOME
Dial-Up

Outside of León, Managua, and Granada, dial-up is usually your only option, and it is often excruciatingly slow. Never mind that the link is advertised as 56KB per second. Experience shows that real speeds are more likely in the 20s or 30s. IBW is the nation's strongest overall Internet provider, offering dial-up service across the country, even in relatively small towns. Dial-up packages run from US$12 a month and up, a cheap way to go, and great if you are traveling around the country with a laptop, as you can find access numbers throughout the country.

Broadband

In Managua, León, and Granada, both IBW and Cablenet (and a few smaller companies) offer cable broadband. Cable Internet is not cheap. Installation fees, which include the sale of a cable modem (don't expect to be permitted to provide your own), are US$40, and the ensuing monthly fees, depending on your bandwidth and speed requirements, can run US$50–100 per month. Many expats grumble that cable Internet companies have oversubscribed their services and the resulting speed of the connections they offer is not very fast, but few grumblers would consider going back to dial-up.

Furthermore, ENITEL now offers DSL service (broadband Internet delivered over phone lines) in a growing number of Nicaragua's major cities. Sold under the name Turbonett, it's even more expensive than cable for the moment but will soon offer greater coverage than cable companies do. There are a few catches: Turbonett comes with a 24-month contract and is available to residents with *cedulas,* not casual travelers tired of dial-up. ENITEL will require from you a proof of income or a bank statement, a copy of some recent utility bills, and a US$50 installation charge. The advertised velocity of the connection is fast: 256KB per second. Find out more at your local ENITEL office.

It is imperative that if you subscribe to broadband services in Nicaragua you keep your virus definitions on your Windows computers up to snuff. Cablenet regularly suffers from viral epidemics that sweep all the Windows computers on the network; management does what it can but is generally less competent in preventing these kinds of Internet annoyances than they should be, and they are unsympathetic to users whose computers have been incapacitated by the latest and greatest Windows trojan. As an alternative, consider using computers that do not run Windows, as they are less frequently targeted by virus producers and thus stand a better chance on Nicaraguan broadband. And obviously, the periodic power outages that have plagued Nicaragua over the past decades will affect your connectivity as well. Even if you are sitting pretty in Granada, a power outage that downs Managua might take your Internet connection down along with it. That is the divine signal that you should step away from the keyboard and pour yourself something cold to drink and prepare to wait it out.

Wireless Connections

We're talking about connecting to the Internet from your straw hut in the boondocks, not the local café, here. For the truly remote, ENITEL offers an experimental wireless service that requires special equipment you lease from the company and a clear view of the nighttime sky. Installation comes with a US$50 fee, but the connection is reportedly faster than satellite services.

COMPUTER USAGE

Electronic equipment's Achilles heel has always been dust and water, and in Nicaragua both are abundant. Besides leaky roofs and long rainy seasons of tropical downpours, the occasional hurricane, and so on, the day-to-day dust that leaks through the pores of your computer will eventually doom it to an untimely death. To get a good idea of how much dust you really have to contend with, tell your *empleada* not to mop the floor one day. By dinner time there should be a fine fuzzy patina of dust from edge to edge. The better you can keep your computer covered the less likely you will be replacing it every two years. Plastic commercial dust covers are a wise investment here more than anywhere, but you can just as easily improvise.

Macintosh

Most of Nicaragua's information superhighway runs on Windows, and more than one *ciber* runs on pirated software. Mac users are not without recourse, however. If you bring a Mac or iPod to Nicaragua, check in with the iMac Center in Managua, which offers not just service and repairs but also sales of fine new Macintosh equipment. Outside of Managua, no Macintosh services are available. The iMac center keeps a modest amount of equipment in stock to deal with repairs, but more exotic problems might require ordering parts from California, which can take 3–4 days via FedEx.

Media

TV, CABLE, AND SATELLITE

Nicaraguan channels are limited to a few homespun news networks, which feature marathons of Mexican or South American *telenovelas* and music videos. If you simply must have your MTV, however, you have lots of

---

DON'T TURN THAT DIAL! THE THRIVING TRADITION OF NICARAGUAN RADIO

Nicaraguan radio is a treasured resource and the backbone of free speech throughout the nation. Whether listening to the news, talk shows, or the local ballgame – or to endless rounds of Mexican *ranchera* music – Nicaraguans like to keep one ear on the radio from dawn to dusk while they go through the morning's chores. If your Spanish is up to it, it's worth your time to tune in, particularly in the mornings when they present the day's headlines.

Contrary to what you're accustomed to back home, you won't hear polished DJs piped in by satellite from some corporate monstrosity that has winnowed down the earth's musical repertoire to a dozen inoffensive tracks. Nicaraguan radio is homegrown, passionate, and rife with raw edges. Don't expect long tirades of glossy, silk-voiced commercials complete with canned jingles either; advertising is frequently read aloud from printed scripts by the same DJs that spin the music. The same goes for the news: While the bigger radio stations in Managua subscribe to wire services, many smaller stations in the countryside simply open up the day's newspaper and read some of the headlines in the most dramatic voice they can conjure up.

There are scores of grassroots radio stations around the country. Take **Radio Palabra de Mujer,** broadcasting out of remote Bocana de Paiwas in eastern Matagalpa. It's radio by women for women, and its programming focuses on shattering the bonds of *machismo* that have defined womanhood in Nicaragua for generations.

In general, expect to hear Nicaragua's most popular songs a little more frequently than you'd like. Nicaraguan radio seizes the current Latin music hits and plays them on infinite repeat until the tune has been scored into your eardrums. Mexican mariachi (or "*ranchera*") music never fails, from Pepe Aguilar to *el rey* (the king) of the genre, Vicente

options for cable television. Estesa offers a package of about 65 channels including both Spanish and English selections, plus the BBC and channels from Spain, France, and Germany. Start with a call to the company's office in Managua. They'll provide you an estimate based on their physical network coverage, and in some cases sales personnel will visit you in your home within the week. If the network doesn't extend down your street things get difficult quickly. They'll provide you the option of paying for it (thousands of dollars, usually) or waiting an undisclosed amount of time before they connect you. In that case, your neighbors will probably come to your rescue with an illicit tap into their own, or someone else's, connection. We're not recommending you use illegal connections to get your *Sex and the City* fix, but we're also not recommending you sit back and wait the rest of your life for Estesa to get their act together.

Of course, you can always bypass all that muckety-muck and beam

Fernandez. The past decade's greatest *cumbias, salsas,* and *merengue* hits are also standard fare, as are the oodles of broken-hearted ballads from Nicaragua's handful of party bands. Urban stations tend to have a little more variety and a lot more Mexican hip-hop and *reggaetón,* while rural stations stick to time-honored classics, *folklóricos,* and *música de recuerdos* (oldies). Also expect a peppering of totally incongruous American music from the 1970s, especially, for unknown reasons, Air Supply, Journey, and "Los Bee-Yees" (The Bee-Gees!).

Consider tuning in short-wave, while you're at it. Shortwave radio is far from dead in the developing world, and Central America receives coverage from several different sources, including the BBC, Radio France International, Radio Exterior de España, and the Voice of America. The frequencies fluctuate widely from season to season, so either surf the airwaves or visit the radio stations' respective websites beforehand. In particular, the **Voice of America** is a decent news source and as close to your well-loved NPR station back home as you'll find (although, in this day and age, you can probably stream your favorite public radio station online). VOA is not simply propaganda for the American government; rather, since the days of World War II the Voice of America has made an effort to report fairly and truthfully even when the truth hurts, as it did during the Vietnam War era. It hosts speakers and musicians and sponsors a wide range of programs.

Radio Exterior de España is broadcast throughout Latin America and the Caribbean. If you can sift through the thick accent, it's a great source of world news and sports coverage, particularly of soccer. Lastly, for a change of pace, check out Fidel Castro's own **Granma** radio service, broadcasting anti-American rants and blistering denouncements of American foreign policy throughout the day.

straight up to the nearest satellite network. DirecTV has offices in Nicaragua and offers coverage across the nation.

NEWSPAPERS AND MAGAZINES

Nicaragua's two major newspapers, *La Prensa* and *El Nuevo Diario,* differ markedly in style. *La Prensa* is older, better established, and, shall we say, a bit more highbrow than its competition. Its editorial bent is decidedly anti-Sandinista and is (still) run by the Chamorro family. Editor Pedro Joaquín Chamorro's assassination by Somoza in the 1970s was one of the final outrages that sparked the Sandinista revolution, but the Chamorros recoiled from Sandinismo soon after Daniel Ortega and company took power, becoming staunch critics of the revolution. The antipathy continues to this day.

El Nuevo Diario appeals to a more working-class crowd and offers up a steady diet of scandals, accidents, and beautiful women to keep the issues selling. Its coverage of popular scandals is often tongue-in-cheek and makes great reading with a couple of Nicaraguan friends looking over your shoulder. You can find both newspapers for sale after 6 A.M. throughout Nicaragua's cities and towns. At C$3 per copy, reading both papers—with a Spanish-English dictionary and cup of coffee at your elbow—is a great way to stay involved with what's happening around you, though international coverage in both papers is limited. Both papers are online, so you can start familiarizing yourself now, a great way to get your Spanish up to par before making the move. There are a few other sensationalistic and/or political rags out there as well, most of which are listed and linked on the main IBW web portal.

For the English-language crowd, *Between the Waves* offers a monthly collection of tourism and activities-related articles that can be a practical addendum to your guidebook. Pick up your first complimentary copy at the airport and look for it afterward at most major hotels and tourist gathering spots in Granada, León, San Juan del Sur, and Managua. And R. Calvet and Associates now publishes an English magazine by the name of *Investments and Tourism,* available for free at many real estate agent offices or online (see the *Resources* section).

TRAVEL AND TRANSPORTATION

Getting around Nicaragua, whether around town, from town to town, or just plain out of town, is easy and cheap, even with the exorbitant gasoline prices of late. If you grew up in the suburbs of any major North American city, you will discover a great deal more available transportation in Nicaragua than you ever did back home. Traveling in comfort and style is a bit trickier and more expensive, but not impossible. Those who have not traveled much in the developing world will find the Nicaraguan roads narrow and full of holes, the traffic frenetic, and the public buses loud, claustrophobic, and quite an adventure. Your perspective will change with experience, as aspects of daily travel that seemed onerous will begin to feel normal, and you too will learn how to cram yourself with a family of five into a bus seat built for two—with enough space to read the paper. Road travel isn't nearly as difficult as it used to be, and with time, your concept of what is "comfortable" will adjust to the realities of living and getting around in Nicaragua.

© JOSHUA BERMAN

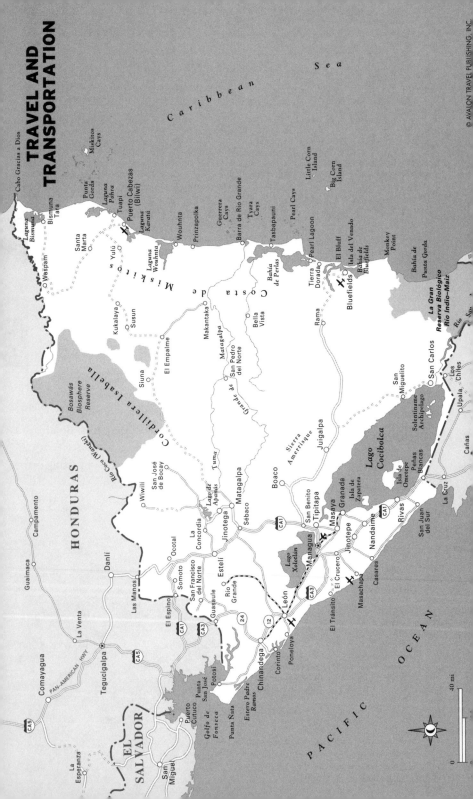

TRAVEL AND TRANSPORTATION

© AVALON TRAVEL PUBLISHING, INC.

Caribbean Sea

Cabo Gracias a Dios
Laguna Bismuna
Bismuna Tara
Punta Gorda
Laguna Pahra
Tuapi
Miskitos Cays
Santa Marta
Waspam
Laguna Karatá
Puerto Cabezas (Bilwi)
Río Coco (Wangki)
Yulú
Wouhnta
Prinzapolka
Laguna Wouhnta
Laguna de Miskitos
Kukalaya
Susun
Guerrera Cays
Barra de Río Grande
Tyara Cays
Pearl Cays
Little Corn Island
Big Corn Island
Siuna
El Empalme
Makantaka
San Pedro del Norte
Bella Vista
Tasbapauni
Bahía de Perlas
Pearl Lagoon
El Bluff
Isla del Venado
Monkey Point
Bosawás Biosphere Reserve
Cordillera Isabelia
Matagalpa
Grande de Matagalpa
Rama
Tierra Dorada
Bluefields
Bahía de Bluefields
Bahía de Punta Gorda
Costa de Mosquitos
Wiwili
San José de Bocay
Lago de Apanás
Tuma
Matagalpa
Sébaco
Boaco
Sierra Amerrisque
Juigalpa
San Miguelito
La Gran Reserva Biológico Río Indio-Maíz
Río San Juan
Campamento
HONDURAS
Guaimaca
Ocotal
La Concordia
Jinotega
Estelí
Río Grande
Somoto
San Francisco del Norte
San Benito
Tipitapa
Masaya
Granada
Isla de Zapatera
Lago Cocibolca
Isla de Ometepe
Peñas Blancas
San Carlos
Solentiname Archipiélago
Los Chiles
Upala
Cañas
Comayagua
PAN-AMERICAN HWY.
Tegucigalpa
Danli
Las Manos
El Espino
Guasaule
Guasaule
Chinandega
León
Managua
Lago Xolotlán
El Crucero
Jinotepe
Nandaime
Rivas
San Juan del Sur
La Cruz
CA1
CA3
24
12
CA1
CA5
La Venta
La Esperanza
EL SALVADOR
San Miguel
Puerto Cutuco
Golfo de Fonseca
Punta San José
Punta Nata
Estero Padre Ramos
Potosí
Corinto
Poneloya
El Tránsito
Masachapa
Casares
PACIFIC OCEAN
40 mi
0
N

Getting to Nicaragua

BY AIR

Nicaragua's national airline, Nicaragüenses de Aviación (NICA), is a member of the TACA Group, and the country is serviced by numerous major international airlines, including Aero Caribbean, American Airlines, Atlantic Airlines, Continental Airlines, Copa Airlines, Iberia, and Sol Air. Most flights from abroad pass through either Miami International Airport or Houston International Airport (or in the case of TACA, through San Salvador). Nearly all European carriers pass through Miami on their way to Nicaragua. American Airlines and Continental both have daily flights to Managua via Miami and Houston, respectively. TACA, LACSA, and SANSA share the Central American market. From Europe, both Iberia and Air France have regular flights into Managua via Miami. Flight time from Houston or Miami is under three hours.

The newest Central American carrier, Nature Air, with regular roundtrip flights connecting San José and Liberia, Costa Rica, with a small airstrip outside Granada, Nicaragua, is growing in popularity. Nature Air flights from San José (55 minutes) or Liberia (25 minutes) are more expensive than the bus but reduce a full day's travel into less than an hour.

Your first impression of Nicaragua will most likely be the still-expanding Managua International Airport (MGA, formerly named "Augusto C. Sandino" in the Sandinista years and "Las Mercedes" during the Somoza era). It's a modern and rather respectable airport with a handful of coffee shops, souvenir stands, money-changing booths, and car rental agencies, and has been undergoing major renovation since the dawn of humankind. Well, maybe not that long, but the ongoing construction at that airport is approaching its 10th anniversary, and there's no sign that it will ever be completed, making one wonder where all that US$30 per person exit tax really ends up.

BY INTERNATIONAL BUS

If you'd rather not fly, traveling from Costa Rica, Honduras, or other points in Central America is relatively inexpensive, but you'll spend the entire day arriving from the nearest capital city, either north or south. All bus lines between Managua and other Central American capitals are based out of Barrio Martha Quezada in Managua and have competing schedules and prices. Several have affiliate offices in other Nicaraguan cities, like Rivas and León. Tica Bus is the most well-established, but King Quality/Cruceros del Golfo, Central Line, and TransNica all compete for a share of the burgeoning bus market, and both quality and timeliness have improved as a result. These buses most closely resemble Greyhound or Peter Pan buses from the United States, and offer air-conditioned comfort, cushy seats, maybe a snack on board, and a movie. Traveling from Managua to either Tegucigalpa or San José will take you the better part of a full day and cost you about US$30.

Getting Around

Since the late 1990s, the major thoroughfares—from the Costa Rican border to the Honduran border via Managua and Estelí, from Managua east to El Rama via Juigalpa, and from Managua to León—have been resurfaced using modern construction equipment and fresh asphalt, and are a high-speed pleasure to ride on. Off these major roads, however, things get less comfortable quickly. Secondary roads that lead from the Panamerican Highway tend to be made of compacted earth and rock, and most of the roads that lead to the Pacific coast suffer from years of neglect. Even the road to Montelimar, Nicaragua's premier coastal resort, could use a little attention.

AIRLINES

Nicaragua's two local carriers, La Costeña and Atlantic Airlines, are both based at Managua International Airport, and between them they offer

© JOSHUA BERMAN

express flight to the Atlantic Coast

ON THE BUS

Big yellow school buses are the mainstay of the Nicaraguan transportation system. Purchased second-hand from North America and lovingly refurbished with bright plastic streamers, translucent window decals, exotic hand-lettered paint jobs, and tough steel rough racks, the modern Nica yellow bus is a source of pride and joy for its loving owner – if "loving" means surpassing its weight capacity with daunting loads of passengers and cargo. Find a comfortable seat, laugh when everyone else laughs, and enjoy the ride.

Should you decide to travel by bus, a couple of tips are worth mentioning. If you are traveling with a lot of luggage, or even just a bulky backpack, the driver's *ayudante* (helper) will want to put your bag on the roof. Having your luggage on the roof (or stowed in the back of the bus) where you can't keep an eye on it is unnerving for most foreign travelers, but it's safer than you'd expect. Even so, hedge your bets by keeping your laptop, money, and other valuables in a smaller bag on your lap. You can try to purchase a second seat for your backpack, but what usually happens is that someone pushes your bag to the side and sits there anyway, or worse, sits on top of your bag. The concept of "I paid for that seat and it's for the use of my luggage" is difficult to express in Spanish and generally unappreciated.

The driver's *ayudante* is usually trustworthy. His job is a remarkable one – keeping track of new passengers as they get on the bus, collecting their fares, helping people find seats, convincing the already-seated to slide over a bit to accommodate someone new, and helping get luggage up onto the roof and then back down again. To do this, he squeezes his way through the thickest of crowds in the aisle, exits the emergency exit at full speed, climbs around the sides and onto the roof, and emits a complicated language of whistles understood only by the driver. In all our years we've found very few *ayudantes* that intentionally tried to cheat us, though in some cases they got distracted and forgot to bring us our change until reminded. Pay attention, but don't lose too much sleep over *ayudantes*. They are by and large on your side. Making friends and giving occasional tips and gifts to drivers and *ayudantes* whom you see regularly during your commute will ensure extra peace of mind and smiles all around.

daily flights to Puerto Cabezas, Waspám, and Siuna in the northeast, Bluefields and Corn Island in the east, and San Carlos in the south. Flights are in single- and double-prop planes and may be a little bouncy at times. Don't be surprised if your pilots (whom you'll practically be sitting next to) kick back and take a nap or read the morning paper after they gain altitude and throw on the cruise control (we're not kidding). Flights within the country generally cost US$60 each way.

TAXIS

There are new Japanese models slowly joining Nicaragua's taxi fleet, but the vast majority remain the same tin-can Russian Ladas that were imported during the 1980s and, miraculously, are still chugging along. In every city except Managua, urban taxis operate on a fixed zone rate, usually no more than C$10 within the central city area. In the capital, however, it's a different story, and you should never get into a cab before settling on a price. There are several new radio taxi companies whose fleets of new air-conditioned cars can whisk you with ease around the city and can be contracted beforehand by your hotel's concierge. Another option is to hire your taxi and driver by the hour or by the day; rates vary widely, but expect anywhere from US$60–80 for a trustworthy driver for the day. Your hotel should be able to recommend someone.

RENTAL CARS

Renting a vehicle might make sense for a week or two when you're scouting out properties, getting a feel for the country, and exploring the coastline, but even if you strike a good deal with the rental car agencies you will want to limit your use of this costly resource. Numerous companies have offices at the airport in Managua and a few in Granada as well. Expect rates of around US$30 per day for a compact car and US$70–120 for a truck, plus insurance and fuel expenses, which are nothing to sneeze at. Weekly rates range US$100–1,200, depending on the type of vehicle and time of year (prices vary between high and low season). Consider using the insurance available through your credit card if you plan on renting a vehicle. Nicaraguan traffic can be chaotic, and more than one unhappy visitor has gotten stuck with a hefty bill after being the victim in a fender bender. Your credit card insurance might cover more than the rental insurance available through the car rental agency.

PUBLIC BUSES

Hundreds of Peace Corps Volunteers, missionaries, and adventure travelers make their way around the nation on Nicaragua's well-developed and slowly improving bus system, and consider bus travel to be an opportune way of getting to know Nicaraguans on their own turf. Nicaraguan buses go everywhere. There's hardly a village on the map that doesn't have some kind of bus passing through at least once a day. No matter where you choose to settle, getting to know the bus system is a good move, just in case, especially in places like Granada and Carazo, where *microbuses* are the most convenient form of transport by far.

Make sure to ask whether the bus you're thinking about taking is an *expreso* or a *ruteada* (an express or local bus), as the difference in travel time can be considerable. Express buses cost a buck more but save you time and sanity as they generally travel directly to the destination city without stopping (or stopping no more than once somewhere along the way), while *rutas* stop for every ... single ... person on the side of the road who flags it down.

DRIVING YOUR OWN VEHICLE

DAILY LIFE

The freedom, comfort, and independence gained by having your own vehicle in Nicaragua comes with a few drawbacks. Such is life. First and foremost is the exorbitant price of gas. Europeans won't be as stunned as North Americans, but even they will find fuel prices in Nicaragua uncomfortably high. Nicaragua gets most of its fuel from Mexico and Venezuela, and transport charges, the vagaries of the international market, and Nicaragua's weak leverage at the bargaining table all add up to expensive gas. We're talking 150–200 percent higher than prices in the United States. Consequently, diesel vehicles are greatly preferred to gasoline engine vehicles.

Second is the challenge of maintaining a vehicle on punishing roads. Expect to have to pay for a realignment and a new set of shocks annually, particularly if you spend much time off the pavement. Toyota, followed by other Japanese and Korean brands, is the king of the heap in Nicaragua, which means it's easier to find replacement parts for those vehicles, albeit more expensive than back home. U.S. vehicles often require parts that must be special-ordered from the factory or from regional suppliers, which means you may have to wait weeks for some parts to be delivered, and then pay extra for them. Should you decide to someday return to the United States, be aware your gasoline vehicle will sell for thousands of dollars less than what it's worth, or not at all.

Also, nationalizing a foreign car (putting Nicaraguan plates on it, see *Vehicle Registration*) can be a nightmare. We've heard horror stories involving customs agents, border runs, storage fees, and impoundings that are reason enough not to try to bring our own car. Plus, the legislation involving importation of vehicles by dealers and by non-Nicaraguans is in flux, and you will get different answers to the same questions depending on with whom you speak. The Nicaraguan government is toying with the idea of banning the importation of any vehicle older than five years, so if you are making your move to Nicaragua in 2007, your car must be a 2002 model or newer, for example. The government hasn't decided whether or

TRAFFIC TICKETS AND ACCIDENTS

Your white (nondiplomatic) license plate and your foreign appearance will attract the attention of traffic police. Police in Nicaragua are known to be fairer and less corrupt than elsewhere in Central America, but with their pitifully small salaries, they are sometimes on the lookout for extra income. Commonly called *"la pesca"* (a reference to fishing), Nicaragua's finest are often seen in groups at intersections and traffic circles, surrounded by construction cones, flourishing bright orange gloves, and pulling over everything in sight for *mala maniobra* (moving violation, literally "bad driving"). Have your papers ready when the officer approaches your window, and get ready to put your Spanish to the test.

The latest method used by police is to confiscate your license and threaten to hold it hostage until you come in next week to pay the fine – unless, of course, you'd rather take care of the matter right away, in which case your attire and vehicle will be quickly assessed to determine the asking rate (probably around US$10). Should you choose to play by the rules, you'll accept a temporary permit after giving up your license, which you'll be able to retrieve by paying the fine at any bank, then taking the receipt to the department of motor vehicles (be-

hind Roberto Huembes Terminal), where they'll have your license. Be aware that there do exist honest Nicaraguan cops who not only won't accept your bribe but will ticket you for the attempt. Also, paying off the police only serves to encourage and perpetuate corruption.

In case of a traffic accident, do *not* move your vehicle from the scene of the crime until authorized by a police officer, even if it is blocking traffic. For lack of high-tech crime scene equipment, the Nicaraguan police force will try to understand how the accident occurred based on what they see at the site. Drivers who move their vehicle at the scene of the accident are held legally liable for the incident – even if you just move your vehicle to the side of the road. Any driver in Nicaragua who is party to an accident where injuries are sustained will be taken into custody, even if the driver has insurance and does not seem to be at fault. This custody will be maintained until a judicial decision is reached (sometimes weeks later) or until the injured party signs a waiver releasing the driver of liability. In many cases, to avoid a lengthy court proceeding and horrifying jail stay, it may be worth your while to plead guilty and pay a fine (which will probably not exceed US$1,000).

not expatriates should be exempt from that legislation. If you are permitted to import the vehicle you will be assessed a tax equivalent to 40 percent of its stated blue book value.

Purchasing a Car in Nicaragua

Given those challenges, you might decide it's smarter just to purchase a vehicle in Nicaragua and not deal with import/export issues. You still have to choose your vehicle carefully, of course, but by purchasing a vehicle locally you can avoid a lot of hassle. Some things to watch out for: First, most vehicles produced for the Nicaraguan market are built without the stringent emissions equipment required in the United States, which mostly precludes you from easily taking your vehicle with you should you leave Nicaragua and return to the United States. It can be done, but it will require costly retrofits that might be more expensive than they merit. Second, importing used American vehicles and selling them on the Nicaraguan market is probably the nation's second most popular get-rich-quick scheme (after casinos). You will be pitting yourself against more than one unscrupulous salesperson and an ocean of used vehicles in varying physical condition. We don't recommend purchasing your vehicle from a lot. Rather, try to look for a vehicle in the company of a trusted Nicaraguan or expat who knows about cars and mechanics, as well as dealerships and popular brands in Nicaragua. Otherwise, caveat emptor.

Whether you buy a vehicle in Nicaragua or take your own vehicle with you, it's worth your time to bring a steering wheel club or other physical deterrent to auto theft (car alarms and sirens are universally ignored in Nicaragua as they are everywhere else). You'll need wheel locks as well—little mechanical pieces that clip over your lug nuts to keep your wheels from disappearing in the night. Take along a set of five and lock down your wheels, including your spare. You won't be able to purchase them in Nicaragua. Unfortunately, there is no such device to prevent the disappearance of external mirrors, radio antennas, windshield wipers, or any other piece of strippable detailing.

What kind of car to drive or buy? Rare is the expat who doesn't drive some sort of sport utility vehicle or truck, and four-wheel drive is almost essential unless you are strictly a city person. All-wheel-drive station wagons are a rarity in Nicaragua, where some roads require more undercarriage clearance than these vehicles provide.

Driver's Licenses

Until about 2005, you were required to acquire a Nicaraguan driver's license if you were not a tourist. That meant, if you got your residency permit you were also required to get a Nicaraguan driver's license. It also meant that if you extended your tourist visa beyond three months you had to have a Nicaraguan driver's license (or stick to buses). But as of 2005, foreigners are permitted to use their foreign driver's license for as long as it is valid. Before you brush this off as one step you won't have to deal with, consider the advantages of having a Nicaraguan license (besides the fun you'll have showing it to your friends back home, of course): It states a case for leniency before the law as you have made an effort to live by Nicaraguan rules and not retain some sort of foreign privilege, and it obviates the need for you to return periodically to your home country to renew your license there. And besides, getting a driver's license is one of the easier bureaucratic processes in Nicaragua.

For the sake of reassuring yourself the requirements haven't changed, start with a trip to the local police department to inquire about a driver's license. Some bigger departments outside of Managua issue licenses, but not all, so the first step is really to confirm whether or not you'll be making a trip to another office to acquire your license. The department can also confirm for you the following steps. Essentially you need your foreign driver's license, a blood test and an eye test, copies of your passport information page and the page where your visa was stamped, and proof of your residency—either your resident permit or the lease to the place you're renting, plus about US$10. Get the paperwork from the police department. It will indicate a bank account in the Banpro bank where you will deposit the money. You will submit the deposit receipt with the rest of your paperwork to get your license. You can have both the blood test and the eye exam performed at the Cruz Roja (the Red Cross) for about US$4 each. Bring the results of those exams, the photocopies of your passport pages, lease, *cédula,* and your Banpro deposit slip to the police department. Once your paperwork is accepted and approved, you will be called into the back room for a photo. About a half hour later, you will be presented with your shiny new Nicaraguan driver's license. Happy motoring!

Vehicle Registration

Registering a Nicaraguan vehicle in your name is, comparatively, a much harder—but not impossible—endeavor. Writing instructions for this process is nearly worthless, because any bureaucrat at any point in the process can make it much more difficult for you at his or her whim. On the other hand, thousands and thousands of people have struggled their way through the system before you, so take heart and read on.

The first step is to purchase insurance. Nicaraguan policies are neither as expensive nor as comprehensive as American auto insurance. Passenger vehicle policies cost about US$85 per year, motorcycle policies about US$60. These policies cover death or injury to other parties but do not cover damage to your own vehicle. Of the several insurance companies doing business in

Nicaragua, SEGUROSSA and INISER are the two most popular. Expats complain equally about both companies but consider the insurance more of a formality than anything else. If you have auto insurance at home that covers you overseas you should consider looking into it, but make clear you need full-time overseas coverage, not a traveler's policy.

The second step is the inspections that ensure your vehicle is road-worthy. You'll complain "but look at all the other junky vehicles on the street!" with indignation and you'll be right, but the situation is slowly changing, and the government is indeed making a concerted effort to remove dilapidated vehicles from circulation. In 2001, "Plan Chatarra" (*chatarra* means "junk metal") nabbed several thousand junky cars in Managua and forced the owners to either pay hefty fines or stop using the vehicles on Managua streets, and a re-registration program in 2005 forced all vehicle owners to reinspect and relicense their vehicles in order to get new plates, which forced a few more junkers off the road. Further such operations are planned every year as an incentive for the owners of those old dilapidated vehicles to invest in some improvements. You need to pass a physical inspection and an emissions inspection, and have someone confirm the chassis and vehicle serial numbers match (an attempt to curb the sale of stolen vehicles, a legitimate concern). You will very likely have to do each inspection in a separate facility—no "one-stop shops" yet, and each stop will have its own payment method. Increasingly, official bureaucratic payments require deposits into an official account to prevent corruption from whisking away the government's revenue into the deep pockets of local officials.

The last step is to take with you to the police station proof of ownership of the vehicle, your importation documents if you imported your own vehicle with you from overseas or the sales documents if you purchased your vehicle in Nicaragua, proof of your insurance, a copy of your driver's license, 2–3 copies of your passport (the information page plus the page with your visa), your *cédula* if you have one, and your inspection reports. They will document your information, make some entries in their computer system, and issue you the new plates. This last step is described in one sentence, but the whole process could easily take several visits to the police station and any number of additional documents they require from you. A few US$20 bills might smooth the road for you, but they might not. Don't be afraid to ask a lot of questions, and better still, take along a Nicaraguan to help interpret the information, as the intricacies of this particular bureaucracy can be daunting.

HOUSING CONSIDERATIONS

Living in Nicaragua means having a roof over your head quite different from the one that sheltered you back home—and we're not only talking about the red clay tiles, corrugated "zinc," and the gap between the wall that invites so many friendly geckos to move in. There are many other aspects to finding a proper home in Nicaragua, and this section introduces and analyzes each one. After assessing the renting versus buying question and the risks of investing in Nicaraguan property, you'll need to know how to go about looking for a place; then, once you move in, you'll have to learn how to manage, maintain, and repair a radically different type of home from what you are accustomed to, not to mention contractors who speak a different language. None of these things pose an insurmountable challenge, but it's important to be cognizant of what living in a Nicaraguan home means. Can you deal with adobe walls, a roof made of clay, and a well in the backyard? How about pervasive dust, termites, and the *ranchera* bar across the street? These are just a few of the many questions you should start asking.

© RANDALL WOOD

RENTING VS. BUYING

A big part of answering this question is assessing how long you think you'll be there, how willing you are to accept the risks inherent in the real estate market of a developing country, and for that matter, why you are going to Nicaragua in the first place. If you are simply hoping to cash in by purchasing a property and then waiting to sell at a profit, then your question has been answered, and renting is not for you—unless that piece of property is nothing more than a patch of wild jungle and you'd like to spend some time in country while it appreciates or is developed.

If you are not heading to Nicaragua to get rich quick, but are more inter-ested in learning about the people, enjoying a relatively low cost of living,

FINDING YOUR *CASA:* CLASSIFIED AD DECODER

The first step in finding a great place is to know what you are looking for. The second is to know what you are looking *at*. Use this guide to navigate Nicaragua's cryptic real estate ads in the newspaper.

Text Stands For	Means	
4H3B	*4 habitaciónes, 3 baños*	4 bedroom, 3 bath
2G	*2 garajes*	2 garages
aa	*aire acondicionado*	air-conditioned
amob.	*amueblado*	furnished
apto	*apartamento*	apartment
area de serv	*area de servicio*	maid's quarters
c/s	*con/sin*	with or without
na	*nueva*	new
parq.	*parqueo*	parking
s/interm	*sin intermediarios*	without intermediaries (brokers)
sem.	*semáforo*	traffic light (used for giving directions)

Managua Neighborhoods	Abbreviations
Carretera Sur	C.Sur
Colonia Los Robles	C.L.R.
Carretera Masaya	C.Mas
Santo Domingo	S.Dom.
Reparto (a name used in many neighborhoods)	Rep.

and basking in the fine weather, then you probably should rent for a while until you're convinced that Nicaragua is indeed where you would like to make your next home—particularly if you are also considering other Central American destinations. Renting is also a valuable option if you are concerned about the uncertainties of politics, the tropical climate, your ability to live far away from friends and loved ones, your Spanish skills, etc. Call it a trial run, and if things work out in your favor and you feel as comfortable, safe, and satisfied as you had hoped, you can make the bigger commitment of purchasing a home, renovating a colonial hideaway, buying a piece of land, or undertaking construction of your own design.

SEARCHING FOR A HOUSE OR APARTMENT

Most potential expatriates begin their housing search online, long before they step foot on Nicaraguan soil, or perhaps immediately after completing their fact-finding trip. In the *Resources* section of this book you will find information for regional real estate agents who can provide housing listings for you. But a large part of your housing search in Nicaragua, like elsewhere, involves leg work. Furthermore, word of mouth in Nicaragua goes a long way, whether you are searching for a property to buy or rent. Make it clear to shop owners, hotel staff, and restaurant personnel that you are in the market for housing. You will be surprised how effectively this method finds you a bevy of neighbors, sisters, and cousins who are interested in doing business. And in a nation where formal methods of communication sometimes fall short, the informal method, a.k.a. "the grapevine" or Jimmy Buffett's infamous "coconut telegraph," is the one that provides the most efficient results. Don't be afraid to chat as you go, and before long the sellers and renters will come to you.

Renting

In more developed markets the rental properties and properties for sale tend to diverge in character. But in Nicaragua's inchoate market, the difference between "for rent" and "for sale" is the intention of the buyer. Don't land in Nicaragua thinking you'll find one-bedroom apartments for rent and colonial palaces for sale and be forced to make a choice, because in reality any given property might be for rent or for sale: If you're lucky, you can find a colonial property for rent just as easily as you'll find a one-bedroom little home for sale. This is especially true since 2000, since many expats have purchased colonial homes in places like Granada and San Juan del Sur expressly for the purpose of renting them out to other expats. If you'd like to start off your exploration of Nicaragua with something that requires little financial commitment, finding one of these properties might be a good first step.

At this point, you will not find many apartment buildings in the style of Florida beachside condominiums or even simple urban multi-unit buildings. With the exception of one work in progress on the limits of San Juan del Sur, only Managua has any apartment buildings, and even there your options are few. But that's not to say there's nothing to rent! Rather, it means that rentals tend to look like everything else: single, free-standing one-family homes and urban colonial-style concrete and adobe homes. Interest is rising among Nicaragua's entrepreneur class in so-called "garden apartment" buildings, in which two-story buildings have four apartments each and cluster around a shared courtyard. This type of construction is common throughout southern Florida, from where Nicaraguan architects have surely taken their inspiration. Notably absent from the Nicaraguan housing market until about 2005 were condominiums and co-ops, time-share rentals, and the like. In the coming decade as places like San Juan del Sur are "developed," keep your eye peeled for progress in this sector.

Because renters and buyers wind up in the same kinds of properties, know what you are getting into and understand how to ensure your potential rental home won't give you undue stress by reading the section below. And don't stress out either about finding a long-term or short-term rental. In Nicaragua, no one draws a distinction between the two, and the terms of your lease will very much be defined by how well you bargain with the property owner. They would like you to stay indefinitely, of course, but we have both rented places for a month or three months at a time and no one has batted

TIPS FOR RENTERS

The Nicaraguan rental market is still nascent and lacks broad institutionality. To the average renter that means you are very free to negotiate with your potential landlord/landlady with regard to the terms of your lease. Nicaraguans frequently ask expatriates for a month of rent up front as a security deposit, but many do not. You may not be required to jump through the hoops you are accustomed to back home either, like personal references, up-front deposits of first and last months of rent, and should these things be requested, feel free to negotiate it down. That blade cuts both ways, though. Nicaraguan law does not provide the legal safeguards for renters that the rental market does in the United States. If you get into a dispute with your landlord, few legal protections – if any – exist to protect you from being thrown out into the street, and should you decide to take your dispute into the court system, an arduous and lengthy process awaits you with no clear hope that the law will protect you.

With the knowledge that you and your landlord will hammer out the details of your lease in the absence of strong legal institutions, take the time to spell out as many contingencies as you can think of and make sure you and your potential landlord agree on them. That means the following: Who will take care of repairs and within what time period? What will happen if a catastrophe (a strong hurricane or earthquake) makes the place unlivable – does that release you from your lease to find a different apartment? How many months in advance must you declare your intention to vacate the property? How many months in advance must your landlord advise you your lease will not be renewed? The more clearly you can spell out these arrangements, the more protections you will be afforded should something go wrong.

Rental prices vary dramatically from region to region and from the countryside to the city. Increasingly, property owners demand payment for rented properties in dollars. This is a not-so-subtle way of writing in a guaranteed rent escalation, as the devaluing local currency doesn't cause a parallel devaluation in the earnings they receive from the rental. You are free to pay córdobas, of course, payable at the exchange rate prevalent at the time rent is due.

an eye at the shortness of the lease. Again, because the rental market is so new in Nicaragua, there's still a lot of room for you to be creative.

PRICES

Again, how well can you bargain, where is the property, and how spacious is it? We have included estimated prices in each of the *Prime Living Location* chapters of this book, but here's somewhat of an overview: In Managua you can expect to spend anywhere from US$100 to $1,500 to rent a variety of homes that run from somewhat uncomfortable single-family homes in not-so-great neighborhoods to luxurious family homes in the best parts of the city. In major towns like Estelí and Matagalpa, there is less variety overall since the market is different, but you can expect to pay US$100–400 a month to rent a single family home. It's harder to estimate prices in San Juan del Sur and Granada because the real estate market is so active there and because such diverse homes are entering the market. But you can expect to pay US$300–$1,000 a month depending on how modern and spacious the home is and perhaps a bit more if the property was recently constructed expressly for the purpose of being rented.

Buying

HOUSING TYPES

Until about 2005, housing in most of Nicaragua consisted of detached single-family homes, frequently but not always built in the Spanish colonial style. But things are changing fast. Although you can still count the number of apartment buildings in Nicaragua on a single hand, very few homes are any higher than one story, and they don't have basements. Managua was a modern city of high-rise buildings before the earthquake of 1972, which left the city in rubble; Managuans rebuilt the city one story high until the early 21st century, when they began to build upward again on the outskirts of Managua. Outside of Managua and the new developments in San Juan del Sur, you'll be hard pressed to find homes that aren't one-story free-standing dwellings.

Colonial Architecture

Most design and construction in the 18th century consisted of adobe (hard-baked mud bricks) or *taquezal*. The latter is an ingenious system of building one-story homes: hardwood posts (often measured sections of hardwood logs stripped of their bark but left round) are placed every seven feet or so, and smaller vertical wooden studs are placed every two feet, making a sort of hardwood timber frame. Small wooden lath cross pieces are then attached very closely up the length of the studs, forming a pocket inside, which the builder can then fill either with mud and adobe, stones, or a combination of both. Finally, to cover over the lath, the builder applies a thick coat of adobe to form smooth walls. The result is the much-loved traditional adobe architecture still present throughout much of Latin America.

© RANDALL WOOD

Flat in front, colonial homes are bigger than they look from the outside.

The colonial design deals effectively with heat by incorporating high ceilings, which allow hot air to rise, and long roofs, which keep the sun (and the rain) off the walls. They typically present a nondescript, flat face streetside but are built around luxurious courtyards inside, around which open patios and rooms are built. The design gives families a convenient and private area around which they can relax and enjoy each others' company, and the open inside facilitates air circulation, which keeps temperatures down. It may seem strange for a northerner to have a home that's open in the middle, but once you get used to it, the boxy, hermetic homes we build in temperate climates may seem like a much less comfortable way to live. In these colonial buildings, the roof is constructed of a wooden riser system and lath on top of which hard clay tiles (*teja*) are set in rows up to the peak of the roof, whose crown is created with a row of upside-down tiles.

Modern Construction

Modern buildings eschew mud and sticks for the material that has changed the face of human settlement worldwide: concrete and concrete blocks. Much of Managua is built of small, concrete block houses that frequently make use of "breeze block" (concrete blocks with formed perforations that permit air to flow through), also found in traditionally colonial cities like Granada and León, particularly in the outlying neighborhoods that formed as the cities grew. Some homes continue to use clay *teja* for their roof, while others go with the quick-and-easy corrugated steel sheets known throughout Nicaragua as *"zinc."* A modern take on the traditional construction is sheets of synthetic fiber board shaped and painted like rows of *teja,* which are lightweight and cool. The synthetic version of the corrugated steel roof is known as "Nicalite" or sometimes "Nicalit" and bears the same curvy surface as its metallic predecessor.

More and more housing developments—particularly on the outskirts of Managua on the road to Masaya and any houses constructed to take advantage of the current housing boom—tend to follow North American designs. Gone is the colonial layout with the courtyard in the center. In its place is a hermetically sealed building with glass windows and air-conditioning units. It's a different approach to moderating temperatures, and a good alternative for those who need air-conditioning and don't mind losing the charm of colonial architecture, while traditionalists disparage the design as inappropriate for the climate.

Materials

First of all, you have to hand it to the colonials, who managed to build charming and comfortable homes using the simple technology represented by adobe and *taquezal:* The wood, mud, and stone that goes into this kind of construction is readily available (although deforestation has made good quality hardwood posts increasingly rare). Adobe homes are always cool and comfortable inside, even in the hot tropical sun, and nicks and cuts in the adobe surface are easily repaired with a minimum of effort. As a result, Nicaraguan farming communities up in the mountains continue to use this technology to build homes. The disadvantage of adobe is that great effort must be expended to keep the material dry. You'll notice the long, sloping tile roofs on homes built of adobe. Their purpose is to shield the buildings' walls from driving rains.

Concrete, while infinitely more convenient than the labor intensive process of building adobe homes (or maintaining them), makes houses hotter as concrete has less insulating value than adobe does. For the record, no one builds adobe homes anymore, but you can still find people who know how to repair them, an important skill in a country where so many homes were built a century ago and have simply been passed from generation to generation.

There is less to debate where *teja* is concerned. The authentic clay tiles, while atmospheric, are a huge hassle. Not only does every tile have to be hand placed, but strong winds, gravity, and the occasional seismic tremor eventually dislodge them, causing incessant leaks, drips, and similar problems. Corrugated steel roofs are no better. Steel roofs get unbearably hot in the sun, leading you to feel like you are being baked alive in your home, particularly if your ceilings aren't high. Corrugated steel roofing is deafeningly loud during Nicaragua's violent rainstorms as well, and in the hot sun it "clicks" as the steel expands around the nails that bind it to the roof beams. The advantage of steel roofing is that it is cheap, ubiquitous, and easy to work with.

In comparison, synthetic alternatives like Nicalite roofing and kin are by far the most amenable alternative. It is lightweight like steel roofing, can be painted to look like *teja* if that's what you like, and doesn't conduct heat the way the steel sheets do. At the same time, Nicalite is quiet when it rains. Its disadvantage is that not all towns have supplies of Nicalite for sale, so you might have to order some from the capital as you build.

The Journal of the Association for Preservation Technology once published an interesting article by Randolph Langenbach that looked at whether adobe and *taquezal* or modern concrete structures are better able to resist earthquakes and found that many of the deaths in the 1972 Managua earthquake occurred in adobe homes that collapsed, killing those inside, but that the cause was deterioration in the wood columns that formed the homes' superstructures. The article went on to say adobe is better at resisting earthquakes than modern buildings because of its inherent flexibility, which permits the buildings to distribute the seismic shock evenly. Nicaragua is prone to earthquakes throughout the country, so this is something to take into consideration.

Bathrooms and Kitchens

Bedrooms and living rooms differ little around the world, but plumbing is often one of the characteristics that set one culture apart from another. As such, the modern Nicaraguan home deals with kitchens and bathrooms in a way you might not be accustomed to. Many Nicaraguans, even in modern cities, cook over wood fires, draw their drinking and washing water from a well, and use a latrine (outhouse) in the backyard as their bathroom. Many homes have an enormous concrete cistern *(pila)* in the backyard in which water is stored and which is drawn down over the course of the day. Other homes maintain a 50-gallon steel drum (many with the original petroleum industry origins clearly visible on the side) in the kitchen from where they get their water. Regardless of whether that's the lifestyle you'd like to lead, it's what you can expect to find when you take possession of a Nicaraguan property and begin your renovation.

Next, instead of a countertop, cabinets, and a sink under which the dishwasher is tucked, you might find a long wooden counter Nicaraguans use to prepare food, along with a freestanding concrete basin and washboard under a water spigot. This structure is called the *pila* or the *lavandero* and is used not only for washing dishes but for laundry. The rugged, corrugated part is for scrubbing, and the deep basin stores a couple of gallons of water, which you scoop out as necessary for your cleaning chores. The best way to get used to one of these contraptions is to spend some time watching how Nicaraguans use them, whether it be by making friends with your neighbors or by paying close attention to your maid as she goes about the daily chores.

The odds are slim you'll be happy with the bathroom in its original configuration either. Accept the fact you'll remodel as you move in. Nicaraguan bathrooms include the same toilets you're used to, but many lack seats and covers, and often are not even hooked up to running water. In this case, you have to get a bucket of water from the basin on the other side of the room and manually flush the toilet by dropping the water into the bowl from a height (repeat or raise the bucket higher for greater effectiveness). If that is not acceptable to you, you'll need to make sure a plumber connects your bathroom to the water lines for you. Even with plumbing, the water pressure is frequently too poor to flush down toilet paper, so don't be surprised to see a small wastebasket of used tissue and be sure to use it yourself, unless you want to face the wrath of an angry and very clogged Nica toilet.

Sound overwhelming? Relax—we've painted the worst-case scenarios (well, not quite: pit latrines are definitely worse). What you find in Nicaragua's housing options could very well be more comfortable than what we've described here, particularly in markets where old homes are being renovated and offered for sale to expats, like Granada and San Juan del Sur. But if you find a lovely old colonial home whose previous owner was born in 1915 and who hasn't kept up with the times, we've made clear what you can expect. Cities like Granada and León all have municipal water and sewer systems, except for outlying neighborhoods where those services have not yet been installed and where you can expect a latrine and a well. Many recently built homes in residential subdivisions now incorporate modern kitchen components formerly unknown to Nicaragua like steel sinks and linoleum countertops, and Managua's middle class is increasingly demanding fancier

© RANDALL WOOD

Clay tile roofs are more complicated to construct than they look.

amenities in bathrooms as well. The catch is, if you are particular about certain elements, like granite countertops in your kitchen or fancy fixtures on the bathroom faucets, you might have to bring them to Nicaragua with you. Same goes for dishwashers and in-sink garbage disposals, which have not yet become part of the modern Nicaraguan home.

INSPECTING A HOUSE: WHAT TO CONSIDER
Location

Hearing about Nicaragua's fantastic locations—Pacific coastline properties, colonial residences in historic cities, lake islands all your own—may be a large part of what has drawn you to Nicaragua, but it is in the more mundane details where you should focus your attention.

Remember, Nicaraguans rise early to start the day, so getting an idea of who your neighbors (and what kind of animals they keep) is an important first step in understanding what your lifestyle would be like and how much noise to expect (hint: expect roosters). Look diligently not just at the property but the surrounding properties as well. Nicaragua lacks any sort of formal zoning laws, so it's perfectly acceptable for your neighbor to start up a pig farm in her backyard if she wants to, and there's little you can do about it. You can't prevent what happens in the future, but you can certainly take a careful look around to see if any neighbors are running businesses out of their homes, and how they will affect you. Come back to see the property at night to find out if anyone is running a *fritanga* (fried food restaurant) out of their home. Never mind how much weight you'll

PROPERTY INSPECTION CHECKLIST

- Air-conditioning
- Bars on the windows, doors
- Easy means of egress in case of earthquake
- Gas stove
- Good plumbing
- Good roof
- Good water pressure
- Off-street parking behind a fence
- Quiet neighborhood, reliable neighbors
- Quiet street, little traffic
- Refrigerator
- Screens to prevent mosquitoes
- Spacious outside patio
- Sunny area to dry clothing
- Washing machine

gain from all the yummy fried food, these places might be too noisy, attract a drinking crowd, lead to trash in the streets and a whole host of hungry dogs. How close are you to a major church or cathedral? The peal of those old bells might be charming the first couple of times and drive you crazy afterward. For that matter, how close is the property to the city's various markets and bus terminals? While convenient, these properties are less restful than you'd imagine.

Next, take a careful look to see if local geographic low spots will lead to stagnant water (and thus malaria-bearing mosquitoes or flies) during the wet season, if the property is breezy enough to keep away the airborne insects, particularly at sunset when the biting insects are after you. Make sure the property isn't on a major thoroughfare. Even certain city streets bear more traffic than others. Avoid city streets with bus routes on them if at all possible, as the noise, pollution, and tumult that accompanies the buses can have a seriously negative impact on your living situation.

Condition of the House

Examine how the house was constructed. If it's an old, adobe structure, what kind of condition is it in? If necessary, have a Nicaraguan friend accompany you to help you understand whether the adobe is in good condition or needs repair. If the roof is of clay tiles, how old are the tiles, and are many tiles chipped, cracked, or missing? If the roof is corrugated steel, do you see any rust spots on the inside that would indicate leaks?

Pay attention to cracks in concrete and fissures in adobe structures that may mean the structure is settling, poorly built, or failing.

Windows and Screens

Look at windows, window glass, and screens. Many Nicaraguan windows are wooden, not glass, so they are either open to the breeze and bugs, or closed to the light. Obviously it's not a serious consideration if the house is colonial and the entire inside is open anyway, but if your house is a modern construction but still has glassless windows, you will need to worry about bugs getting inside your home. Screen windows are not as common as they should be, but screened windows will dramatically improve your lifestyle, especially in Granada, where the lakeshore breeze carries along with it a swarm of little gnats throughout several months of the year. For the same reason, take an up-close look at where the walls meet the roof. Some Nicaraguan homes' roof beams sit on top of the walls with a five-inch gap between the surface of the roof and the top of the wall. It's good for ventilation but bad for insects (and for theft as well—a friend of ours was burglarized one day while he was out; after following the footprints he realized they'd entered his home by actually lifting the roof off of the wall and sliding in).

Plumbing

Check the water supply to make sure there is decent water pressure. Then ask the neighbors on both sides if the water pressure drops at any point during the day (*"se va el agua durante el día?"*). More than one neighborhood is connected to pumps that run only in the morning and evening, which is why so many Nicaraguan families fill up their *pila* and barrel in the morning to guarantee a source of water for later in the day. Take a careful look at the bathroom facilities and make sure the outflow from the shower is connected to the city sewer system and doesn't just run out of a pipe at the bottom of your property (and check your neighbors' properties for the same reason).

Wood and Termites

If Nicaraguan builders don't use wood, it's because in the tropics and subtropics, termites proliferate so easily that nothing built of wood can be expected to last longer than a few years, and what the termites don't terminate, the humidity will. You are unlikely to find a wooden home anywhere but on the Atlantic coast, but poke your fingernail or a penknife into the wood of window sills and anywhere else you find wood exposed, to ensure

HOUSEHOLD EXPENSES

The kind of expenses to expect upon moving into a Nicaraguan home or apartment include household help (maids and night watch-people), utilities (water, sewer, telephone, and electricity), and, if you're buying a home, taxes. Expats moving to Nicaragua for the cheap lifestyle have the rudest awakening when it comes to utilities. Overall Nicaragua is a less expensive place to live, but Nicaragua imports the bulk of the energy it produces in the form of petroleum products for the production of electricity. Given rising petroleum prices worldwide, Nicaragua's electricity costs far more than it does back home. You can find more detailed information about what kind of general expenses to expect upon moving to Nicaragua in the *Finances* chapter.

that it isn't rotten. Termites eat the soft inside of wooden structures but leave the hard exterior and the painted surface. More than one home owner has been surprised to find an otherwise perfect-looking wooden beam had been chewed hollow inside by termites. You can frequently spot termites by the wood dust that drops to the floor where they've been working, which often gets caught up in spider webs. Keep your eyes open!

Electricity and Wiring

Expats all have a crazy wiring story to tell. Randy's is the bathroom light switch in a building in Managua that consisted of two exposed wires with bright copper tips. To turn on the light, one was expected to reach over the puddle of water on the floor and hook one exposed wire around the other. After a fat blue spark shot out of the connection, the lights would come on. Many of the haphazard jobs you find are the result of the "good-enough-for-now" mentality that pervaded throughout the civil war and has been hard to shake loose since. Taking a good look at your home's wiring will help you understand if you are at risk of electrical problems. Lots of electricians are available to help you, should you need to address any issues, but communicate clearly what you want to avoid hiring someone who intends to replace bad wiring with more of the same. Don't forget to glance at the fuse box. How many amps was the house rated for? Most Nicaraguan homes are rated for fewer than 100 amps, which means you won't be able to run many electronic devices simultaneously, much less heavy-draw items like air-conditioning. That was acceptable a decade ago when most Nicaraguan families had no reason to use anything more complicated than a couple of light bulbs, a refrigerator, and an electric fan, but if you intend to run a big television, computer equipment, a hair dryer, and a washing machine, your old Nicaraguan system might not be able to withstand that kind of stress. If for any reason you are not sure or not confident assessing your electrical system, find an electrician to do it on your behalf.

Lastly, note which major appliances, if any, your home contains. It's likely it only has a refrigerator, and might not have even that. You will never see a dishwasher or garbage disposal, but might rarely find a home with a washing machine (certainly not a dryer, as everyone just hangs their clothes outside in the sun).

PROPERTY OWNERSHIP: THE RISKS
Political Risks

As far as risk goes, your first concern is likely the political risk that has characterized Nicaragua since the early 1990s and perhaps earlier. Nicaragua has enjoyed a stable economy and peaceful transition of governments since 1990 when the Sandinistas turned power over to the government of Doña Violeta Chamorro. But every time elections roll around, both Nicaraguans and expats get a little antsy. The worst-case scenario, as most people paint it, would be a return to power of Daniel Ortega, whose government will then immediately begin to confiscate the property of every expat in town. But if you take the time to talk to Nicaraguans and the local expat community, you will find very few people who seriously believe that particular scenario would ever occur. Nicaragua in the 21st century is not the Nicaragua of the 1980s, nor are any of its political parties or personalities unchanged. The Nicaraguan government has extensive political and economic commitments to other nations as well as to its own people not to engage in activities so economically devastating as the confiscation of foreign-owned property. The authors do not claim to have any inside information with regard to the political situation, but the mood on the street is clearly that while it is smart to pay close attention to Nicaraguan politics, there is little serious popular concern that an incoming government will expropriate your land.

Economic Risks

The economic risk of investing in Nicaragua receives less attention but deserves more. It's clear that prices for housing and land have risen exorbitantly since 1995, and many analysts expect prices to continue rising in the future. But are Nicaraguan housing prices outstripping the real value of property on the market? Assessing that question should be part of the due diligence process you undertake on your fact-finding trip. If politics are the first topic of conversation on every expat's tongue, the fear of a "housing bubble" in Nicaragua is the second. Keep things in perspective: It is ultimately a deeply personal assessment as to whether the price you pay to buy property in Nicaragua is worth the risk of investing in a foreign country as well as whether you would be happy living there in the first place. If you are satisfied with the price you pay for a home or piece of land, then you should not be concerned even if prices drop. But by all means, ignore the hype of "the next Costa Rica" or "last real estate bargain on earth" type of talk. It's not that you can't find a good deal in Nicaragua, it's that you should pay attention to the quality of the properties you investigate and ignore the hype.

Legal Risks and Property Titles

This is potentially the most nerve-wracking and salient concern shared by prospective buyers. Bad plumbing, after all, can be dealt with. But you do not, for any reason, want to be dragged into Nicaragua's court system, which is one of the most corrupt and bureaucratic in Central America. The big issue at hand is clear title to the property.

But first, some history:

Land before 1979 was not evenly distributed among the population. While in the cities everyone essentially held the title to their land, out in the countryside vast tracts were the property of the wealthy aristocracy *(terretenientes),* many of whom left much of their land fallow and unproductive. Meanwhile, poor landless farmers were forced into a virtual indentured servitude for salaries on which they could barely survive. A major platform of the Sandinistas after their 1979 revolution was addressing this egregious social injustice, and true to their promise, they launched their land reform by confiscating wealthy landowners' property and distributing it to the poor. They started with the properties of the former dictator, President Somoza, who by some accounts owned most of the land worth owning, then moved on to the estates and homes of his friends and business allies—and for good measure, the land of expatriates and foreign investors as well. The Sandinistas redistributed this land to poor Nicaraguans throughout the country (keeping some of the nicer properties for themselves: Daniel Ortega, to this day, lives in a Managua home he swiped from a North American).

Fast forward to 1990, with the collapsed Sandinista government and socialist Nicaragua converting back to a market-based economy. Some properties reverted to former owners, some did not, and some Nicaraguans sold their re-acquired properties for quick cash. The result is a system in which three people might have legitimate claim to the same plat land (and a couple more might show up to try to claim it also, sometimes by paying fake taxes on the plot to "prove" it is theirs).

The land problem is less of an issue in cities like Granada, León, and Estelí, and more of a problem in the countryside. But expats everywhere nervously await the day some supposed former owner of their property shows up to "claim" it, whether their claim is true or false. The interloper is more likely to have powerful friends than you are in the court system, so you are at a marked disadvantage that you can only hope to address with some well-placed bribes. How much will it cost you to get your problem fixed? How much have you got?

Your first step in addressing potential legal problems is to duly investigate the history of the property, at least back to 1975, either by yourself or with the help of a Nicaragua-based consultant who specializes in both title research and guiding you through the local legal system. Your second step is to purchase title insurance. Before 1999 no one was willing to offer title insurance to property investors in Nicaragua, but that changed when the Florida-based First American Title Insurance Company entered the market. First American's comprehensive policy covers ownership issues, liens, mortgages, contracts, options, and other encumbrances on titles, plus fraud, forgery, and rights of access to and from the land. Having a policy of this type is an important step in your legal defense should you encounter a problem. Still, title insurance is new to Nicaragua and relatively untested. Before purchasing a policy, find out exactly what you are protected from and in what circumstances. Start the conversation by ensuring that you'll be covered in the Nicaraguan court system and go from there, possibly painting some worst-case scenarios for your agent to address.

Building Your Own Home

Building your own home in Nicaragua is probably the best way to ensure your tropical paradise will satisfy your every whim. But this is no casual undertaking. In general, expect to pay US$40–50 per square meter of house, but it's the price and time contingencies endemic to any construction project that will make you tear your hair out in frustration and cause this estimate to vary wildly. Assuming you know something about construction and have a design with which you are satisfied, and assuming your Spanish is fluent or nearly so, and assuming you can find an engineer or architect that both knows how to build appropriately and is well enough connected to keep the petty officials off of your back, Nicaragua is a land of opportunity. Construction companies of this caliber are increasingly available in Nicaragua as the real estate boom progresses, but you get what you pay for. This is one area where you should not simply choose the lowest bidder.

Remember: In a land where business opportunities are few and far between the system concentrates on people extracting money from you at every possible opportunity. Knowing that you will do anything to advance your project and your dream home to the next stage of the process, every petty bureaucrat in the district will attempt to put up road blocks that you

© RANDALL WOOD

Building from scratch is one way to get what you want.

DAILY LIFE

can overcome only with kickbacks. (Check the *Resources* section for listings of architects and construction companies with whom you can begin to establish a relationship, and proceed cautiously from there.)

Let it be said that lots of expatriates have built, do build, and will continue to build their dream homes in Nicaragua. But it takes patience, the will to navigate the political system, a sense of humor, and dogged perseverance, not to mention a little bit of experience or familiarity with construction to ensure you are getting what you want. Your first step is to talk to the expatriates in the community or area where you intend to make your home, and your second step is to talk to the architects and builders that will make it happen.

For construction or even just renovation, the nation's best source of amenities is Camino Oriente on the outskirts of Managua before you get to the Plaza Siman. This age-old strip mall is the place to go for furniture, countertops, lighting fixtures, and more. The Camino Oriente consists of about a dozen small shops that cater to the new homeowner, so make an afternoon out of it and look around.

PRIME LIVING LOCATIONS

© RANDALL WOOD

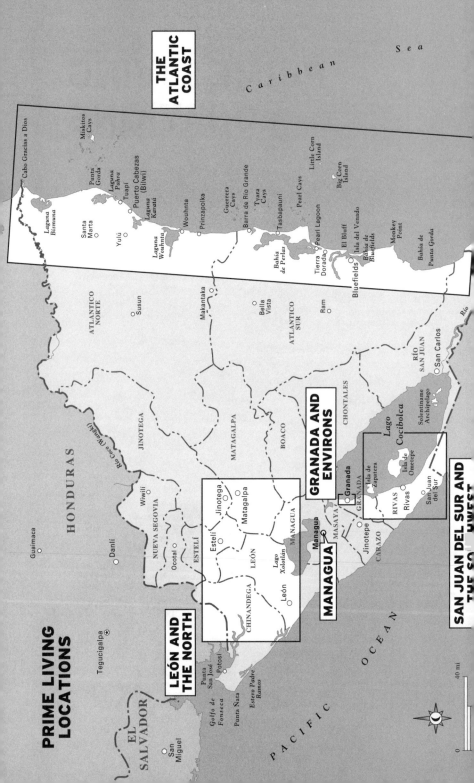

PRIME LIVING LOCATIONS

THE ATLANTIC COAST

LEÓN AND THE NORTH

GRANADA AND ENVIRONS

MANAGUA

SAN JUAN DEL SUR AND THE SOUTHWEST

EL SALVADOR

HONDURAS

Tegucigalpa

Guaimaca

San Miguel

Danlí

Ocotal

Wiwilí

NUEVA SEGOVIA

ESTELÍ

JINOTEGA

Cabo Gracias a Dios

Miskitos Cays

Punta Gorda

Santa Marta

Laguna Bismuna

Laguna Pahra

Tuapi

Puerto Cabezas (Bilwi)

Yulú

Laguna Karatá

Laguna Wouhnta

Wouhnta

Prinzapolka

ATLÁNTICO NORTE

Susun

Makantaka

Barra de Río Grande

Guerrera Cays

Tyara Cays

Pearl Cays

Little Corn Island

Big Corn Island

Bahía de Perlas

Tasbapauni

Pearl Lagoon

Tierra Dorada

El Bluff

Isla del Venado

Bahía de Bluefields

Monkey Point

Bahía de Punta Gorda

Bluefields

Bella Vista

Ram

ATLÁNTICO SUR

San Carlos

RÍO SAN JUAN

CHONTALES

BOACO

MATAGALPA

Matagalpa

Jinotega

Estelí

LEÓN

Lago Xolotlán

León

CHINANDEGA

Punta San José

Potosí

Golfo de Fonseca

Punta Ñata

Estero Padre Ramos

MANAGUA

Managua

MASAYA

Jinotepe

CARAZO

MASAYA

GRANADA

Granada

GRANADA AND ENVIRONS

Isla de Zapatera

Lago Cocibolca

Solentiname Archipelago

Isla de Ometepe

RIVAS

Rivas

San Juan del Sur

SAN JUAN DEL SUR AND THE SOUTHWEST

Río

Río Coco (Wanki)

PACIFIC OCEAN

Caribbean Sea

40 mi

0

OVERVIEW

Once you decide to really start looking for a place to call home, Nicaragua seems like a big place. But you can concentrate your effort on regions and make a big task into a series of smaller tasks. If you heard any mention at all of Nicaragua back home, you probably heard about the two places that are receiving the lion's share of the attention: the colonial city of Granada and the beachfront around San Juan del Sur. Those two areas should be where you spend most of your energy and attention. But there's lots more, depending on what you are looking for. Outside of Granada is the impressive island of Ometepe, and just north of San Juan del Sur are Rivas and Tola. To the north of Managua, León is every bit as colonial as Granada is, and Estelí and Matagalpa offer a rustic lifestyle unlike even what you'd expect in Granada. A good strategy for getting to know the different regions is to start with the popular areas—Granada and San Juan del Sur—and then branch out a bit to get a feel for the alternative options. If you intend to retire in Nicaragua you can safely branch farther afield,

© JOSHUA BERMAN

but if you need to work in Managua you have fewer choices. Managua houses a good many of the expats who find themselves in Nicaragua for work-related reasons.

GRANADA AND ENVIRONS

As both the first town that Spain's *conquistadores* established in Central America and the epicenter of Nicaragua's current tourism boom, Granada is a brightly painted city of extremes: old yet new, relaxed yet active, exotic yet comfortable. Nowhere else in Nicaragua will you find the colonial architecture, community spirit, and breathtaking landscape that Granada offers to both the casual and extended visitor. From either your hotel balcony or the veranda of your newly purchased colonial getaway, your view of Granada features a sea of red-tiled roofs and church steeples, the verdant slopes of Volcán Mombacho, and the breezy expanse of Lake Cocibolca. Outside of Granada proper the Laguna de Apoyo is a cerulean swimming hole inside a forested, ancient volcanic crater with low-key communities living both at water's edge and at the crater's lip above; between the two the trees are full of monkeys. And Mombacho itself is increasingly gaining attention for its quiet and reclusive lifestyle and the relatively cool climate. Foreigners who choose Granada and the gorgeous regions on all sides enjoy being part of the casually growing clusters of colorful foreign characters who congregate in the city's many restaurants, cafés, bars, and plazas. Granada has charm, creature comforts, and a bustling real estate market. It also offers volunteer opportunities, a cultural smorgasbord of sights and entertainment, and no shortage of nearby tourist activities (kayaking, hiking, swimming, crafts shopping). Granada is popular for good reason, and this is reflected in the number of expats and tourists—and the relatively high price of rentals and real estate.

SAN JUAN DEL SUR AND THE SOUTHWEST

Nicaragua's dramatic Pacific southwest is being billed as the best remaining real estate on the Pacific coast. That may be true: The southwest Pacific's innumerable bays and hillsides remain largely undeveloped, but they are the focus of more than a dozen real estate agencies crowding the streets of San Juan del Sur, the small fishing village where all the action is centered. Nearby, sleepy and colonial Rivas is rife with potential but remains to this day nothing more than a regional commercial center and the place where San Juan residents go to run errands. Then there's La Isla de Ometepe, Nicaragua's "Oasis of Peace," rising from the waters of Lake Cocibolca in the form of two lush, magical volcanic cones. If this breathtaking volcanic island draws your attention, you're not the first: the Nahuatl people made it the cultural center of their Nicaraguan home centuries before the Spaniards arrived.

The Pacific coastline rivals and even surpasses Granada in terms of development, construction, and business. Tourism development, real estate rustlin', and even the construction of retirement communities and golf courses are all being spearheaded in this geographically exciting and diverse corner of the country. What's more, in addition to the reckless profiteering and negligent bulldozing that normally define such investment activities, there are a few socially and environmentally responsible projects that are searching for more sustainable development solutions than have been practiced in the past. As such endeavors succeed, they stand to become important models for the rest of Nicaragua and beyond, just as Costa Rica pioneered and showcased a practice that came to be known as "ecotourism."

MANAGUA

Boisterous and bustling, Nicaragua's resilient, vibrant capital is at once a daunting, chaotic urban center and a country village where everybody knows everybody else. Nowhere else in Nicaragua can you find the diversity of entertainment and nightlife that Managua offers, and rather than wait for Saturday, Managuans enjoy the *fiesta* life most nights of the week. You'll enjoy better-stocked supermarkets, a richer diversity of restaurants with cuisine from around the world, and a wider array of stores, shops, and services. Want to catch a dance performance or a bit of theater? Managua's the place. Don't be mistaken; most travelers avoid Managua at all costs except for the occasional foray for banking, medical, or entertainment purposes. But like it or not, this is where the business community, the nongovernmental and development organizations, and all the embassies are, and the city has hosted an expat community for decades. You likely won't write home about how much you adore living in Managua, but if other reasons compel you to settle down there, you'll find before long that Managua's got quite a bit to offer; learning how to find your way around can even make it feel like home.

LEÓN AND THE NORTH

Just northwest of Managua, Nicaragua's second most popular colonial city is off the radar screen of most foreigners hoping to settle in a colonial city, yet León offers much of what makes Granada special, including colonial architecture and long avenues of clay-tiled roofs. León's streets bustle with the day-to-day activity of a regional commercial center and the exuberance of the city's thousands of university students, who fill the cafés with the buzz of politics and optimism. León's history is as long as that of Nicaragua itself, and if the atmosphere seems intense there, it is because the city lies in the shadow of a commanding and striking range of volcanoes called Los Maribios (Nahuatl for "The Giants"), which are prone to rumble and burp from time to time. León, the northwest regional capital, is only a short drive from the beach and is the gateway to Nicaragua's most productive region, where the fertile, volcanic soil produces grains, vegetables, and export crops, and whose lush fields of sugarcane distill into fine, flavorful rum.

Shifting north and east of Managua, the broad, low fields around the great lakes rumple upward into untidy foothills and, eventually, the blunt mountain ranges that make up most of Nicaragua's wild center. Estelí, Matagalpa, Jinotega, and the rest of Nicaragua's northern *departamentos* are rife with adventure, mystery, and a quiet sort of solitude that lures the casually intrepid traveler far from the well-trodden tourist paths of Central America. These hills are often cool in the evenings, misty in the mornings, and home to hundreds of small villages and communities, some prosperous and others struggling. If you are eager to avoid the land grab in southwestern Nicaragua and instead seek the simple lifestyle the frontier offers, you might find the north calling your name. Up in these hills, it's still possible to plant a couple of acres and get away from it all, and although you may feel like a pioneer, you're not the first: Cuban immigrants who left the island after Fidel's revolution now make up part of the population of Estelí, where they grow tobacco with ancestral Cuban seeds; a generation earlier, German immigrants bound for the California gold rush chose Matagalpa, where they introduced coffee, the cash crop that has defined Nicaragua's economy ever since.

THE ATLANTIC COAST

Nicaragua's Atlantic coast is separated from the rest of the country by a long, torturous drive or a short one-hour flight; either way, the massive eastern portion of the country is worlds away from anything else. The few easily reached salt-and-sugar white-sand beaches and turquoise waters are exactly as you'd expect them, but the mixed Caribbean culture is uniquely Nicaraguan. The region's major towns—Bluefields and Puerto Cabezas—though sleepy and isolated, can be rough, primarily because of hard economic times and a certain lawlessness that pervades in a region first settled by marauding pirates; and most of the long, wild coastline is swampy and inaccessible, so you'll probably find yourself looking around Pearl Lagoon and the enticing Corn Islands. To live on Nicaragua's Atlantic side, you'll need to be comfortable on the outskirts of society—and a great deal more self-reliant than elsewhere in Nicaragua. More than one foreigner has devised a comfortable and pleasant lifestyle here, proving it's possible. On the other hand, don't fool yourself: This is not the Caribbean of comfortable resort hotels and package tours. You'll make the Atlantic coast your home because you like a simple, rustic lifestyle, not because you want to sit back and coast. With the risk comes potential, and Nicaragua's Caribbean potential is enormous.

PRIME LIVING LOCATIONS

GRANADA AND ENVIRONS

The warm hub of Nicaragua's tourist and real estate scene, the enchanting old city of Granada—and all its amenities—is surrounded by fantastic natural features, including the world's 10th largest freshwater lake and several stunning volcanoes and crater lagoons. The region is easily accessed from either Managua or Costa Rica, and the landscape flows gently into Masaya and the Pueblos Blancos just to the west. But the city itself is the big draw. Expats love Granada's quiet, provincial atmosphere, the colonial architecture and warm tropical colors, and the picturesque landscape on all sides. Granada's position on the lakeshore guarantees its broad horizons and a fresh breeze—two things the burgeoning expat community has come to enjoy in great numbers. This community is equally a draw to the city, as a growing number of restaurants, clubs, and services are appearing to cater to this exciting crowd. It's not just about the city, though: Granada is surrounded on all sides by natural splendor and interesting side trips, so don't miss the opportunity to explore outside of the city limits.

© JOSHUA BERMAN

CLIMATE

Granada's weather is decidedly tropical but humid by Nicaraguan standards, thanks to the warm waters of Lake Cocibolca. Expect temperatures in the mid-30s °C (90s °F) throughout much of the year, with evenings dipping into the low 20s °C (70s °F). December through April is the dry season, when Granada gets dusty and a bit uncomfortable; May through November comprise the rainy season, when afternoon showers are the norm and the days are pleasant if a bit muggy. The narrow streets and heat-absorbing adobe tend to radiate a great deal of heat in the early afternoons, when a quick stroll downtown can feel like a lap through the rotisserie chicken oven. Early mornings are the coolest, and you can expect your neighbors to take advantage of this by rising early to set into the day's pot-clanking, music-blaring chores. After a couple of months in Granada, you will likely decide it's easier—and more practical—to join them than complain about the noise.

Granada City

More a sleepy country town than an urban center, yet still a great place to dine out, enjoy a bit of nightlife, and appreciate both the colonial architecture and unparalleled surrounding landscape, Granada is the most popular of Nicaragua's towns among tourists and expats alike. With a bit of imagination it's not hard to picture what it looked like back in the 18th century (hint—except for the Internet signs on the plazas and SUVs on the narrow cobblestone lanes, it's not too different). In fact, architecturally, Granada is hands-down the most attractive city in the nation. Long a regional commercial center and home to Nicaragua's powerful merchant and landed families, Granada stayed aligned with the Spanish crown in the 19th century, and Granadinos (as they are known) have, since independence, remained more conservative than their revolutionary compatriots in León. Granadinos are also renowned for their pride and have enacted legislation to ensure the classic appearance of their town stays that way.

That colonial charm permeates every corner of the city, from narrow streets that run from the lake's edge past rows of cool, dark colonial homes set around green interior courtyards, to the broad parks and immense, colorful cathedrals that punctuate the skyline of red clay-tile roofs. By Nicaraguan standards, Granada qualifies as a populous city, but by any other standard on earth it's really a village, with neighbors who know each other and quiet, little-trafficked streets. That residential feel is just one reason

PRIME LIVING LOCATIONS

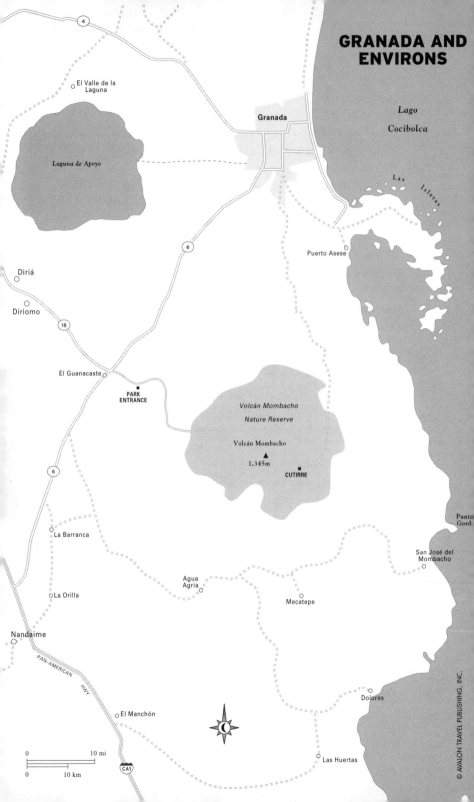

GRANADA AND ENVIRONS

4

El Valle de la Laguna

Granada

Lago Cocibolca

Laguna de Apoyo

Las Isletas

6

Puerto Asese

Diriá

Diriomo

18

El Guanacaste

PARK ENTRANCE

Volcán Mombacho Nature Reserve

Volcán Mombacho
▲
1,345m

CUTIRRE

6

Punta Gorda

La Barranca

San José del Mombacho

Agua Agria

La Orilla

Mecatepe

Nandaime

PAN-AMERICAN HWY

El Manchón

Dolores

Las Huertas

0   10 mi

0   10 km

CA1

© AVALON TRAVEL PUBLISHING, INC.

expats are drawn to this colorful destination in numbers matched only in the beachfront communities of San Juan del Sur. In fact, Granada's expat scene thrives like no other in Nicaragua. Since the late 1990s more and more hotels, restaurants, coffee shops, wine bars, and the like are foreign-owned and -run. That means you'll have a better chance of finding good brie or a glass of French merlot in Granada than you will elsewhere in the nation; it also means you won't exactly be roughing it with the locals as much as you would in one of Nicaragua's lesser-visited regions. Granada is also a mini-epicenter of both Spanish-language schools and volunteer opportunities: Numerous teen centers, schools, orphanages, and foundations are always pleased to have a helping hand.

Lastly, because Granada is such a hot spot among expats, you can expect a busier-than-average real estate market and more budding agents than you would think possible. One foreign resident described the fluctuating real estate market as having a "cowboy atmosphere"; that is to say, the rules are being defined as the market progresses, but Granada remains open to the adventurous risk taker who is not put off by the developing world characteristics with which Granada still struggles (solid waste management, for one). Housing prices have risen dramatically over the past half decade relative to the rest of the nation as investors have purchased, renovated, and re-sold colonial properties that were Nicaraguan family–owned for centuries. Quaint, colonial fixer-uppers are still readily available in Granada, but the clock is definitely ticking in this fast-and-furious market.

THE LAY OF THE LAND

Only an hour's drive from Managua International Airport (and only 10 minutes from a new airstrip up the road), Granada proper is a small red-tile and adobe village that extends just a kilometer or two in each direction and hugs the western shoreline of Lake Cocibolca. Forget about suburbs—you'll know when you've left the town by the call of the cicadas and the sight of broad fields.

Designed in the 16th century, Granada's urban layout is decidedly co-lonial. The main cathedral and government buildings occupy two sides of the central plaza, around which a simple grid street system holds Granada's hotels, restaurants, and other businesses. South of the plaza is the boisterous open-air market. Two small creeks, Arroyo Aduana and Arroyo Zacateligüe flank the city's northern and southern boundaries, more or less; both have been canalized and neither is pretty to look at (or smell). Granada's effective western boundary is Avenida Arrellano, which runs south from Carretera

PRIME LIVING LOCATIONS

EXPAT PROFILE: DONNA TABOR, QUEEN OF CALLE CALZADA

Donna Tabor's journey from Pittsburgh, Pennsylvania-based television producer to the Nicaragua project coordinator of Building New Hope is an ongoing adventure that has taken place in Granada for nearly a decade. During this time she has alternately served as Peace Corps Volunteer, bed-and-breakfast proprietress, community organizer, and adopted mother to countless Nicaraguan street children. Donna's role in her Nicaraguan neighborhood is ever-evolving and, as she keeps collaborating with new and old friends as they pass through Granada, the activities of Building New Hope continue to benefit Nicaraguan children in new, empowering ways.

Why is Granada a great place to live?

Granada is a nice place to live for a lot of reasons. I can't say that it's "great" — or that there aren't other places I wouldn't enjoy as much or more, but for various reasons, I'm committed to living here, probably for a long while. The best part about Granada is its historical charm, growing access to amenities to which spoiled foreigners are accustomed, the continual flow of international visitors, and a relatively stable community of expats.

What is the expat community like in Granada?

Many are here to enjoy the new culture and to give back to the community. It's heartening to join in with people who want to help develop projects that will enhance Granada for everyone — e.g., planning a small library, helping street children, etc. We also have a small group of expats who are concerned about animal mistreatment and are taking steps to protect stray dogs as well as alleviate the overpopulation of unwanted animals. One expat has organized a mosaic class for street boys, helping them to learn a craft and to sell them to tourists. Another group has designed a "Reading in the Schools" program for elementary grades. And, of course, others are here in a frenzied search for cheap real estate, bargains, big money in little time, etc.

Still, Granada is in a class of its own; there's no other community like it in Nicaragua. It is nearing first world: international restaurants, a country club, Internet cafés on every corner, and now a Subway franchise! We also have a small but blossoming artist community, and there are classes such

Masaya, the principal highway leading to Masaya and Managua. Granada's eastern boundary is the great lake itself, responsible both for the city's fresh breeze and its above-average humidity.

At the southern end of the city's lakeshore is the Complejo Turístico and Malecón, a quiet sort of park with a scattering of outdoor restaurants where you can enjoy fresh fish and the afternoon breeze. Just south of that is Puerto Asese, a stretch of municipal docks and restaurants where you can find boat service

© DONNA TABOR

as yoga, karate, kayaking, crafts . . . and services one wouldn't expect like massage therapy, reflexology, pedicures, website design.

I feel lucky to have been a part of the start-up process of a growing community. It is a creative endeavor for some of us. In a way, it has a frontier feel to it because newcomers who want to start businesses have a wide open choice of niches — we need nearly everything here (except another real estate office!).

What are the drawbacks to living in Granada?
For a lot of people here, the heat and humidity rate are the biggest problems. For those of us coming from a faster-paced culture, the irresponsibility and lackadaisical attitude of the local and national governments are irritating. I'd say it is "unacceptable" except that as foreigners, we have no choice but to accept it — no one wants our vote.

Other drawbacks include inadequate health care, erratic infrastructure (who knows when there will be lack of electricity or water, or for how long), garbage-strewn streets, cruel attacks on and lack of attention to animals (the street dog population is horrendous; we are soon opening a clinic to attempt to curb this), the horse droppings on public streets (smell as well as sight), the lack of attention to homeless kids in desperate need of help, and the absence of police assistance when needed. And, unfortunately, cheap living and desperate poverty attract undesirable foreign residents (a.k.a. "the dead pecker brigade"), whose disgusting exploits give the rest of the community a bad name.

to the gorgeous aquatic sanctuary of the Isletas, actually volcanic debris that Volcán Mombacho coughed up centuries ago. Looming over it all is mighty Mombacho itself, officially dormant but a portentous part of the landscape just the same. Mombacho's slopes contain rich organic coffee plantations, protected cloud forest and hiking trails, and several popular "canopy tours." The whole upper part of the volcano is a frequently visited tourist destination, and is a must-see whether or not you decide to call Granada home.

HOUSING

Granada's quiet colonial charm and small, negotiable neighborhoods make it wonderfully small-town. Colonial homes tend to be big and spacious, particularly by American standards, as they are built around breezy interior courtyards. Even modest homes can be as big as 335 square meters (3,600 square feet) including the courtyard.

Granada is booming as confidence in Nicaragua grows and as the Nicaraguan economy strengthens, and properties don't stay on the market for much longer than two weeks. City regulations will dictate that colonial homes remain colonial, so you won't very likely be able to radically renovate your property, but because most expats are drawn to Granada precisely for the architecture, that only affects the precious few who might otherwise be tempted to raze the colonial home and replace it with something modern and atrocious.

The true bargains disappeared ages ago, but new properties enter the market every day. In some cases these are colonial classics in a poorer state of repair than the first entries to hit the market, and they will require a handy sort of person willing to accept the responsibility of fixing up the home to make it livable. In other cases the homes are less traditionally colonial than you might hope for, but are offered at more reasonable prices. And lastly, some of these properties have already passed through foreign hands, been gorgeously renovated, and are now back on the market. You will find few bargains in this category as you'll be dealing with savvy folks who are well aware of both the real estate market and your desire to find something lovely in Granada, and they'll drive a hard bargain. Still, you might well decide in the tide of rising property values it is worth your while to snap properties like this up.

Low-priced properties tend to come with warts that require specialized construction expertise. Remember: In a colonial city you cannot possibly know the internals of your home's wiring and plumbing system. The closer you get to the plaza or the lakeshore, the higher you can expect prices to be. Choice colonial buildings in good shape, particularly if they've been recently renovated or if the previous owner is foreign, can run over US$200,000, and even places that require full restoration can cost you over US$100,000. If that's steep for your taste, ask about properties in the outskirt barrios where smaller colonial adobe and tile homes with simple facades cost US$60,000–100,000.

Where to Live

The area between the park and the lakeshore was the first to be developed and the market is now concentrating on areas a bit farther away from the action, which contain homes just as gorgeous as those that have already changed hands. These barrios include the long stretch on both sides of Calle El Caimito (which runs parallel to the city's popular main drag and leads to the lakeshore) and the less populated northern half of the city, which terminates with the city's curious railroad museum and the Parque Sandino. South of the Arroyo Zacateligüe there is very little action at all. Part of this protected land belongs to the popular lakefront tourist complex, but much of the rest lies fallow.

As you travel away from the city center the architecture changes from colonial adobe and red tile to concrete block and corrugated steel roof, which is not nearly as enticing but is much more accessible financially. This is particularly true of the southwest quadrant. Similarly, the lakeshore land just north of the city on the road to Malacatoya isn't as attractive as you'd think it is: Much of the land is either low enough to be swampy or otherwise ill-suited for building.

No matter where you look within the city limits, spend a day or two hanging around each neighborhood to get a feel for it—that means walking the streets and resting in its various open spaces and cafés from dawn until evening.

The above information notwithstanding, Granada is full of surprises, and once the locals find out you are in the market they may be able to turn you on to some pleasant properties where you wouldn't expect them. Similarly, a growing number of families have decided to circumvent the real estate agents and simply hang a "for sale" ("*se vende*") sign out. Walking the streets is the only way to discover these bargains. Another way to settle into a colonial place is to look for dilapidated properties in need of work (caveat emptor—it should go without saying). Adobe is tough to work with and you'll need the expertise and labor of specialist contractors to get your property in order. Sometimes "restoring" old adobe places means tearing down walls and rebuilding them either from scratch or using concrete and more modern materials. This gets expensive fast.

More difficult than dealing with repairs can be striking a deal with the seller. Granadinos are well aware of the boom and know how to drive a hard bargain. If they're selling it's probably because they intend to relocate to Miami or California, and they're hoping the sale of their home will finance the trip. You will have the strongest offer if you spend 3–4 weeks in town getting to know the market, looking around, and talking to other expats who have bought before setting out to find a property. Nicas are impoverished but not stupid and know very well the expression about a fool and his money (hint—you're the one with the money).

Remember, Granada is one of the focal points of Nicaragua's ongoing real estate frenzy, so finding an agent won't be a problem, and some very well-respected international agencies already have offices in Granada. Start your research online before making your first trip. Century 21 and Re/Max are just two of the real estate companies that offer listings on their websites. Century 21 and Brenes Morales have offices in Granada. Century 21, through its GPS (Granda Property Service), also sponsors occasional real estate all-inclusive tours in which licensed agents show you around properties in Granada and elsewhere over the course of three days.

Rental Apartments

Clean, secure, unfurnished apartments go for US$250–450 a month, though the market is leading to higher prices in this category relative to a couple of years ago. These prices are comparable to Managua but much higher than elsewhere in the country and show no signs of dropping. If you are in town to search for properties and you expect to work on a 3–4 week timeframe, you'd do well to strike a deal with your hotel, many of which are willing to let you have your room at a long-term rate. They are less flexible during the busy seasons (around Christmas and from June to August), when they are just as able to rent the rooms out at full price.

GETTING AROUND

Granada was built on a level lakeside plain at the foot of Mombacho. It is an eminently walkable city, and you can stroll from one end to the other in less than half an hour—though that time could grow significantly if you are invited to sit and chat with your Nicaraguan or foreign friends whom you are sure to meet.

If the heat's got you down, there are other forms of transport as well, including taxis and three-wheeled "pedicabs." A quainter ride is the horse and carriage service you can find at the plaza (choose a carriage pulled by a well-fed and healthy-looking animal only). This is a

© RANDALL WOOD

a three-wheeled "pedicab"

great way to explore the city while still feeling your way around—strike a by-the-hour deal with the driver and simply cruise the streets to get a look at the neighborhoods.

There are several car rental agencies in Granada, located at the gas station at the entrance to town (and in greater numbers at the airport in Managua). Having your own vehicle is a great way to get to and from the lakeside Complejo Turístico or for jaunts out of town and to the capital. But in choosing to drive you choose to deal with traffic, poor drivers, and Granada's sometimes limited parking.

You can just as easily get around by public transportation. Very comfortable and convenient minibuses ply the highway between Managua, Masaya, and Granada, departing from a terminal half a block south of the central park. Slower "local" buses (yellow school buses) service the rest of the region, leaving from the Shell Palmira (on the south side of the city just past the Palí supermarket).

Las Isletas

Granada's Isletas are a treasure, still awash in bird song and forest canopy and simple to reach via a gorgeous and comfortable boat trip from the shores of Granada. The peninsula and the 365 granitic (and mostly lushly vegetated) islets constitute a volcanic upchuck from nearby Volcán Mombacho, which blew its top 20,000 years ago. Inhabited since pre-Columbian time by the Nahuatl, who prized the the islets for excellent fishing, the Isletas remain to this day a fun tourist destination for day trips, picnicking, and swimming excursions, and for the record, the fishing is still not bad.

THE LAY OF THE LAND

The peninsula is shaped somewhat like a hooked thumb that extends in a graceful backward curve from the lakeshore. Along both sides a labyrinth of islets both great and small make for fun boating and exploring. The islets closest to Granada are the ones that bear the greatest part of the archipelago's population, which hovers around 100 people, which is to say the shorebirds—particularly the brightly colored oropendulas and *chorchas*—still outnumber the humans in this exotic locale. The farthest islets are the least visited, but geography and vegetation conspire to provide a breathtaking diversity of landforms throughout the archipelago, and two islets can be radically different even if they are separated by no more than a couple of meters of water.

THE MAN WHO WOULD BE KING: WILLIAM WALKER AND GRANADA

Should some Realtor take you by the hand and whisper in your ear, "this property dates all the way back to the Spanish!" snarl back, "Let's go ask William Walker, shall we?" Granada's most infamous and least noble resident, William Walker changed the history of Nicaragua with a swipe of his gilded saber and permanently altered how Nicaraguans greet their American neighbors to the north – that is, with open arms but with their eyes open. For that matter, he permanently altered the Granada skyline, by burning the city to the ground and pissing in the ashes. Your colonial home dates back about 150 years at the most, or was one of precious few survivors.

The year was 1853, and Nicaragua's Liberals and Conservatives were once again at each other's throats in a fierce competition for political power. The Liberals saw a chance to beat the Conservatives once and for all with some hired foreign guns, and they invited American adventurer, white supremacist, and filibuster William Walker to join them in the battle in Nicaragua. He accepted, and within the year they realized they'd created a monster.

Walker, the self-proclaimed "Grey-eyed Man of Destiny" from Nashville, Tennessee, arrived with a band of 300 thug mercenaries he'd rounded up in the tough neighborhoods of San Francisco and promptly led the Liberals to a rousing victory over the Conservatives. But he had no intentions of going home. Two years later he usurped power, arranged for elections that he rigged to his advantage, and declared himself the president of

WHERE TO LIVE

There's only one way to get familiar with this gorgeous region, and that is to charter a boat and driver for lazy afternoons poking about the archipelago. Not a bad way to spend a day, regardless of how your property search turns out! Some islets do become available from time to time, but it's not as easy to settle down in the Isletas as it is to feather your nest back in town. These days the Isletas are the playground of Nicaragua's powerful political elite, and the property records read like a "Who's Who in Nicaragua": Pellas, Chamorro, Jerez, Alemán, Bolaños, and so on. That makes it not as easy to find a property here as you'd think, and prices run higher than they do in nearby Granada. Unimproved islets near shore can start at US$55,000 with no structures on them. If you find an *isleta* for sale, you'll need more than just a lot of cash and patience to see through the deal. Check carefully to see if any local laws prohibit developing the islet. Some islets are considered "protected" and others have had restrictions placed on them by powerful neighbors who don't want any company. To live here, you'll need your own boat, as ferry service is geared more

Nicaragua. His goal was to make Nicaragua a slave state loyal to the American south's nascent confederacy.

The United States, at the brink of civil war, officially recognized Walker as president of Nicaragua. Walker reinstituted slavery and declared English the official language of the country. But Walker did what no Nicaraguan leader has been able to accomplish since: He united the people. In a rare moment of fear-inspired solidarity, the Nicaraguans temporarily forgot their differences, banded together, and with the help of the other Central American nations and some financing from Cornelius Vanderbilt (who had lost his steamship company to Walker), defeated Walker at the Battle of San Jacinto on September 14, 1856, now a national holiday. Not long afterward he was captured and executed by a rifle squad in Honduras. The Liberals fell into disgrace, and the Conservatives effectively ruled the nation for the next 30 years.

The scars Walker wrought on the nation run deep. As he and his men fled Granada they paused long enough to burn the city to the ground and plant a sign that proclaimed "Here was Granada." You can still see scorch marks on some buildings in the city. On the highway leading north from Managua to Estelí you'll find a statue commemorating the victory over Walker's troops by a mobilized populace at San Jacinto. And deep inside every Nicaraguan is a secret distaste for loud, bold Americans with ambitious plans and a confident gait. William Walker's own account, *La Guerra de Nicaragua*, tells his fascinating story in no uncertain terms. Just be careful who sees you reading it.

for tourists than residents, plus a generator to provide electricity during the Isletas' frequent power outages. These are things you should consider bringing with you from overseas, as good quality fiberglass boats are extremely rare in Nicaragua.

GETTING AROUND

The Port of Asese is your point of departure for all points in the Isletas. There is regular boat service from the port, and the captains of these 20-seat wooden launches know the islands well. As a tourist you can simply ask to be let off at an islet for swimming and establish a time to be picked up again. The captain will get you as close to shore as possible, then disappear over the horizon, leaving you free explore, nap, and enjoy the afternoon. Be ready for the return, as these boats make several stops picking up passengers from the various islets on their way home and won't want to sit around waiting while you get your gear together. But for serious exploring or property searching you are better off striking a deal with a boat and captain to take you exploring through the islets on a daily or by-the-hour rate. These captains know more about the history and the ownership status of these islets than the authors, and striking up a conversation with your guide as you navigate the channels that separate these 365 jewels is a great way of familiarizing yourself with what's available.

Laguna de Apoyo

Due west of lively, bustling Granada but fundamentally different in every way from geography to lifestyle, the Laguna de Apoyo is exotic and other-worldly. A well-loved and frequently visited swimming hole and day-trip resort, Apoyo is actually a long-submerged volcanic crater that formed 1.6 million years ago in the most violent volcanic event in Nicaragua's prehistory. The crater is as close to bottomless as you could hope to find in Central America: Not until the 1990s did scientists with special equipment map the crater's floor more than 200 meters down; the lake is one of a handful in Nicaragua that now host unique and specially adapted fish species found nowhere else on earth. A half dozen pleasant eateries and hotels line one part of the shoreline inside the crater, and the entire limpid landscape can be enjoyed from the spectacular rural hamlet of Catarina, perched at the crater's lip high above, which also enjoys a gorgeous view of red-roofed Granada off in the distance.

Though you won't escape earthquakes *anywhere* in Nicaragua, the Laguna de Apoyo has trembled more recently than most places, so turn your back to any real estate agent who neglects to mention the risk of the occasional tremor. The last one was in 2001; it originated under the town of Catarina and shook the cauldron so violently the lake waters actually sloshed from side to side. The vibration caused several local homes to crumble to the ground and led to rumors that the water was boiling.

THE LAY OF THE LAND

Apoyo consists of two inhabitable areas separated by a steep slope: the slim beach at the lake's edge down at the bottom and a narrow band of homes along the crater lip, accessible most easily from the town of Catarina. To reach the lakeshore, look for the turnoff on the road that connects Granada to Managua. The road climbs through some small rural settlements, passes a guard post where you will be charged a dollar to access the "tourist facility," and then snakes wildly downward into the belly of the crater. At the bottom of the road you'll find the popular Norome

© RANDALL WOOD

The Laguna de Apoyo is best appreciated from up high.

hotel and a handful of restaurants, guesthouses, and a private home or two (including one that belongs to former president Alemán, who had the audacity to pave the public road up to the entrance of his home and no farther).

The rest of what is popularly called the Laguna de Apoyo is accessible from a completely different point: From Granada take the road that leads toward Nandaime and turn right on the road toward Catarina. From Managua head toward Masaya and then follow signs toward Catarina. The town of Catarina is beautiful and charming in its own right, but it's also the gateway to one of the few residential developments underway in the region, Rancho Monterrey. Because most of the crater's interior is neither suitable for development nor available for ecological reasons, the lip of the crater outside Catarina is where you'll find all the action.

WHERE TO LIVE

Rancho Monterrey is one of the few areas on the Catarina side where you can expect to find a place to live. This is newly developed construction, not renovated colonial properties. In fact, nowhere in this area will you find "authentic" adobe colonial houses, although a few of the modern homes being developed are designed with colonial-esque features—interior courtyard, pillars, and red-tile roofs.

In choosing to settle on the Laguna de Apoyo you are giving up the conveniences of relatively cosmopolitan Granada with its markets and transportation links, not to mention the restaurant scene. But in exchange you gain a cooler, more pleasant climate, a gorgeous view of the lake and Granada, and a bit of solitude. Ecological restrictions rightly limit the amount of property available for development here, so besides the random homeowner who has put their property on the market, the prospective home buyer will be limited to options in Rancho Monterrey until some other well-connected developer successfully opens up a new swath of land for construction. Homes in the little town of Catarina are very Nicaraguan but reasonably priced. If you can find anything here you can expect it to cost you about US$30,000 and noticeably lack the amenities you'd expect from a modern North American home, like hot water. The new developments on the crater cost quite a bit more, of course: Prices start just shy of US$200,000.

Down in the crater land is at an extreme premium: There's not much space to develop the interior of a volcanic crater given the steep landform. But Norome has lots and small homes for sale on its property. These tend to go for about US$130,000.

GETTING AROUND

It's easy enough to get to Catarina via bus, but very difficult to get to the bottom of the crater with anything other than your own private vehicle. Count on driving if you are interested in this region, and for the trip down to the lake's edge, obviously, check your brakes first. Once you've arrived in either area, your own two feet are all you will need to get around, as the compact nature of the developed area makes for easy exploring.

PRIME LIVING LOCATIONS

Volcán Mombacho

You can hardly miss Mombacho—it towers over the city of Granada like a sleepy, gap-toothed menace on the southern horizon. Mombacho is only a kilometer or two outside of the city limits—too close for comfort if it weren't a long-dormant volcano that forfeited its strength the day it blew its top. A few sulfur vents and thermal springs remain, but the mature age of the cloud forest at the top indicates just how long the mountain has been silent.

THE LAY OF THE LAND

The Mombacho volcano is developed under a program of hybrid land use. From 850 meters (2,800 feet) above sea level down, the slopes of Mombacho are carpeted with lush coffee plantations and smaller farms; above 850 meters it is a nationally protected nature reserve and a verdant bit of cloud forest home to monkeys, small mammals, and a plethora of birdlife. Mombacho's greatest challenge is transportation and access. The roads that circle the slopes of this sleeping giant are unimproved, and during the rainy season they become rutted mud pits that trucks hauling out the coffee harvest churn up into a froth. The main road from the highway is in decent shape but

© RANDALL WOOD

Granada City, with Volcán Mombacho in the background

services only the mountain's primary coffee plantation and the Mombacho Nature Reserve at the top.

WHERE TO LIVE

Most properties for sale in this area tend to be on the mountain's lower slopes. Granada real estate agents run the listings for small farms available on the slopes of Mombacho, when they arise, but increasingly these farms are being purchased, hacked into smaller residential lots, and resold. It would be wise to visit the property in the rainy season before committing. Farms can entail up to 50 hectares (125 acres) and cost several hundred thousand dollars depending on the ease of access and the quality of the coffee growing there. Smaller residences hitting the market in 2006 are priced below US$100,000.

GETTING AROUND

With the exception of the tourist track that leads from the highway up to the reserve at the mountain's summit Mombacho is free of good roads. Some smaller tracks lead around the volcano's lower perimeter's northern and southern flanks, and you will need a respectable four-wheel vehicle to make use of either, more so in the rainy season. The best way to explore this area is in the company of a local or a real estate agent who knows his or her way around this fascinating but difficult to access region.

SAN JUAN DEL SUR AND THE SOUTHWEST

Nicaragua's southwest corner was the first part of the country to attract a curious community of beach-seeking foreigners. Some have settled in the small port of San Juan del Sur while others prefer the dozens of barely developed bays and beaches nearby, where property continues to change hands at a quick rate. Though Nicaraguan residents of San Juan (locals' affectionate abbreviation for the town) are still transforming their home from full-time fishing village to the nation's premier Pacific coast destination, it remains unassuming, nonchalant, and remarkably *tranquilo*.

If you haven't heard of San Juan del Sur yet, you will. It's long been a sort of traveler's retreat, offering quiet coastal charm and a community rich with expats and passers-through who appreciate the laid-back coastal lifestyle, best enjoyed with your feet up and a cold drink in one hand. But increasingly, San Juan del Sur has grown into a veritable real estate feeding frenzy as investors, now confident that Nicaragua's war-torn 1980s

© JOSHUA BERMAN

are long behind, scoop up stunning Pacific properties and develop their dream homes, start small businesses, or just enjoy the view.

Though the energy is building to a crescendo, San Juan del Sur for the moment retains the lethargic beach town feel that has characterized it for centuries. The real action turns out to be not the port town itself, but rather the unfettered landscape on both sides. The enticing coastline that flanks the town to both the north and the south is gradually developing from overlooked and inaccessible scrubland to highly appreciated and rapidly modernizing beachfront property.

How far will the renovation of this hot real estate market extend? It's hard to tell. Not far away from San Juan del Sur is Rivas, the provincial and tame capital city of the region but really a sleepy town, a cultural icon that still exudes much of the colonial charm endemic to Central America: broad streets and open skyline, a friendly village laid out in the colonial tradition, around a central square and cathedral. But Rivas lags in the shadow of brassy, bold Granada, which has garnered the lion's share of attention among would-be residents, and lies forgotten while the coastline to its west undergoes a transformation.

Just over the horizon, alluring and mysterious Isla de Ometepe remains virtually untouched by all the nearby hype and surprisingly isolated from the rest of the nation. Ometepe is proudly Nicaraguan and even proudly Nahuatl, as this is one place where the indigenous pre-Columbian culture left its greatest imprint. Certainly its links to its indigenous past are more apparent, from the legends and stories in which it is immersed to the petroglyphs that emerge from misty fields across the twin volcanoes. But Ometepe's relative isolation, including the sporadic ferry access over occasionally rough waters—not to mention a very bumpy and poorly maintained road—has helped to keep the island largely as it has been for centuries.

Though the entire area is only a few hours' drive south from Managua or Granada, many of the the first foreign visitors to San Juan del Sur, Rivas, and La Isla de Ometepe came from the opposite direction, from Costa Rica. For them, happening upon Nicaragua's southwest coast must have felt like stepping back in time, where tourist-friendly services were few but opportunities and friendly faces were plenty. The region has come a long way in terms of services since then. San Juan del Sur finally has its own bank branch, for example, but things still happen slowly here, on their own version of "Nica Time." Expatriates looking for a cheap version of Costa Rica will be disappointed that San Juan del

Sur isn't as modern, tourist-ready, or as polished; but those folks who are willing to sacrifice shine for a better deal and a more honest experience will be quite content.

CLIMATE

Weather in Nicaragua's southwest follows the same pattern as Managua. The wet season is May–November and you can usually expect afternoon showers during this time. October and November are the really rainy months and afternoon showers can be downpours. The dry season is December–April and is usually characterized by clear skies and starry nights. Expect high winds in January. San Juan del Sur experiences two extraordinarily busy tourist seasons when even Nicaraguans flock to the beach during Christmas and Semana Santa (Easter week). Temperatures are warm and pleasant throughout the year here.

San Juan del Sur

Don't let the real estate brokers tell you the land is "undiscovered"; it just hasn't been discovered recently. San Juan's first tourist boom occurred in the 1850s, when the village served as a major stopover for California-bound gold-rushers. Its perfectly protected bay and delicious supply of seafood provided a pleasant break for many a weary, fortune-seeking adventurer (and for many a broke, homeward-bound failure as well). Travelers in those days took clipper ships from New York or Baltimore to Nicaragua's Caribbean coast, then steamed up the Río San Juan to San Jorge, crossed the peninsula through Rivas by horse cart to San Juan del Sur, and boarded another clipper ship bound for California, fame, and fortune. But San Juan del Sur's fortune dried up when the gold did, and the town faded back into obscurity. After a 150-year respite, the town is once again a primary part of the adventurer's scene—just ask around the many beach bars where travelers trade stories over heaping plates of fish and shrimp, and where the clink of the ice in your glass is an all-too-natural companion to the lapping of waves on the shoreline.

San Juan del Sur and nearby communities are home to about 18,000 Nicaraguan inhabitants. Temporary residents include a near-constant stream of backpackers, well-to-do Nicaraguan weekenders, and an increasing number of big-spending foreigners, many of whom come for a few weeks to laze around the restaurants and half-heartedly scout the coastline for long-dreamed plots of paradise. Others arrive with surfboards under their

PRIME LIVING LOCATIONS

© JOSHUA BERMAN

Grand views are the norm along the southwest Pacific coast.

arms in search of the famed local waves, which a year-round offshore breeze carves into curls; still others come to fish, sail, or dive. Long-term expats include Spanish-language students, ambitious hoteliers, creative community developers, and the requisite handful of prospectors and scavengers.

THE LAY OF THE LAND

San Juan del Sur lies at the western terminus of a 26-kilometer (16-mile) road that extends from the Pan-American Highway at an intersection known as "La Virgin," just south of the city of Rivas and a few kilometers north of the Costa Rican border at Peñas Blancas. Central San Juan del Sur is limited to about 10 square blocks by a broad crescent bay on one side and steep hills on the other. And though a steady progression of vacation homes—some muted, some a bit garish—has begun to climb the steep hillsides on the outskirts, the town's centerpiece, the bay, ensures lots of open space and a broad horizon, which make for stunning sunsets. By foot, you can cruise San Juan del Sur from one side to the other in a couple of minutes. San Juan del Sur proper is compact and easy to navigate. From San Juan, a single dirt road winds south to the even smaller fishing village of Ostional, where no tourist facilities exist, but a long strip of beach puts you within spitting distance of Costa Rica. Another unimproved road extends north behind the coastline, granting access to a string of beaches, bays, settlements, and headlands. You'll need a personal vehicle to explore the properties on both sides of town: Although major improvements to the road began in 2006, ongoing construction and several low-water stream crossings dictate a four-wheel-drive vehicle.

WHERE TO LIVE

You have two basic choices: Either live in the town of San Juan del Sur as near to the water as you can get, where you will enjoy a small but clever expat community and lots of bars and restaurants, or try your hand at an

THE "BEACHFRONT" BLUES: NICARAGUA'S COASTAL LAW

If one thing is certain about Nicaragua's beachfront property, it's that *nothing* is certain. The infamous Coastal Law remains a mystery even to Realtors, no two of which were able to agree for us on its status. In a nutshell, the Coastal Law would prohibit anyone – yes, that includes you – from owning land within 50 meters of the high-tide mark anywhere along Nicaragua's coast. Those properties would be leased but not sold to potential investors and the leases could be modified periodically. Or maybe it's 200 meters from the coastline. Or maybe the law was shelved and will be dealt with at some point in the future. Or maybe it's been killed, a wooden stake driven through its beastly heart.

It is popularly presumed that Nicaraguan lawmakers wrote this particularly malicious law precisely because it would generate fear and uncertainty, and they could then rely on handsome kickbacks from foreign investors for the favor of not passing the law. A precedent certainly exists: Both Mexico and Costa Rica have similar legislation in place. Should a law of this persuasion come to be, the Nicaraguan government will almost certainly have to provide a grandfather clause to facilitate the compliance of the dozens of coastal properties that already belong to someone or other. In the meantime, be wary of beachfront properties in general, which have a much higher risk than other properties inland.

PRIME LIVING LOCATIONS

outlying community north or south of San Juan del Sur proper, and spend lots of lazy afternoons back in town visiting friends. These are two undisputedly different undertakings.

First of all, despite the beauty of San Juan del Sur's charming bay, many expats grumble that it is best enjoyed on the other side of a cold beer while plunked down in your deck chair, rather than splashing in its waters. The bay's natural shape leads to less tidal mixing with clean ocean water than other points along the coast, and from time to time the bay water grows stale with pollutants from the fishing ships (at other times, storms or tides force waves of cool, fresh ocean water in and the cycle begins anew). And the bay's floor drops off slowly and lazily, so at 50 meters (165 feet) off the coast the water is still only waist deep. It's a great, safe place for kids to splash around in, since the waves are infrequently strong, but if you are adamant about an early morning swim you might be better off in one of the small communities outside of San Juan proper.

San Juan, despite its small size, is the heart and soul of a decent social scene, and if you opt for one of the countless nooks and crannies of the

EXPAT PROFILE: CHRIS BERRY

When California lawyer Chris Berry first arrived in Nicaragua in 1988, it was aboard his sailboat, *Pelican Eyes*. Chris wandered ashore in San Juan del Sur and, eventually, wandered into tourism when it arrived in town a decade later — first by taking the odd visitor on sunset sails, later by opening Pelican Eyes Piedras y Olas, one of the classiest hotel-restaurants in the country and a source of employment for more than 150 Nicaraguans. After making the commitment to stay and be a part of Nicaragua, Chris met fellow expat and retired Red Cross nurse Jean Brugger; together they founded the A. Jean Brugger Education Project, a nonprofit that, in addition to anti-litter and environmental campaigns, provides scholarships, uniforms, school supplies, and job training to dedicated students in the San Juan del Sur area. Chris's experiences obtaining citizenship and starting a business had to be improvised in a very different Nicaragua than now exists and are thus irrelevant considering today's new systems, but his advice to would-be expats is as pertinent as ever.

Why is San Juan del Sur a great place to live?
It's a coastal resort town, fishing village, and dynamic tourist industry, all in a 100-plus-year-old community.

What are the drawbacks to living there?
Our mission statement is to benefit this community with employment. However, we've almost reached the end of our ability to draw from it. That means importing workers. To maintain equilibrium we must train more San Juan folks. That costs money. Big circle. It will work out but growth here now has surpassed qualified employee reserves.

What is the expat community like in San Juan del Sur and how is it different from those in other parts of Nicaragua?
I don't know the expat community, except as United States and Canadian Warden. I would say it's the same as most Latin countries: a combination of people living month-to-month and investors with commercial plans.

What was the biggest hassle in purchasing your land?
This land was acquired meter by meter and it has taken nine years. There isn't a hassle or obstacle I haven't experienced. The process has been streamlined and institutionalized and is much easier (and more

coastline outside of town, you will find yourself commuting back in to do your shopping, passing through the market, or enjoying a meal with your colleagues and neighbors—and even the most curmudgeonly misanthropes will want to chat with their fellow expats after a few weeks of solitary confinement in gorgeous but hard-to-reach Pacific paradises up the coast.

Most prospective expats begin their search with an extended stay in San

© CHRIS BERRY

expensive) these days. Title insurance, where donated or confiscated lands aren't at issue, is available from First American Title.

How do you feel about the cost of living? Are you living cheaply compared to back home, or is it not such the great deal that people say it is?
If you wish to live at a high U.S. standard with all U.S. products and services, the cost of living is high, but still lower than in the United States. If you are willing to compromise on certain things, the cost of living is perhaps 35 percent cheaper.

Any surprises? Any advice along the lines of "I wish someone had told me . . . ?"
Yes: Bring certified copies and originals of every legal document you could ever have dreamed pertained to your life, every bit of info about you and your family. Trying to figure it out after you get here and sending for birth and death certificates, etc., is really quite difficult.

Any other advice for someone thinking about making the move?
Learn Spanish. Learn the culture. Commit to spending 10-25 percent of your budget on locals. Commit to integrate, not segregate. Enjoy your life and share that luxury. Let people see you smile. Avoid the temptation to complain about the system here with other expats. Systems are systems. They suck in most places. You are no longer in the United States or Canada. Don't ever, ever, ever say, "It isn't like this in the States." The moment that comes out of your mouth, go back to where it is like that: the States.

PRIME LIVING LOCATIONS

Juan del Sur town, where a number of long-term rental, townhouse, and time-share options are available through various individuals and hotels in all price ranges (US$50–1,000 or more per month). There is a small, well-off neighborhood north of the river that is almost entirely a playground for Nicaragua's elite, including former presidents who occasionally fly in by helicopter (when they're not under house arrest in their other palaces, anyway). From the beachfront, glance northward at the luxury estates being built on that hillside ridge. It's called La Talanquera, and the recently built properties are owned largely by Nicaragua's wealthy (and the odd U.S. basketball star).

Likewise, the ridge tops of the steep headlands that form the San Juan Bay (and other bays north and south of town) are increasingly covered with fancy customized homes. You will also find several gated communities on the hills above town, including Paradise Bay and Villas Viscaya, and a few more going up just outside of San Juan del Sur in both directions.

Within San Juan del Sur, the name of the game is to get as close as you can to the water's edge. After all, you didn't travel this far just to live inland. But there's a catch: The entire bay side of the road that follows the bay belongs to the national government (not the San Juan del Sur government) and cannot be purchased but only leased in long-term arrangements. Southward from town, the shoreline quickly folds upward into a rocky promontory, on the other side of which you'll find the rapidly developing Paradise Bay, a 56-hectare (138-acre) cluster of developed properties with water, major utilities, and a paved road. Your third choice is to look at properties right in town. No matter where you set up shop in San Juan del Sur you will still be no more than a five-minute walk from the water's edge.

There are gorgeous condos being built at Piedras y Olas on the eastern edge of town as well as Portofino at Talanquera on the north side of the bay, and a growing number of developments are offering time-share properties or even fractional time shares.

You'll have a hard time getting land exactly on the beach. In addition to the phantom Coastal Law (see sidebar, *The "Beachfront" Blues: Nicaragua's Coastal Law*), much of the waterfront property is either tied up in huge family farms that haven't yet been carved up or belong to powerful Nicaraguan families that have no intention of selling out. That means much of what's for sale is found on the bluffs overlooking the water or has access to the water via a little trunk road. This is a rapidly evolving market, so talk to your Realtor and keep your ear to the ground for developments as they happen.

Prices

Renters can find a three-bedroom place within town for about US$375 a month plus utilities. But once you decide to purchase, prices get harder to pin down, as this market is changing so quickly. You could pick up a furnished condo for around US$180,000 in 2006, but appreciation on these properties seems to be running at more than 30 percent per year, and in

PRIME LIVING LOCATIONS

some places it's closer to 100 percent. Bubble or great investment? We can't tell. Lots in places like Yankee Beach and Playa Papayal run US$20,000–100,000, but a lot of the price difference is dependent on how good the view is and how easy it is to reach the property, plus whether or not any utilities are available.

GETTING AROUND

Getting to San Juan del Sur is a piece of cake on well-paved roads from Granada or Managua. It's an under-three-hour trip by express bus, taxi, or hired vehicle. Once you reach San Juan del Sur you won't need a taxi to get around town, though in Rivas you'll find lots of them trolling for passengers for the easy last leg of the trip. San Juan is small enough that you can walk just about anywhere you want, but feel free to make use of the open *ciclo*-taxis (three-wheeled bicycle taxis), a fun way to cruise up and down the beach road.

To travel up and down the coast, you'll need a sturdy car, sturdy legs, or a decent mountain bike. You can rent bikes at plenty of budget hotels in town. Taxi drivers lounge around the market and can take you up and down the coast, but be sure the vehicle is in good condition and, in the rainy season, has four-wheel drive. Ask around your hotel or favorite bar about turtle tours and water taxis. Reliable, friendly private taxi services abound—ask your hotel for recommendations.

North Along the Coast

The long-promised coastal road providing easy access and electricity to the scores of spectacular beaches and ocean-vista hillsides has ensured a continuing development boom around each of the bays, beaches, and headlands along this long stretch of beautiful coastline. This includes private plots, gated communities, even a golf course with fairway plots and views of the ocean. Meanwhile, the road remains a promise, not a plan, and clever expats deal with transportation by their own means. It's still a bumpy, rutted ride to scout this section of the country. As you'll see, that hasn't slowed anybody down.

THE LAY OF THE LAND

This area can be divided into two rough sections: the beaches just north of San Juan del Sur (accessed via the road to Chocolata) and those to the west of Tola (accessed by driving through the city of Rivas). If you're really

PRIME LIVING LOCATIONS

serious about scouting, you'll need a reliable driver with a sturdy vehicle and some INETER (Government Land Studies Institute) topographical quads. Most real estate agencies have maps that highlight their own properties, occasionally against a photocopied background of the proper quad map. Following are a few of the more well-known beaches listed as you'll find them traveling from south to north.

Playa Marsella is pleasant, breezy beach, with good snorkeling around the rocks (watch the currents). The resort at Marsella is perched way above the beach; cliff-top cabins, restaurant, and properties boast incredible views. Playa Madera offers one of the most consistent and easy-to-access surf breaks; increasing upscale development may threaten the campgrounds and budget accommodations that have been around for years. The road (if you make all the correct turns) will take you to a parking lot right on the sand.

Bahía Majagual is home to a low-key budget eco-lodge by the same name that resides on a spectacular stretch of beach. Hidden at the end of 12 rough kilometers (7.5 miles) from San Juan del Sur, Majagual was once frequented by high-ranking Sandinista officials; a few *generalísimos* are still holding on to nearby pieces of property. Continuing north along the coast, Playa Ocotal is where you'll find the much-hyped Morgan's Rock Hacienda & Eco Lodge, a high-end eco-resort at the vanguard of Nicaragua's upscale tourism market.

Ten kilometers (six miles) west of Rivas is the agricultural community of **Tola,** gateway to the steadily improving shore road and a string of lonely, beautiful beaches that make up 30 kilometers (19 miles) of Pacific shoreline. Until very recently, you would have been the only foreigner on any of these beaches, but the word is out, land prices are rising, and numerous developments are going up. Being developed are private properties, not tourist facilities, so this area remains a propitious region in which to build your dream home, not look for a hotel room.

Playa Gigante is the first beach you come to after Tola, named after a geological formation called Punta Pie de Gigante (The Giant's Foot). This is a beautiful crescent beach well off the beaten track. The community of Gigante consists of a few dozen poor homes and about 500 locals. February–May (especially on Sunday), you have a great chance of buying fresh fish right off the boat, which you can cook up Nica style (with rice, salad, and plantains).

Another quiet and poor beachfront community, **Las Salinas** has a lovely beach with several waves popular among surfers, plus a few expat-owned "surf camp" places to stay, the owners of which may be happy to talk real estate with you. There are also nearby hot springs. **Guasacate** is one of Nicaragua's better beaches but remains virtually unvisited and undeveloped. It's a huge stretch of sand with access to the famed Popoyo surf break. Hopefully the recent construction of wealthy private homes won't complicate the development and use of the beach for the public. The entrance to Guasacate is 6.5 kilometers (4 miles) down the first left-hand road after crossing a bridge in Las Salinas and is paved the whole way.

Most of the deserted beaches in the 10-kilometer (6-mile) strip between Las Salinas and El Astillero don't even have names. **El Astillero** itself is a fishing village full of small boats and is, in fact, the first safe boat anchorage north of Gigante. North of El Astillero the road turns inland away from the coast. Accessing the beach anywhere along this area requires a boat and a lot of dedication. Ask around in El Astillero. There are plenty of underemployed sailors and fishermen that would be glad to strike a deal with you if you're interested in exploring the coastline.

WHERE TO LIVE

Most first-timers to the area, especially those lured by investment opportunities on the Internet, will probably end up in one of the handful of gated communities, billed either as vacation or retirement getaways; such places offer well-maintained, fully furnished homes with less risk of title and management problems than if you are looking on your own. The most popular developments include Rancho Santana, Rancho Los Perros, Iguana Beach and Golf Resort, and Guacalito de la Isla, all offering lots, condos, and clubhouses in secure isolation from the big, bad world outside. The advantage is that these developments offer lots that are ready to build and include water hookups from a private well and electrical hookups off the community line. In this remote stretch of landscape, that sets you a long way forward in the race to build your dream home. Lots in these communities run from US$45,000 to well over US$400,000.

There is plenty of land outside those walls as well but it is disappearing fast in what earlier expats disparage as "the land grab" and recent expats laud as "a great investment." How much longer any open land at all will be available on this choice coastline is anybody's guess. Regardless of whether you choose to settle down in a gated community, hack your own piece of paradise out of the hillside, or renovate an existing house in town, the trick is to think about what the area will look like 20 years from now. If you wanted it to be easier, you wouldn't be in Nicaragua, remember, and by choosing Nicaragua over other countries you are trading price for convenience. Keep it all in perspective.

GETTING AROUND

The road out of San Juan del Sur is halfway decent until the community of Chocolata, where it deteriorates. Buses still run north from Chocolata to Rivas (when the road is not flooded out), but it's quicker to drive around through La Virgen and Rivas to continue to points north of San Juan del Sur and west of Tola. Rent a car with four-wheel drive in Managua, or hire a local car and driver, preferably one who is bilingual and well recommended. Otherwise, there are sporadic buses out of San Juan del Sur and Rivas, as well as dozens of eager taxi drivers. Another option is to go by water. Real estate agencies or surf tour operators can arrange this or you can locate your own water taxi by asking around the beach bars. Finally, top-of-the-line places like Rancho Santana are more than happy to pick you up in Managua by helicopter and fly you in style to the coastline (you and two passengers fly for US$400 one way).

South Along the Coast

Slightly more accessible than the coastline to the north, and every bit as spectacular, this length of coastline includes numerous beaches and a growing number of developments. There are a few scattered eateries, gated communities, and the beautiful La Flor Wildlife Refuge, where endangered populations of sea turtles arrive each year to lay their eggs in the sand under the protection of armed soldiers.

From San Juan del Sur, you'll first pass through Barrio Las Delicias, which includes the sports stadium, cemetery, and friendly suburban folks, and leads you to a fork in the road known as "El Container." Go right here and walk another kilometer to Playa Remanso. There are no services here, so come prepared with water and food. In addition to its consistent but mediocre beach break for surfing, Remanso has a long, interesting shore that is fascinating to explore at low tide—look for bat caves, tide pools, blow holes, and plenty of wildlife. Walking 30 minutes farther south, you'll hit Playa Tamarindo, followed by Playa Hermosa. A bit farther is gated access to the new development at Yankee Beach. Continue to find Playa el Coco, the aforementioned wildlife reserve, and, eventually, the village of Ostional.

WHERE TO LIVE

Again, there are a couple of developed residential communities and a lot of land in between, but this area is still a diamond in the rough. The first foreign settlement was probably German-owned **Parque Marítimo El Coco,** 18 kilometers (11 miles) south of San Juan, where day-trippers are welcome to eat in the Puesta del Sol restaurant and take a look at the properties, which include fully furnished homes. Another gated option, closer to San Juan del Sur, is **Cantamar Playa Yankee.** Prices are changing drastically as foreigners flood this market. At printing, lots were available starting at US$40,000 and up, but expect prices to be higher than that as the market fluctuates. Lots with homes on them sell for US$200,000 and up but are harder to find than empty properties with no structures built on them.

GETTING AROUND

South of San Juan, transport is better than in the other direction. Wider dirt roads to the communities of Ostional, Las Parclas, and Escamequita also run through barrios outside of town like Las Delicias. There are plans to pave this road, all the way to Costa Rica, though it is still not clear when this will happen, or who will pay for it. The same transport options exist as for those mentioned to the north of San Juan del Sur.

Rivas

As the most important commercial and transportation hub in southwest Nicaragua, you would think that "The City of Mangos" would have eagerly jumped aboard the tourism and development bandwagon. You'd be wrong. Built on the thin isthmus of land between Lake Cocibolca and the Pacific coast, Rivas is the only major city south of Granada before you hit the Costa Rican border. Nearby San Jorge is the port town on the lake, and the ocean lies due west past Tola, out of sight beyond several low ranges of overgrazed hills. It is a strategic placement, which has been inhabited and fought over since the first Nahuatl and Chorotega inhabitants settled here; the area was a crucial stopover for gold-rushers en route between the Atlantic and Pacific, and was the site of battles involving William Walker's troops in the 1850s, land-hungry Costa Ricans, and most recently, between Sandinista and National Guard armies in the 1970s.

Alas, Rivas, a hot, low-lying colonial city of 45,000 near the windswept shore of Lake Cocibolca, is seen by both expats and travelers alike as

© RANDALL WOOD

Rivas's cathedral witnessed the Gold Rush.

somewhere through which they must pass on their way to the Isla de Ometepe or San Juan del Sur, or as a "necessary evil" when they have banking, communication, or shopping needs that can't be fulfilled elsewhere in the area. One expat in San Juan went so far as to call it the "Nica version of Cleveland." We don't think it's that bad, actually; Rivas is hot, sure, but it is friendly and more languorous compared to Granada. Rivas also exhibits some truly charming colonial architecture, visible in several 18th-century churches, and boasts a museum and quick access to the Pacific coast, La Isla de Ometepe, and Costa Rica. The mayor's office is trying to offer incentives to buy and build in Rivas, so if you like the humid weather and don't care too much about (or can't afford to purchase) beachfront property, Rivas is a pleasant—if innocuous—place to renovate and settle into a colonial home.

THE LAY OF THE LAND

Rivas is a city built on a gently rolling landscape common throughout the narrow isthmus that barely separates Lake Cocibolca from the Pacific coast. It spreads westward from the highway—you'll know you've entered Rivas when you go through the traffic circle on the highway.

The town's colonial center is only three long blocks from the highway, where the impressive Iglesia Parroquial de San Pedro towers over the tree-lined park to its west. As you leave the church behind you and proceed westward, the land gradually slopes down toward the market and main bus terminal and beyond. In fact, from the highway west the land descends gently into the sea, though from Rivas it's still quite a few miles away.

East of the highway Rivas's pleasant baseball stadium overlooks traffic. Newer developments are starting to appear east of the highway, but they are without exception marginal neighborhoods.

Outside of Rivas, rough roads lead down to La Chocolata and eventually San Juan del Sur (but for the latter destination the main highway is the better route), along both sides of which small family farms of up to four hectares (10 acres) sustain herds of cattle and crops of sugarcane.

WHERE TO LIVE

If you decide to call Rivas your home, the city is your oyster. Only two caveats are worth mentioning: The four blocks around the central park are the liveliest at all hours of the day (and night), and you would do well to avoid properties on the main drag that connect the highway to the bus terminal, as the bus traffic will slowly drive you insane. Better, quieter, and more attractive urban properties are found in the southern and eastern parts of town or on the small farm parcels outside of town. Within the city limits of Rivas, expect small, one-family homes to cost US$20,000–40,000. When real estate agents discuss Rivas with you, they are more likely thinking of the beachfront communities sprouting up along the Pacific coastline. (These areas are discussed under the *North Along the Coast* section and cost far, far more.)

Rental prices strongly depend on your ability to bargain. Locals are eager to make a killing off of expats who are looking to rent. You should be able to rent a simple home for US$300–600 per month, but you should get prices from several potential landlords to see if the prices offered are appropriate for the market.

GETTING AROUND

Rivas is about two hours southwest of Managua and an hour or so from Granada, though times vary depending on your mode of transport. Express buses ply these routes all day, and shared or private taxis between Rivas, San Juan del Sur (25 minutes), and the Costa Rica border are readily available and very cheap.

Isla de Ometepe

Nicaraguan to the core since the days the Nahuatl first decided to call the twin peaks of this volcanic island their home, Isla de Ometepe remains to this day an enchanted place comfortably removed from much of the rest of the nation, but still very much the cultural heart of Nicaragua. Few visitors to this island community fail to rave about it. Ometepe is an island composed of two joined volcanoes—one active, one dormant—which rise dramatically from the waters of Cocibolca. Inhabited since pre-Columbian times, Ometepe is awash in Nahuatl myths and legends. Long before the Spanish arrived, the islanders considered Ometepe sacred, inhabited by the gods, and today a palpable sense of mystery and magic permeates day-to-day life. But regardless of Ometepe's rich history, its present is equally fortunate. Ometepe's volcanic soils are deep and rich with nutrients, and Ometepe enjoys more rainfall than neighboring Chontales and Boaco (on the other side of the lake); as such, Ometepe's steep slopes are carpeted with lush virgin forest and thriving expanses of plantains, avocados, mangos, and coffee. Adventurous and sometimes dangerous trails lead to both craters, abundant with wildlife and rare vegetation.

Ometepe enjoys a rapidly developing budget tourism scene but still lacks facilities and hotels that would attract a wealthier set of travelers. It's clear why developers think La Isla de Ometepe will be "the next big

Ometepe's fantastic lakeshore is relaxing and clean.

thing," but the boom has yet to happen, which means you may still have time to get in on it. What is keeping Ometepe from the swarms of eager expatriates and would-be future residents? Its isolation, for one. Ometepe is connected to the rest of the world by semi-regular ferry service, but only one ship in the fleet carries vehicular traffic, and bad weather has been known to shut down service to the island altogether until the weather clears. But once you're on the island the near total lack of services and perhaps the periodic threat of Ometepe's north half—Volcán Concepción—erupting have conspired to keep Ometepe relatively free of the real estate boom ongoing across the lake in Granada. Still, it's nearly impossible not to gaze across at Central America's most exotic island and think "how amazing would it be to live there?" You're surely not alone in that thought.

THE LAY OF THE LAND

Most of La Isla de Ometepe's approximately 35,000 residents live in or around its two port towns, **Moyogalpa** on the west (where San Jorge ferries will let you off) and **Altagracia** on the north side of Volcán Concepción. The cramped isthmus that unites Volcán Concepción and Volcán Maderas is called Santo Domingo and is where you'll find Ometepe's fancier hotels and lodges. A single road wends its way around the lower circumference of Concepción, connecting Altagracia, Moyogalpa, and the many villages in between. From "Empalme El Quinto" on Concepción's northeast side a branch road leads over to the Volcán Maderas side, and spurs lead to Maderas's north and south coasts. At present, the eastern side of Maderas requires hiking boots and a sunny afternoon.

WHERE TO LIVE

The two port towns and their outlying communities make the most obvious first choice for expats, as existing properties have been developed and the potential for creative eco- or adventure tourism is the highest. Wander among the existing hotels and restaurants in these two sleepy port towns to get a feel for the present situation and then fill one of the local economy's many vacant niches with a small place of your own. Moyogalpa, in particular, has extensive rural "suburbs" of single family farms. The track from Moyogalpa eastward toward the *empalme* and eventually Altagracia is the most trafficked (by Ometepe's standards, this is still just the occasional vehicle), and a steady progression of small fishing villages all consist of small concrete homes at the lake's edge.

FERRY SCHEDULE TO AND FROM SAN JORGE

SAN JORGE-MOYOGALPA

Departure Time	Ferry Name
9 A.M.	Karen María
9:30 A.M.	Reyna del Sur
10:30 A.M.	Ferry Ometepe
11:30 A.M.	Señora del Lago
12:30 P.M.	Santa Martha
1:30 P.M.	Reyna del Sur
2:30 P.M.	Ferry Ometepe
3:30 A.M.	Reyna del Sur
4:30 P.M.	Señora del Lago
5:30 P.M.	Ferry Ometepe

MOYOGALPA-SAN JORGE

Departure Time	Ferry Name
5:30 A.M.	Karen María
6 A.M.	Señora del Lago
6:30 A.M.	Santa Martha
6:45 A.M.	Ferry Ometepe
7 A.M.	Reyna del Sur
11 A.M.	Reyna del Sur

Concepción's backside (the northwest face) is wilder and the road is poorer, tying larger farms and smallish banana plantations together. This is a more likely area to find a farm of a respectable size. The isthmus between the two volcanic cones is most apt for the would-be beachfront hotel owner, as several interesting establishments already dip their toes into the water on the north side. Lastly, Volcán Maderas is the less active volcanic peak (dormant, actually), but the road to Balgüe is a bone-cruncher, and the road along Maderas's south shore is rougher still. If you like the look of the land, start your visit with a stay in one of the area's two popular eco-lodges, the Albergue Ecológico El Porvenir or the Hotel Hacienda Merida. From there you can explore options and inquire about would-be property sellers anxious to try their hand elsewhere.

© RANDALL WOOD

11:30 A.M.	Karen María
12:30 P.M.	Ferry Ometepe
1:30 P.M.	Señora del Lago
4 P.M.	Ferry Ometepe

The Ferry Ometepe is the safest and biggest ship. All times on this schedule are subject to change. For the most up-to-date schedule, or to be sure that your boat is running, call Ometepe Tours (tel. 563-4779).

PRIME LIVING LOCATIONS

GETTING AROUND

Ferries from the dock at San Jorge run regularly all day—some have room for vehicles, but the competing boat companies are very unhelpful about giving out information when it doesn't involve their boat. For the best ferry information, go to the Ometepe Tours information booth near the pier gates—they're the most honest of the bunch and can arrange all kinds of transport and tours once you're on the island. As soon as you disembark from the ferry in the town of Moyogalpa, there is no shortage of vehicles: slow buses, hired taxis, and pickup trucks. Fast boat transportation between Granada and Ometepe exists every few years, and will hopefully be available again soon, depending on rising demand. In the meantime, there are a couple of slow boats each week that make the trip when the waves aren't too big.

Volcán Maderas

Once you're on the island, if you haven't dragged along your own vehicle you are resigned to the infrequent, overcrowded vomit-buses (all right, they're not that bad, but an awful lot of vomiting does seem to occur) that ply the route between Altagracia and Moyogalpa counterclockwise. Note that on Sunday it is better to assume that these buses don't run at all. The locals frequently hitchhike and you are free to do so as well, as the island's small-town feel keeps Ometepe rather free of violent crime.

MANAGUA

Once a nondescript fishing village in the years when León and Granada battled for domination of the nation's political and commercial power, Managua grew to become the most modern and well-developed city on the Central American isthmus—until it was reduced to rubble by the earthquake of 1972, followed by a revolution in its streets, a civil war, and various economic and urban crises from which it only really began to recover in the late 1990s. Today, Managua embodies numerous contradictions as Nicaragua's largest, most dynamic, and least loved city. Managua is the most prosperous and the most derelict, the city that offers the most amenities but exudes the least charisma. Managua is at once a major city whose historic downtown remains frightfully empty, while new businesses sprout like mushrooms along its periphery.

Managua doesn't charm at first glance, or even second glance. But if you can look past its traffic, its chaotic sprawl, and its bland, concrete architecture, Managua may win you over before you know it. Managua's

© JOSHUA BERMAN

greatest charm is its small-town feel in an otherwise big city. Managua is enormous, but it is a city of barrios, each of which has its own personality and function. Most foreign residents and well-off Nicas spend the majority of their time in only a couple of select neighborhoods, making Managua far smaller and more manageable than they'd expect.

Many a foreigner has visited Managua on other business, decided they would never live there, and wound up doing so anyway. Because, like it or not, Managua is where the jobs are. For a variety of practical reasons, embassies and consulates, multinational companies, export-import businesses—plus the development, aid, and NGO communities—are all headquartered in the capital. So say what you will about Managua, it's home to hundreds of foreign nationals; once you've settled into their burgeoning community and discovered how to get around, you may very well decide that Managua isn't so bad after all.

The Lay of the Land

Managua grips the south shore of Lake Managua, also known as Lake Xolotlán, and in fact, popular legend calls Managua "the bride of Xolotlán." The land rises gently to the south to a small range of hills that overlooks the city and divides the Managua watershed from the pineapple plantations of Ticuantepe. Due south of Managua those hills rise in a crescendo to the blustery highlands of El Crucero, which enjoys a cool climate in remarkable contrast to Managua's. El Crucero is actually a long-extinct volcano that forms just one of the many pinnacles in Nicaragua's volcanic ridge, and its lush volcanic slopes bear thick crops of coffee and bananas. To the east of the city lie broad sugarcane plantations that feed the rum distilleries outside of León, while just northwest of the city is the astonishing Chiltepe peninsula, which interrupts the otherwise smooth lakeshore of Xolotlán. Chiltepe is formed from a pair of volcanic peaks, both of which now cradle volcanic lakes of clear fresh water where they once belched fire.

But before anyone tries to sell you lakefront property in the nation's capital, let's just say "the bride" could use a bath and a manicure. Lake Managua has been biologically dead for decades, the victim of half a century of uninspired environmental policy and the tenacious abuse of the industries that prospered just long enough to devastate the lake before collapsing. Managua's *malecón* is a lakeside boardwalk that sports a couple of Ferris wheels and small eateries. Take a stroll along it some

"TO THE LAKE, UP, AND UNDER THE COCONUTS": UNDERSTANDING MANAGUA DIRECTIONS

When we received an enraged letter from a reader decrying our ineptitude for not including street names on the map of Managua in *Moon Handbooks Nicaragua*, we responded by agreeing that this would have been a grievous error indeed – if there actually *were* street names in the capital! Managuans have their own way of finding their way around and it does not include such prosaic details as avenues and addresses. In the few instances in which street names and house numbers exist, they are ignored.

Rather, addresses in Managua begin with a landmark (either existing or historical) that is then followed by a description of how many *cuadras* (blocks) should be traveled and in which direction in order to reach your destination, which may further be distinguished by the color of the building or type of tree growing nearby. Somehow, it works. To understand how, remember this: north is *"al lago"* (toward the lake); east is *"arriba"* (up, referring to the sunrise); south is *"al sur"* or *"a la*

montaña" (to the south); and west is *"abajo"* (down, where the sun sets).

Some other key phrases are *contiguo a* (next door to), *frente a* (across from), *casa esquinera* (corner house), and *a mano derecha/izquierda* (on the right/left-hand side). Also note that *"varas"* are often used to measure distances of less than one block; this is an old colonial measurement just shy of a meter. Here are a few examples, with their translations, to help get you started:

De la Plaza España, tres cuadras abajo, tres cuadras al lago, casa esquinera. (From Plaza España, three blocks west, three blocks north, corner house.)

De donde fue el Sandy's, 200 varas arriba, frente al gran hotel. (From where Sandy's used to be, 200 meters to the east, across from the big hotel.)

De Tica Bus, una cuadras arriba, media cuadras al sur, a mano izquierda, busca al flaco Irlandes. (From the Tica Bus station, one block east, half a block south, look for the skinny Irishman.)

afternoon to notice not a single boat plies the waves of Lake Managua. There's nothing to fish for.

The city of Managua is essentially flat, with the exception of a couple of unique features, like the Laguna de Tiscapa, a drowned volcanic crater in the center of the city, on top of which sits an incongruous collection of attractions, including a monument to Augusto C. Sandino, the ruins of Somoza's palace, and a "canopy tour" that sends tourists zipping over the lake on steel cables. With the exception of Tiscapa, however, Managua's myriad barrios blend into one another with little rhyme or reason, and for that matter, without any road signs. If you find it confusing to make your way around Managua, you're not alone. Aside from Managua's unique system of directions (see sidebar, *"To the Lake, Up, and Under the Coconuts": Understanding Managua Directions*), few neighborhoods have characteristics so salient that you can distinguish one from the other—unless, of course, you've grown up there and can see the subtle differences invisible to the newcomer's eye.

CLIMATE

"Hazy, hot, and humid with a chance of showers." That's Managua's weather forecast for the foreseeable future. Managua, at 12° North latitude and a paltry 30 meters above sea level, is about as close to the center of the earth as you can get in Nicaragua and, consequently, it is hot. Managua's rainy season runs from mid-May through late October, during which time bright sunny mornings give way to overcast skies and afternoon showers that send maids scurrying to bring in the wash. By evening the air, though still humid, is cooler and pleasant, and you can sleep through most of the year under nothing more substantial than a light cotton sheet. Beware April and May however, when, at the tail end of the dry season, Managua stifles and the heat radiating off the road can cook you in your shoes. Managuans with access to pools tend to congregate there when possible, and they make a trip to the beach in April for Semana Santa.

Follow Managuans' lead if you make the capital your home, and lie low during the hot hours of the day, when only "mad dogs and Englishmen" roam the streets. Instead, pop out in late afternoon to finish up your chores, and then enjoy the evening out with friends.

Where to Live

The most attractive and safest neighborhoods with the thickest tree canopies are, unsurprisingly, the areas to which the expatriate community flocks. The main neighborhoods are **Las Colinas** and **Santo Domingo** in the south of the city and **Carretera Sur** in the southwest. Increasingly, Managua is expanding southward and eastward toward Masaya, where former farmland is being developed into smart little communities with modern amenities like curbed roadways and even the occasional sidewalk! While this is still a nascent real estate trend, look for increasingly nice properties along this **Carretera Masaya** corridor.

PRIME LIVING LOCATIONS

© RANDALL WOOD

A one-story city: Much of Managua is at ground level.

SANTO DOMINGO

Santo Domingo is, without question, home to Managua's finest properties and nicest homes. It is marginally nicer than Las Colinas, which also offers excellent quality homes and properties. The difference is that Santo Domingo is slightly quieter and the lots tend to be more wooded, so you get a bit more privacy. More than one ambassador makes Santo Domingo his or her home, as do a lot of the executive staff of the major development organizations. Santo Domingo is simply a great place to live. It is a bigger neighborhood than it seems at first glance. You enter it off the south side of Carretera Masaya at the city's outskirts. Tucked quietly at the entrance to Santo Domingo is the unobtrusive Ministry of Agriculture and a private school. It stretches westward and climbs the hills back behind an old military base, however, and on the second tier of Santo Domingo, smaller properties enjoy a surprisingly nice view of the capital below. Santo Domingo is off the beaten track even by Managua standards. Its roads do not make a good shortcut between any two other places, so it receives less traffic than do other neighborhoods, and the traffic that plies its streets tends to be the hulking white SUVs of ministry and embassy staff.

Not surprisingly, Santo Domingo isn't cheap. A nice home with modern appliances and a decent piece of property could easily cost you what a similar property would be worth in a place like Indiana or Colorado. Expect to pay upward of US$100,000 for decent properties in this neighborhood. Rentals are sometimes, but not always, available. Embassies like to rent for their staff in this neighborhood, and they typically pay US$1,000–2,000 per month for fancy family homes with three or more bedrooms, staff quarters, ample living quarters, oversize bathrooms, and large backyards for entertaining. There are no apartments or apartment buildings, and the locals are happy to keep it that way. But ask around and you might be able to find a family interested in renting out a wing of their house or a room to a suitable tenant with good credentials and an easy smile. Unfortunately, the Realtors don't carry these kinds of opportunities in their listings; your best way to latch onto a room in this neighborhood is by word of mouth or through a friend. If you are employed by an embassy, NGO, or foreign mission of some sort, your contacts there will serve you well.

LAS COLINAS

Across Carretera Masaya from Santo Domingo, Las Colinas is a bit less shaded, but the houses are every bit as nice as their cousins on the other street. Las Colinas (The Hills) attracts the same crowd as Santo Domingo: wealthy Managuans and expats connected to embassies and NGOs. Las Colinas is every bit as luxurious as Santo Domingo, and its properties are every bit as palatial, with similar prices for selling and renting. Las Colinas was laid out after the earthquake of 1972 by architects and planners that had spent a good amount of time in the United States, and it shows. The homes, the streets, and the lots all bear a striking resemblance to something you could find in California (except for the enormous barbed wire-topped fences that demarcate property boundaries). Plus, in a clear reference to the United States, Las Colinas streets all bear names, which—believe it or not—confuse Nicaraguans. Randy lived here for several years and, when registering for his driver's license, reported a street name and house number to an unbelieving clerk at the Police Office who corrected him, "no, your address should be 'from the bank, two blocks to the lake, three blocks up.'" In addition to street signs, Las Colinas boasts a good elementary school and day-care center, enough speed bumps to keep traffic down to a minimum, and a handful of embassies and consulates for countries that decided to avoid the cacophony of Managua's raucous downtown.

Because of Las Colinas's proximity to Barrio Renée Shick (named after a fallen Sandinista revolutionary), which is a rough neighborhood even by Central American standards, you'll need to choose your jogging routes carefully.

Las Colinas and Santo Domingo boast luxury homes.

© RANDALL WOOD

CARRETERA SUR

Managua's third popular expat neighborhood is, like the other two, on the city's outskirts, thus avoiding a bit of the confusion, heat, and noise endemic elsewhere in the capital. Carretera Sur is the highway that leads from Managua south through El Crucero to Jinotepe, Diriamba, and the Pueblos Blancos. It rises steadily from Managua, so each property is a bit higher than its neighbor to the north and a bit lower than its neighbor to the south. Managuans refer to properties on the Carretera Sur by kilometer number, and the highway is well-marked with white and black kilometer stones.

Carretera Sur's advantage is the quality of its properties, each of which is more like a little *quinta* (small, personal farm) than a traditional lot in a developed neighborhood (though you can find the latter as well). If you decide to make Carretera Sur your home you can easily find a property that includes a nice home and an acre of coffee, hardwoods, or fruit trees. Your property might be accessible only by a dirt road from the highway or overlook one of the jagged valleys that penetrate the hills south of Managua. There is no doubt that homes along Carretera Sur, due to their elevation above the city, enjoy more pleasant evening breezes and cooler afternoons than do the properties in either Santo Domingo or Las Colinas.

In exchange, you sacrifice a bit of the neighborhood feel that predominates the other two areas (even with the high walls and armed private security guards of those areas, there really is a community!). Because Carretera Sur, as a neighborhood, is defined as the properties on either side of the highway, it is linear and a bit disjointed. Your street will be the same primary means of egress from Managua's southwestern corner as the buses and vehicles bound for points south. The noise factor is mitigated by the size of the properties, but once you drive your vehicle out of your driveway and reach the edge of the highway, expect to have to step on the accelerator hard and nudge your way out into traffic. Also, certain sections of the highway are prone to the diesel groan of trucks and buses downshifting to slow their velocity as they approach the city limits. All this is to say one property differs very much from another on Carretera Sur, and no description of the properties there can suitably be generalized to the rest of the neighborhood.

When investigating a property on Carretera Sur it's worth your while to take a careful look at your neighbors both uphill and down to gain an understanding of how they are using their land. Because of the broken terrain and the occasionally steep slopes, inappropriately developed construction projects uphill can negatively impact your property or your home, from dust to noise to mudslides to flooding due to newly built upstream structures. For that matter, knowing what your neighbors are like is good advice no matter where in the world you decide to call home.

Expect prices to run from US$100,000 to as high as US$300,000; rentals, when available, hover around US$1,000 per month.

CARRETERA MASAYA

Carretera Masaya is the major thoroughfare that links Managua to Masaya (and then Granada). It's a major road, as Managua goes, but in 2003 the national government made resurfacing and upgrading the road a major priority, and travel between these two important cities is now radically improved. As late as the second half of the 1990s, once you passed Las Colinas and Santo Domingo on your way out of town you entered a bucolic farming zone that lasted right up to the city limits of Masaya, then again between Masaya and Granada. But slowly those farms are being developed into small housing communities that eschew the traditional downtown Managua philosophy that "quick enough is good enough" for properly designed parcels of evenly spaced and often wooded lots on paved streets with curbs and either city water or wells. These properties are the haunt of Managua's young professionals, 30- and 40-somethings that grew up in Managua's traditional neighborhoods but have decided to move out to the suburbs instead and commute back to Managua. Anyone will tell you that sooner or later Managua and Masaya are going to connect into one mega-village with more urban elements at the western side and more rural elements at the eastern. The development along Carretera Masaya reflects this philosophy, and by designing new properties and neighborhoods, Nicaragua's architects, planners, and real estate agents can abandon the sometimes insurmountable problems faced by Managua proper.

Your first step is getting to know the neighborhood. Drive from Managua west toward Masaya and you will encounter a blizzard of real estate signs for named, gated communities. These new developments are the most exciting prospect in Managuan real estate. Built by reputable development companies and designed to the standards of Nicaraguans that spent a decade in Miami and want a little more for their money, the developments usually offer two or three models of homes, all set in a gated community with a night watchman, a private water supply, and sometimes other amenities. Houses tend to be two or three bedrooms with a bathroom for each room, plus separate living quarters for the maid. These development communities, known in Spanish as *urbanizaciones,* number in the dozens as this book goes to press, but increasingly, the farm land south of Managua is being converted into these communities, with names like Bosques de Capistrano, Michaelangelo, Villas Porto Novo, and Villas Puertas de Hierro, and represent the future of Managuan development as the city creeps inexorably toward Masaya.

Any attempt to provide a comprehensive list of these neighborhoods would date this book before it ever hit the shelves, as these communities open for business, fill up, and finish construction all in a six-month period. Your first step is to cruise the neighborhood and visit not only the *urbanizaciones* themselves but also the developers promoting them, as they will be able to direct you to their other properties as well. You are only a phone call away from making a deal. This is a rapidly developing and energized neighborhood with high appeal for the crowd that needs to be in Managua but doesn't want to live there, and for those that are unwilling to pay the higher prices that predominate in neighborhoods like Santo Domingo and Las Colinas.

In general, expect prices to run around US$60,000–120,000 for a single-family three-bedroom home with a pleasant design and a green lawn on all sides. You will be hard-pressed to find properties for rent in this neighborhood, as it is so new that most inhabitants are settling in themselves.

OTHER MIDDLE-CLASS NEIGHBORHOODS

Managua's increasingly embattled middle-class neighborhoods are centrally located in the city and include Los Robles, Barrio Tiscapa, and El Dorado. None of these neighborhoods are particularly unpleasant to live in and, on the contrary, offer a reasonable lifestyle in comfortable homes with traditional amenities. None, however, is exceptional, which is to say, none will provide a tremendous opportunity to write home to friends and family bragging about your sweet new "lifestyle." On the other hand, choosing the middle-class route gives you an unparalleled opportunity to get to know your *capitalino* neighbors, who will be much more willing to accept you as a member of the community than they would if you lived in an uppity expat enclave. That is to say, what you sacrifice in terms of exceptional living conditions will be more than recompensed with your inclusion in the day-to-day lives of ordinary Managuans, which in fact may be your goal—especially if saving money and improving your Spanish are also priorities.

Los Robles

Occupying both sides of Carretera Masaya close to Managua's center, Los Robles is still a name that resonates with a bit of class, and more than one government minister calls Los Robles home. Houses in this neighborhood have more land than do the properties elsewhere in Managua, and though the properties are contiguous, the buildings are not adjacent, which makes this neighborhood a bit quieter than other parts of the city. The small, winding streets that form this neighborhood are a pleasant change of pace from the more linear neighborhoods that dominate elsewhere, and everybody has a tree or two on the front lawn, making Los Robles relatively shaded, even at noon. Los Robles is also the site of several of Managua's more well-loved restaurants and cafés, including La Casa del Café and La Cocina de Doña Haydee. In Los Robles your neighbor might be a tropical bed-and-breakfast, the owner of a small business, or a middle-class family of five. Prices vary wildly depending on the quality of the house, size of the lot, and neighbors, but you can expect to find a single-family home in this neighborhood for US$60,000–100,000. This is a pleasant neighborhood in which to rent, due to the abundant restaurant and entertainment options; accordingly, single-family homes for rent tend to run in the US$400–700 per month range.

Barrio Tiscapa

Barrio Tiscapa barely registers on the map, but it is convenient, highly central, and safer than most. Tucked in between Managua's largest bookstore

EXPAT PROFILE: MONICA DRAZBA

Nicaragua has become home for Monica Drazba after 25 years of living and working in the aquaculture business in Latin America. She left the United States for Mexico in 1980. Starting shrimp farms, living in large cities and remote beach towns, and starting and raising a family in four different countries has kept Monica and her family on their toes, adjusting to new places, new schools, and new people. Living in the third world has afforded her the opportunity to be a stay-at-home mother, volunteer in local charities, and only do occasional consulting work. She now works at the U.S. Agency for International Development as the acting executive officer, while continuing to do seafood sanitation consulting and writing on a part-time basis. Her husband, Larry, is general manager and partner in the largest shrimp farm in Nicaragua, a vertically integrated business that processes six million pounds of shrimp per year.

Why is Managua a great place to live?
Managua is a small town inhabited by more than a million people. It's almost impossible to not meet a friend at the supermarket, at the dentist, or in line at the airport. Once you've settled in and made your peace with quirky roads, no street signs, psychopathic bus drivers, electric bill shock, and dealing with immigration and customs, it's pretty comfortable. Assuming you've got the income, supermarkets are well-stocked with a variety of local and imported items at fairly reasonable prices. Produce is varied, and local fruit is amazingly inexpensive. My experience with medical care has been good, and the new Metropolitan Hospital will make you feel like you're in the States, only at one-tenth the price. There is a plethora of movie houses, an excellent theater that hosts local and international concerts and productions, a wild nightlife of clubs and casinos, and some very good restaurants. The pace is relaxed, crime is still low, though, unfortunately, rising. Most feel very safe on the streets. Managua is home to several country clubs and fitness centers, and a beautiful golf course is only minutes away.

What is the expat community like there and how is it different from those in other parts of Nicaragua?
In Managua the expats are a far smaller, almost an insignificant presence within the enormous local population, unlike in Granada. I like this. The group here is made up of working expats with their spouses and families, and only a very few retirees. There are American, Canadian, and German teachers in abundance at the international schools, embassy and development assistance personnel from all over the first world, and American women who have married Nicaraguan men and are now living in Managua. These latter are expats with far closer ties and dependence on the local economy. Unlike in other cities in Nicaragua, the community here is a working community, so the lifestyle is not the tourist-on-the-beach style, but the everyday life of those who go to work in the morning and come home to dinner (prepared by the maids) in the

evening. Expats raise their children here and go to weddings, baptisms, and funerals. All in all, it is a full life for those who call Managua home.

How did you find your home?

We began to move here in 1995 when finding decent, large housing was very difficult. After a fruitless search and a tearful trip back to Guatemala (where I was living), we decided to purchase a lot in a very good section of Managua. The cost was very reasonable compared to land prices in other capital cities in Central America – less than one-fifteenth the price of comparable land in Guatemala City! We built a large home, with sufficient space for four growing children, my giant book collection, and furniture and antiques picked up in Guatemala, Mexico, and Ecuador. Building the house was quite a lot of work, but surprisingly took less time (six months) than researching the land title before purchasing the property. We're examples of the time and money every knowledgeable buyer must spend to ensure that the land being purchased is really owned by the seller. The construction industry 10 years ago was still in its very weakest stages after the Sandinista epoch, so building this house was difficult. Today, it would be far easier and far more expensive. This was a great investment and the land has tripled in value over the last nine years.

Any surprises? Any advice along the lines of "I wish someone had told me . . . ?"

I always warn those who move here to purchase a high-clearance vehicle; four-wheel drive is less important than your car's ability to drive over vicious speed bumps, rocks, and the occasional curb when there's trouble up ahead and you need to get out of traffic (no kidding). The price of electricity is a shock! (No pun intended, well, maybe a little one.) This was a very unpleasant surprise; indeed, Nicaragua has the highest energy cost in Central America.

© MONICA DRAZBA

Monica (center) with the rest of the Drazba family

(HISPAMER) and the University of Central America ("La UCA") and only a block or two from the popular Metrocentro shopping mall, Barrio Tiscapa is just difficult enough to drive through that it is not a major thoroughfare, and it remains quiet and residential. Properties in this neighborhood sell for US$40,000–80,000 and rent for around US$300–500 per month.

El Dorado

El Dorado is a fairly nondescript middle-class Managuan neighborhood whose claim to fame is that it is safer than most neighborhoods at the same socioeconomic stratum. El Dorado is not far from Mercado Roberto Huembes in the heart of downtown Managua. Homes are concrete blocks and frequently contiguous, with small enclosed backyards and enclosed parking spaces out front. Many of your neighbors in this neighborhood will be Nicaraguan families that fled to Miami during the years of the Sandinista revolution and returned with their savings to buy clean, orderly little homes. You will not have many expat neighbors, but your dollars will certainly stretch farther, and you can expect to get to know lots of Managuans on every side. Small, clean homes in El Dorado regularly fetch US$40,000–60,000 and rent for less than US$300 per month. The nicer homes are the ones with more ample backyards.

Getting Around

You have three ways to get around Managua—no, make that two. Managua is served by an extensive, convoluted, and dangerous public bus system conspicuously devoid of marked stops or published routes: This is the option that should be discarded for all. While bus travel between cities is essentially safe in Nicaragua, Managua's city buses, called *urbanos,* are not. On the off chance you do take a Managuan bus, stay near the front so the driver can keep an eye on you, keep nothing of value in your pockets, and pay close attention to your surroundings. Even middle-class Managuans refuse to use *urbanos,* and with good reason. That leaves taxis and your own vehicle.

TAXIS

Taxis are cheap, ridiculously easy to find, and usually safe, provided you make good decisions and keep your wits about you. Long gone are the days of the late 1990s when red-plated (registered) taxis competed with white-plated *piratas* (unregistered taxis) for fares. Managua finally pressured the illegal operators to either register for red plates or be forced off the road. That still left 14,000 taxis in operation, which means you will not have to worry about finding one: They'll swarm around you like flies as soon as you step forward from the curb. Taxis cost from US$1 (C$20) to US$5 (C$85) depending on how far across town you are traveling. A day of errands can certainly add up, but it's well worth the price considering how convoluted and difficult Managua's street system is, allowing you to simply read off your destination to the driver and sit back for the ride. Remember: When hailing a cab take a good look at the state of the vehicle. Agree on the price before stepping into the cab (at which point all your bargaining leverage vanishes). The bargaining typically goes back and forth no more than three times (unlike in Asia), and once you've agreed on a price, the deal is done. The more reputable cab companies have better maintained vehicles, and private cab owners that take pride in keeping their vehicle clean and shiny are more likely to offer good service. Yes, you can expect to pay these folks a little more, and it's worth every dime.

DRIVING IN MANAGUA

Finally, for the brave, the foolhardy, and the well-insured, driving yourself around Managua is infinitely more comfortable than taking taxis—and infinitely more stressful. Still, all expats in Managua agree having your own vehicle is well worth the trouble, so you'll wind up behind the wheel sooner or later. Here's how to do it.

First, bone up on your offensive driving skills by taking your own, um, crash course by driving around New York City, Boston, and Washington, D.C. The skills you pick up will come in useful in Managua, where the drivers are more aggressive, the traffic patterns less predictable, and the road conditions more precarious. Next, save yourself the headache of starting from scratch and spend your first couple of weeks using the taxi system so you can learn how to navigate, paying close attention to the routes chosen by your driver. Managua's lack of street signs is your first challenge, but once you get to know the city's major landmarks you will be ahead of the game. Half the battle of driving in Managua is knowing which lane to be in, and experience is the best teacher. As when driving in Manhattan, you are generally rewarded by staying aggressive in your driving decisions; the weak and the meek are quickly trodden upon. Be bold but cautious, and fasten your seatbelt. Because traffic often prevents any buildup of real speed, Managuan traffic accidents infrequently result in death, but fender-benders are par for the course. Keep your eyes on the road and good luck!

LEÓN AND THE NORTH

Nicaragua has not one classic colonial city but two, and while Granada basks in fame and adulation, life in less renowned León goes on much as it has for centuries. Surrounded on all sides by fertile fields of corn and sugarcane and laid out on the warm plain beneath a row of immense volcanoes, León's streets speak of majesty and history. The city as a whole is one of Nicaragua's three most important cities and should not be overlooked by either the casual traveler or potential long-term expatriate.

You'll cross into the broad area we refer to as "the North" as soon as your vehicle leaves Managua's city limits and begins its upward rumble, ascending steadily through dry hills that erupt into taller green peaks. The air cools perceptibly and the pace of life slows. Political leaders and regimes have come and gone, farms have prospered and failed, rivers have risen and dried. But above all the rhythm of the land in the vast countryside of Nicaragua's wild north is the rhythm of the harvest, and as surely as the

© RANDALL WOOD

one of León's several gorgeous churches

sun will rise tomorrow, Nicaragua's rugged farmers and ranchers will rise before dawn to begin the day's chores and provide for their families.

By way of orientation, glance at a map and take note of the place names: Estelí, Matagalpa, Jinotega, Jalapa. In lieu of the pantheon of the Catholic church's well-known saints, you find hard, indigenous words that trip on your tongue and evoke Nahuatl defiance and cultural pride. Nicaragua's north is no more indigenous than anywhere else (unlike in countries like Guatemala or Bolivia, where indigenous cultures remain clustered in certain geographic regions), but the hard mountain spirit of Nicaragua's earliest ancestors lives on in the campesinos that call the north home. They live harder lives than their cousins south of Managua. They are more dependent on farming, cope with less-developed roads, and put up with wells whose water tables are farther down. They are more dependent on the luck of the harvest and receive less from their elected officials in Managua. Like most upland folk, they are hardy and resilient and live life as fully as they can.

You might draw a few stares if you settle in any of these locations, as the locals will be surprised to see you joining them, but provided you make an effort to know your neighbors and seem to provide more benefit than problems, you will be quickly welcomed as a valuable part of the community. And while you'll live a simpler lifestyle than you would in a more developed town like Granada, you might find the cooler weather alone makes it worth your while.

PRIME LIVING LOCATIONS

CLIMATE

Nicaragua's northwest experiences a more prolonged dry season (November–April, rainy season May–October) than anywhere except the north-center, which is truly arid. But in contrast to the cool nights of the mountains, the lowlands of León and Chinandega can get sticky and hot. The least comfortable months in this area are April and May, when temperatures can soar to just over 38°C (100°F). During this time, locals take advantage of the early mornings and late evenings and choose lightweight, breathable clothing.

León and Region

Cornerstone of the fertile northwest volcanic plains that produce most of Nicaragua's sugar—and all of its booze—León is the second oldest city in Central America. Settled by Francisco Hernández de Córdoba and his band of *conquistadores* not once but twice, the whole city is a testament to the colonial lifestyle that characterized Latin America in the 17th and 18th centuries. Here, the buzz and enthusiasm of a vibrant student community permeate the very fabric of a city rife with grand churches and cathedrals, the vestiges of a proud indigenous community, and neat adobe homes set on narrow streets.

For the record, the first try at establishing the Spanish imperial presence west of Lake Cocibolca is now called "León Viejo" and is found not far from the sleepy provincial town of La Paz Centro on Lake Managua's southwestern shore. Lake Managua was still a limpid pool lush with vegetation and fish in those years, but Volcán Momotombo on the other side of the lake shook regularly and in 1610 erupted violently, so the locals decided it would be better to relocate a little farther to the west. Hernández de Córdoba never made the trip: His hand-chosen governor, Pedrarias Dávila, had him decapitated his second year in power. Old León was forgotten and gradually subsided beneath the sediment of history, to be rediscovered in 1966 by archaeologists from the National University (UNAN). In 2000 they found the headless cadaver of Córdoba himself (Dávila's cadaver as well) and placed them in a carefully tended mausoleum.

León has always played an important and formative role in the nation's history and was a bastion of the liberal movements that started pressing for independence from Spain in the 19th century and contributed greatly to the overthrow of dictator Somoza in the 20th century. Blame those uppity students. The Leoneses are justifiably proud of their charming

PRIME LIVING LOCATIONS

town, lined with traditionally designed homes that look out onto vistas unchanged over the centuries. León's cathedral is a masterpiece and the largest cathedral in Central America. Some of the nation's most beloved sons, including Rubén Darío, are buried within. But a dozen additional churches make striking landmarks for easy navigation through the city, and each is worth visiting in turn. León's eastern neighborhood of Subtiava used to be an indigenous villa that served the colonials at its side and to this day smells vaguely of rebellion.

León is certainly the centerpiece and economic anchor of Nicaragua's northwest, but it's also the gateway to more gorgeous Pacific coastline. Lots of Leoneses enjoy summer homes in the beach towns of Poneloya and Las Peñitas. But farther off the beaten track in otherwise forgotten bays and estuaries like Estero Padre Ramos and Playa Aserradores, long, vacant tracts of beautiful Pacific beachfront properties lie undeveloped, ticking off the days until some major hotel chain or group of adventurous investors reshapes the area into something quite different.

THE LAY OF THE LAND

León is characteristic of all of Nicaragua's northwest in that it was formed eons ago when the mighty Cordillera Los Maribios (the Maribios mountain range, Nahuatl for "Giants") began washing sediment out to the sea. The entire region is a broad, fertile, and essentially featureless agricultural plain that lies at the feet of the aforementioned volcanic giants. So great is this mountain range's environmental influence that east of the range the landscape changes entirely and even the vegetation types differ. The land slopes gently down to the Pacific Ocean and slopes even more gently down in the northwest to the Estero Real (Royal Estuary), where land and water blend almost indistinguishably in a morass of mangroves and saw grass. This low-lying area around the estuary, punctuated by the little village of Puerto Morazán, suffered greatly during Hurricane Mitch, which inundated the village up to the church's steeple.

León proper is a bright and charismatic city whose only downfall is perhaps the heat, which at the tail end of the dry season can be oppressive. The only point at which the city's elevation changes dramatically is where the Río Chiquito passes through the city limits and the streets plunge down on both sides to meet it. Elsewhere, the landscape is rather uniform.

West of the city, the Pacific coastline is less regular than it is around San Juan del Sur's stretch of bays and points. At Corinto, Jiquilillo, and Aposentillo the land folds in on itself into quiet bays and estuaries rife with waterfowl and plant species. These bays are hard to get to, one of several factors that have kept this gorgeous area relatively undeveloped.

WHERE TO LIVE

Less ostentatious and self aware than Granada, the city of León is every bit as gorgeous, if colonial architecture is your cup of tea. Don't be fooled by the drab exteriors of the homes that line the old part of León's city streets: Behind the tall wooden doors are high-ceilinged interior courtyards that make colonial Spanish architecture such a delight to live in. In León the many students pursuing degrees in medicine, engineering, and economics at UNAN-León and other schools lend a palpable sense of excitement to the city's dozens of cafés, restaurants, and bars. León is a bigger city than it looks at first, and there are lots of different areas smaller than a neighborhood, each with its own local character. Homes are a bit bigger and more ornate in the city center, say in a five-block radius from the cathedral of León and the city's main park, which is León's commercial center as well. You'll find quieter digs to the west and southwest of the park. As León center blends into Subtiava the architecture changes from more traditional courtyard-type houses to more modern fare. Properties toward the river at the south end of town are less attractive than you'd think because the river still carries away a fair bit of the city's solid waste.

León is encapsulated by a road that goes on to connect Managua to Chinandega, relieving the city from some of that traffic, but outside of the city you can find larger homes built on family farms, or at least big nonurban lots. This is actually one of León's fastest-developing neighborhoods, as the land within the city limits is at a premium and no one intends to build upward. León's housing market is still not very affected by the boom in the south, which means you'll find more reasonable prices here. Expect to pay US$30,000 for a three-bedroom home in the city and up to US$100,000 if the structure more closely resembles the kind of home you'd find in a place like Florida. Renting is even more reasonable: Within the city you can spend US$500 per month for a one-family home and up to US$800 if it's a colonial-style home.

The region's two premier beach towns, **Poneloya** and **Las Peñitas** are relaxing vacation destinations anyway, but they swell to capacity during Semana Santa in April, when toasty Leoneses come to dip their heels in the cool Pacific surf (Poneloya boasts some very good surfing waves, but the requisite undertow that accompanies them means you should swim here with caution). Both towns have well-developed communities that treasure their environment and their neighborhood camaraderie. Properties in these

EXPAT PROFILE: OLIN COHAN

After two years living in a remote beach village in northwestern Nicaragua, where he helped establish an environmental education curriculum in the communities around the national wetland reserve Estero Padre Ramos, northern California native and social worker Olin Cohan moved to León in 2003, where he started a nonprofit organization called UniversitÁrea Protegida (UAP). UAP (www.eii.org/uap) is a scholarship and training program for Nicaraguan university students with a focus on supporting ecological research, environmental education, and youth development in rural communities throughout the country. When we caught up to this enterprising 30-year-old, Olin was opening a small hostel in León (www.tortugaboluda.com) to help maintain his own expenses and be able to continue to work with the local university (UNAN León) on the development of UAP.

Why is León a great place to live?

There are many reasons why León is a great place to live. It is big enough to have a variety of things to do, and small enough to recognize people on the streets. It is also the academic center of Nicaragua, which gives the city a young, intellectual *onda* (vibe). In all my travels throughout Latin America, I have not found another city like León. People are proud of this city's revolutionary history, and continue to smile – through good times and bad.

What are the drawbacks to living there?

The heat is often unbearable. The firecrackers at all hours of the night on fiesta nights can get old, but it is also a reminder of where you are.

What is the expat community like there and how is it different from those in other parts of Nicaragua?

There are a handful of expats who have chosen León as their base, but not a ridiculous amount to make the city feel overtaken by foreigners. There is a good mix of travelers, those of us who have decided to stay, and locals. Even in the backpacker hostels, you still see a lot of Leoneses enjoying the scene. It seems like the expat community stays in touch, but most of

districts go for US$35,000–75,000 depending on how close to the beach the house is located and in what condition the structure is in.

It's easier to rent than to buy along the Pacific coast of León since the communities are geared toward tourism. You can expect to pay about US$400–800 per month for small homes in Poneloya or Las Peñitas if you establish your price in the down season (the rainy season). From January to April prices rise along the coast due to city slickers looking for beach time in the hot season and you can expect to pay up to US$200 or more, especially if the place has easy access to the sea.

© OLIN COHAN

us have our Nica friends and families as our principal hangout source.

Do you rent or did you buy?
I recently bought a house in León after renting for years. It came about by chance and I decided to make the investment instead of continuing to rent. I have moved around a lot, from renting rooms with families for as little as US$35 a month to sharing houses with friends and workmates for US$350 a month (divided among us all). Buying the house in León was relatively simple compared to other things I have done in Nicaragua. The process took about a month. I am fortunate to have a friend who is an experienced lawyer who did the paperwork for a good price. The previous owners were great and understanding and helped along the way to make the transition smooth.

Any surprises? Any advice along the lines of "I wish someone had told me . . . ?"
I could have used some warning about buying a vehicle. I bought a lemon when I first moved to León after two years on buses. I thought it would make life easier, but it has been nothing but problems. I wish someone would have told me to take more time buying a vehicle and to spend more for something reliable. Nicaraguan roads take a toll on vehicles, and an extra thousand bucks at the start will save you a lot of time and money down the line.

PRIME LIVING LOCATIONS

Outside of these two beach towns you'll have to be a bit more creative and intrepid, as this area has not yet experienced the intense pressure and institutionalization of a real estate market that the land surrounding San Juan del Sur has. You'll need to start with a reconnaissance trip along the coast, preferably with a Nica friend who can help you get oriented, and follow that up with a trip to the mayor's office of the region you're interested in to find out what is available and what it will take to purchase it. That leaves room for capriciousness on the part of the mayor's office, but steadfast determination and a keen sense of justice may see you through the negotiation (stick to your guns and press for what's fair).

GETTING AROUND

Two major roads connect León to Managua. Named Carretera a León Vieja and Carretera a León Nueva, the former is a pitted, all-but-totally deteriorated affair slated for major renovation in 2007, while the latter is an already-renovated asphalt speedway along which most traffic between these two cities is routed. As you cruise between points A and B, just for fun, count the bridges over which you pass, bearing in mind every single one of them was washed out during Hurricane Mitch (1998) and has subsequently been carefully replaced or rebuilt. Buses (not the *rutas,* which take forever) leave Managua's Mercado Israel Lewites several times per hour, arriving in León about 90 minutes afterward. But, provided you don't take your eyes from the road in the frenetic and unpredictable traffic along this stretch of highway, it's an easy drive. León is the hub for transportation throughout Nicaragua's northwest shoulder, and you can find transportation here to take you into the hinterlands of Chinandega all the way up to Volcán Cosigüina. Note that after El Viejo, the road deteriorates rapidly and a four-wheel drive vehicle will be much appreciated. The roads that lead west toward the beach aren't necessarily in great shape either, and you are expected to have the tools on board your vehicle to fix flat tires, etc., if the need should arise.

Within the city of León, though you could easily walk from neighborhood to neighborhood with little trouble, you will find both an aggressive community of taxi drivers and a growing fleet of *ciclo*-taxis manned by entrepreneurial young men. Buses to León's popular coastal resort towns Poneloya and Las Peñitas depart from León's western bus station in the neighborhood of Subtiava.

Estelí City and Region

Estelí is very much a cowboy town, and the epicenter of proud, peaceful communities of farmers and cattle ranchers. Volunteers and foreign development workers enjoy Estelí as a pleasant alternative to Managua: Its multiple supermarkets offer a variety of food and merchandise including foreign goodies and imported tastes, its main streets offer a wide selection of restaurants and shops, and you can run all your errands in one fell swoop and on foot! This latter might be Estelí's charm relative to Nicaragua's capital: that you can find a place to repair your watch, buy a custom-fit pair of shoes, and eat at a decent restaurant, all while avoiding the chaos and tension of Managua. Furthermore, Estelí is surrounded on all sides by interesting attractions that increasingly draw international travelers and backpackers. These range in variety from the sylvan beauty of the cloud forest at Miraflor, where you can even hope to see the elusive yet unrivaled quetzal (Nicaragua's rarest bird), to the refreshing swimming hole at Estanzuela and the Tisey Reserve, where you can splash under a mountain waterfall and hike a new network of trails. A bumpy ride down into the valley west of Estelí will take you to San Juan de Limay, where you can visit artisans who carve the delicate soapstone sculptures that line the shelves of Nicaragua's best crafts markets. This is also home to Nicaragua's Cuban-descended tobacco growers and cigar rollers, who produce and market some of the world's most acclaimed brands of *puros*.

© RANDALL WOOD

Cowboy culture runs strong in Estelí.

THE LAY OF THE LAND

Estelí proper is a neat, well-organized city of north–south and east–west streets that have even been named and numbered, a true rarity in Nicaragua (even though no one bothers to use the names, resorting to the traditional "from the gas station, two blocks west" system). It is pressed between the Estelí river to the west and the Panamerican Highway to the east, and now spills well over the highway onto the eastern side, where new neighborhoods are rapidly developing character of their own. The city sits at about 800 meters (2,600 feet) above sea level, so it's cool and pleasant year-round, relative to the tropical lowlands, and in January it can get downright chilly (a flannel shirt or light sweater would be just about right).

Estelí was built at one of the points where the Estelí river valley is the most sweeping; to the north, the land grows rougher and the river is pressed into narrow valleys. The hills climb to both sides of the river and the highway, which travel essentially in tandem, as the river flows northward and joins the Río Coco, whose ultimate destination is the Caribbean. Those mountains make for some beautiful landscapes, and the myriad valleys differ from each other in many ways. To the north of Estelí you'll find tobacco fields on both sides of the river valley, some of which were buried under loads of thick sand during Hurricane Mitch. The landscape lowers as you proceed northward through Condega to Palacagüina, then builds again as you approach Somoto and Ocotal, reaching its peak along the Honduran border. Nicaragua's highest point is near Ocotal at Pico Mogotón (2,106 meters/6,909 feet).

West of the city, the department of Estelí climbs to an abrupt peak and then drops in a cascade of smaller foothills to the dry valley of San Juan de Limay, whose inhabitants struggle to eke out a meager existence on subsistence crops, to the desolate plains north of León. These lowlands alternate between sunburned and swampy, draining slowly to the north at the Estero Real and to the south into Lake Managua.

East of Estelí the hills continue to climb up to the the cloud forest of Miraflor and the delightful mountain town of San Rafael del Norte, where Augusto C. Sandino and his troops first practiced what would later be called guerrilla warfare, way back in the 1930s. Long gone is Sandino, but not the zeal for the principles he stood for: autonomy, independence, and justice. San Rafael is somewhat of a gateway to the green coffee plantations that lie to the north in La Rica and San Sebastián de Yalí, where only the harvests of bananas rival the quantity of sacks of dried coffee beans flowing out to the markets for export.

WHERE TO LIVE

Within the city limits, Estelí has several different neighborhoods of similar characteristics. Expatriates stationed there prefer the neighborhoods just north and south of the central park. As you move away from the highway, property values drop, doubly so once the pavement ends and the street turns to dirt. The new neighborhoods being developed on the east side of the highway are certainly rougher in character but offer more possibilities for development (not to mention larger lots). To purchase a single-family home in this area you will pay about US$50,000 in the city, but you can rent a single-family home for an easy US$300–500 per month.

Outside of the city limits, Estelí is cowboy country, and where you wind up will depend largely on what you're looking to do with the land. Remember that between Estelí and points east rainfall is more constant and land is a bit more fertile, but the protected area of Miraflor is responsible for the tree cover that dominates that region's microclimate, and it's not for sale. North and east of Estelí the landscape is much drier and the hillsides more eroded; this land is far less suitable for development and offers fewer possibilities. The landscape moistens once you hit San Sebastian de Yalí, with its coffee and banana plantations, all the way to San Rafael del Norte, which can get downright soggy in the rainy season. But with rainfall comes rough roads. You could easily carve a little farm out of the gorgeous landscape around these two areas, but you'd be resigning yourself to a self-sufficient lifestyle. If that appeals to you, kick in the four-wheel drive and go exploring. Small family farms, when available, run US$90,000 and up depending on the fertility of the soil and the proximity to water, not to mention how much rainfall it receives. You will have a hard time renting anywhere out of the city limits, unless you're willing to pay for a room or two in someone's house. It is also difficult to find rental farms. Your best bet is to make connections with people in the city and see if somebody has a cousin or an uncle out in the countryside who would be willing to do business with you. In Estelí everyone has family out in the countryside, so the trick is finding someone interested in leasing their property.

GETTING AROUND

Estelí is easy to get to and from thanks to its keystone position on the Panamerican Highway. In fact, you can hardly avoid it. Once you're in town, taxis from point to point will cost you less than a dollar, which is a useful trick for getting to popular just-out-of-town getaways like La

Casita, the organic and whole foods restaurant on the town's southern border. Otherwise, you can easily walk the city's streets, which are laid out in a simple grid pattern and are even numbered, in stark contrast to Managua. For trips to areas outside of Estelí city, buses depart from two terminals located alongside the highway. Any cab driver will get you there, and walking to either bus terminal is a bit of a hassle anyway.

Matagalpa City and Region

Matagalpa city, lovingly nicknamed La Perla del Septentrión (The Pearl of the North), has long been the heart of Nicaragua's vibrant coffee industry and a hard-working little commercial center surrounded on all sides by rolling blue-green hills awash in the crisp mountain air of Nicaragua's highlands. Well over a century ago German immigrants bound for California and Alaska transited the Central American isthmus at Nicaragua only to find their economic prospects were just as good in the rich, fertile soils of Matagalpa as they would be in the Yukon, and many of them stayed on. Katherina Braun gets the credit for establishing Nicaragua's premier export industry, however. Returning from the market with a sack of coffee beans she decided to plant a few in the garden, and Nicaragua's foray into rich, bold export coffee had begun. Today, coffee grows on over 10,000 hectares (25,000 acres) of Nicaragua's mountainous uplands, contributes an average of US$140 million per year to the economy, and employs more than 200,000 people, nearly a third of the agriculture workforce (13 percent of the national workforce).

Like Estelí and Chontales, the department of Matagalpa bore the brunt of the civil war during the 1980s, and though the war is long past, the memories of that difficult decade still run fresh under the surface of society. No one is feeling particularly rancorous, but many families lost sons and hus-

© JOSHUA BERMAN

Matagalpa's streets are steep.

bands (and a few daughters as well), and everyone is glad to just leave the war behind them.

If Matagalpa has an Achilles' heel, it's water. Deforestation and contamination have made both drinking water and water for irrigation the region's most precious commodity. Piped water schemes that intend to pump water from as far away as Chagüitillo (at the base of the hill) up to the department capital will hopefully remedy this situation; in the meantime, the prospective long-term resident would do well to ask as many questions about the quality and reliability of the water supply as possible. The water shortage is an issue in the city, not in the countryside, where residents have their own wells and catchment basins. If your interest in the region is for a little plantation of your own, you will very likely find the water problem has been dealt with.

Matagalpa city has several attractions of its own, including a number of colonial-era churches and cathedrals, the most extraordinary of which is La Catedral de San Pedro de Matagalpa, a disproportionately large cathedral when it was built in 1874 and still the most prominent building in the valley: You can see it first as your vehicle crests the road into town long before you circle into the valley floor. In town, a pair of discos, a small modern movie theater, and regular cultural presentations make Matagalpa an interesting place to call home, even if the region's peace and tranquility—best enjoyed from the porch of your house—are its most salient characteristics.

THE LAY OF THE LAND

Matagalpa is an extensive region, with varied topography from the foothills and rice fields around Sébaco to the backcountry east of La Dália (where the road struggles eastward to Nicaragua's wildest interior and eventually emerges on the Atlantic coast), to the coffee highlands that blend northward into Jinotega. The city itself nestles into somewhat of a river valley, with bold, rounded hills on all sides. Matagalpans like to remind you that theirs is the most hilly department, and their city is no exception to that characterization: You'll build up lots of muscle traversing the ups and downs of Matagalpa city. Outside of the city, every little mountain valley is different; they run the gamut from nondescript to spectacular, such as the gorgeous cliffs at Peñas Blancas (1,445 meters/4,741 feet) or the waterfalls at Santa Emilia. The city of Matagalpa runs essentially from north to south, with the highway forming the city's western terminus. Shanty towns inhabited by Matagalpa's coffee labor pool ring the hillsides on all sides of Matagalpa.

PRIME LIVING LOCATIONS

WHERE TO LIVE

The city of Matagalpa offers nondescript but occasionally roomy concrete homes arranged along the city streets which rent for about US$300–500 per month and sell for about US$50,000 (they sell for more if they have a good source of water). With few exceptions, these homes have tiled or concrete floors and street parking. The areas around Matagalpa's two parks are the most lively and exciting: **Parque Darío** at the south end and **Parque Morazán** at the north. Homes get less exciting architecturally as you head toward the east of the city, but prices drop dramatically as well.

Matagalpa's charm lies outside of the city, where you can avoid its vexing water problems and get your hands on a piece of farmland. Avoid the Sébaco area, which is largely owned by Nicaragua's chemical-dumping rice monopolists and whose farm soils are poorly suited to crops outside of wet rice anyway (they're muck). Better land for farming, for a coffee plantation, or for a little piece of "peace and quiet" are found east of the city along both sides of the **highway to El Tuma** and beyond. Access to water and the size of the property are the two forces that drive prices outside of the city. A small family farm might go for US$100,000–300,000 depending on accessibility, availability of water, and fertility of the soil.

GETTING AROUND

The city of Matagalpa sprawls a bit more than other cities in its class, so hopping the occasional taxi here is a good way to get around. But you are perfectly able to get around on foot if you'd like to, particularly if you're confining your housing search to certain areas within the city, like the city blocks around the Catedral de San Pedro de Matagalpa in Parque Morazán. Otherwise, it's worth your while to explore this part of Nicaragua in your personal vehicle.

Jinotega City and Region

As you travel from Matagalpa eastward to Jinotega you may be concerned about finding yourself farther from basic services and cosmopolitan city life. Concentrate on the landscape instead, which grows more rugged, more verdant, and in our opinion, more inspiring. The Jinotega region is less developed and more wooded, receives more rainfall annually, and suffers few of the problems that intense cultivation and more densely populated settlements have caused western Nicaragua to face. In that regard, the department of Jinotega is truly the frontier, both socially and physically.

THE LAY OF THE LAND

As your vehicle lumbers east out of the city of Jinotega and threads its way through the rough mountain landscape of the Cordillera Isabella (the Isabel mountain range), you enter a landscape where the land is truly yours to work, but where your ability to sustain yourself economically and physically will alone determine your lifestyle. East of Jinotega the locals largely plant subsistence crops or cultivate shade-grown coffee and vegetables. In fact, the Pantasma Valley provides well over half the fresh vegetables—carrots, broccoli, potatoes, and more—consumed in Nicaragua daily. It's not hard to understand if you take a trip out east to explore: These hillsides are still well-watered, and the soils are deep and rich. Jinotega is Nicaragua's largest department, and as such it incorporates a wide variety of landforms, from the truly wild and little-visited Bosawás reserve (it's more wild than reserved) to a number of stunning waterfalls reachable only by truly epic backpacking trips, to some of Nicaragua's more isolated peaks, to mile after mile of hillside farm. Jinotega is also the most mountainous department, and only upon reaching the department boundary with the RAAN do the hills begin to subside into the lowland tropical pine savannas that stretch eastward to the Caribbean coast.

A cerulean gem cut from the wilds of eastern Jinotega, the Apanás Reservoir is a particularly gorgeous area. The artificial reservoir was created by damming up the waters of the Río Tuma in 1964 and forcing them to flood a broad river valley just north of the city of Jinotega. Today the Lago Apanás reservoir supplies the water to the twin turbines at Asturias, which produces 15 percent of the nation's hydropower. The hydroelectric power system is in serious disrepair, as much needed capital improvements have been delayed for decades and the lake slowly fills up with river sediments—the bane of any reservoir—but for the casual land owner the lake is valuable because it provides not just a source of drinking water and a source for irrigation but because the landscape around the lake is so beautiful. Never mind the wide skyline and the auburn sunsets, Lago Apanás is a breeding and feeding ground for dozens of species of migratory waterfowl.

WHERE TO LIVE

The city of Jinotega is compact and well laid out, and easier to understand than some other cities, like Matagalpa, whose hilly landscape has led to a more sprawling city plan. Jinotega is wedged in between the highway and the Río Jinotega, and the streets are oriented in an essentially north–south fashion according to the colonial design: a park, cathedral, and municipal offices at the city center, and residential and commercial areas radiate outward. A little stream, the Quebrada Ducuali, threads through the city but has been channelized and often shunted underground through large parts of the city. Urban Jinotegan properties are similar to those you would find in the other cities of Nicaragua's north: concrete block houses and walled-in grassy lawns or courtyards out back. The homes are either adjacent or nearly so, with small concrete or ceramic tile sidewalks out front and a driveway or garage alongside the home. Most neighborhoods are built along streets of *adoquines,* Nicaragua's ubiquitous concrete paving stones, but newer and poorer neighborhoods growing quickly on the east side of the highway have dirt streets and poor drainage.

The closer your property is to the town square the more valuable— and the older—it will be. The southern end of town is sprawling quickly through the valley. Here, while homes are newer, roads are unimproved and many of your neighbors will be of lower income status. Expect to pay US$50,000 for a small home in the city limits. Some of the newer housing developments at the south end of town are cheaply built and cost less, but they are to be avoided, even if you do love a good bargain. You can rent anywhere in Jinotega for about US$300–500 a month.

The advantages of living in the city are the better access to services, but with the exception of basic health care, telephone, and piped water, Jinotega offers little in the way of services. If you've come this far north of Managua, you are very likely looking for a quiet, bucolic existence. In this regard, Jinotega excels. Directly north of Jinotega in the **Valle de Tomatoya** you'll find a thriving artisan community and smallish homes set on small farms. The **Lago de Apanás** area of Jinotega is a decent 45-minute trek eastward from the city on the road to Pantasma. The road that traces the south side of the lake is better quality, as it is a main thoroughfare be-tween Jinotega and points east, while a similar but less-used road traces the northern perimeter of the lake.

GETTING AROUND

Jinotega is linked to Matagalpa and—believe it or not—to Estelí by public bus service. Buses bound for Matagalpa leave from a terminal alongside the high-way at the south side of town. Buses to Estelí via a very bumpy road through San Rafael del Norte leave from the north side of town by the market. From Jinotega you can also find transportation to the eastern hinterland, including such legendary and far-off locations as El Cuá and Bocay, two names that made it into the news frequently during the war years of the 1980s.

In town, you are really confined to either your own two feet or your personal vehicle. Having your own vehicle, preferably one with four-wheel drive traction, is the best way to explore the southern end of town where the pavement stops; elsewhere, Jinotega is perfectly navigable on foot. Once you settle into your new digs, however, you are likely to do what everyone else does; namely, buy a horse.

PRIME LIVING LOCATIONS

THE ATLANTIC COAST

People use the expression "the Atlantic coast" in different ways. In Managua, anything east of Jinotega is sometimes considered the Atlantic coast, meaning the entirety of the two enormous autonomous regions of RAAN and RAAS (Región Autónoma del Atlántico Norte and Atlántico Sur, respectively). We are referring specifically to the Atlantic littoral, including the port cities of Bluefields and Puerto Cabezas, the coastline immediately around Bluefields, and the two Caribbean islands of Big Corn and Little Corn. The Nicaraguan Atlantic coast comprises a lot more territory than that, of course, but these are really the only accessible areas for foreigners. And we'll say it right up front: For a variety of reasons, listing the Atlantic coast as a "prime" living location is a stretch. The low number of expats living there is testament to this. Still, if you are intrigued, pay a visit and see what you think. In a couple of years, it may be a whole new ballgame.

The Nicaraguan Caribbean is another world, by any leap of the imagination. For decades it was another nation in spirit. It was colonized by the

© RANDALL WOOD

British, not the Spanish; the locals grew up speaking English, and more than one African slave transported to the New World ended up on this "Miskito Coast" on a plantation of one sort or another. The English, true to form, left existing indigenous leaders in place but co-opted them and their kingdoms, and the Miskito people in particular became unofficial British troops, armed to the teeth with new muskets (from whence they get their name) and sometimes sent westward to kick the new Spanish settlements in the arse. The English were joined by German Moravian missionaries, whose distinct architectural touch is readily apparent to this day in the little white churches of Bluefields and Pearl Lagoon.

British colonialists vacated the Atlantic coast in 1860, when American businesses began to trickle in to harvest timber and bananas. The brief economic boom transformed Bluefields into a sort of gold-rush town whose economic strength has never again been matched. So it's clear why, when the Americans filtered back home and in 1894 Nicaraguan president José Zelaya marched an army from Managua to "integrate" the Atlantic coast, the locals viewed it as just one more in a long series of unappreciated occupations. While Nicaragua's Atlantic coast has been a grudging "part" of the rest of Nicaragua ever since, the "Spaniards" from Managua—the word is used to this day—never completely subjugated the region, which retains a vibrant and enthusiastic culture very much its own.

One reason the coast remains relatively uninfluenced by Spanish Nicaragua is the poor state of the infrastructure that unites the two regions. Bluefields is unequivocally the gateway to the Nicaraguan Caribbean, yet the trip from Managua to Bluefields means many hours on a road that before 2004 was a rutted bone-breaker, followed by an hour trip down the Río Escondido to the coast. Alternatively, the Atlantic coast is served by two airlines that run Cessna-type single- and twin-prop eight-seat planes back and forth from the capital. Puerto Cabeza (called simply "Port" by its English-speaking locals) is at the far end of a road that has definitely *not* been rehabilitated and that becomes functionally useless in the rainy season. And for the record, no road at all links one Caribbean city to the other: Both Bluefields and Puerto Cabezas are essentially outposts from Managua and practically islands unto themselves.

The Atlantic coast is without doubt a rustic, isolated corner of the world, and lately it's seen more than its share of trouble as a result of Colombian drug traffickers that stop in the numerous cays and islets on their way north to Miami. But it's a hard place to resist: a turquoise and sugar-sand marvel with a Latin character all its own. For those who are tired of the rat race

ATLANTIC COAST FLIGHT SCHEDULE

The following flight times have changed little over the last six years or so, but it is always worth checking and reserving your flight at least a few days in advance, more if during peak travel times like Christmas week, Semana Santa, or Palo de Mayo.

AIRLINES
Atlantic Airlines
Managua: tel. 222-5787 or 222-3037, fax 228-5614
Bluefields: tel. 572-1299 or 572-0259
Corn Island: tel. 575-5055 or 575-5151
reservaciones@atlanticairlines.com.ni
www.atlanticairlines.com.ni

La Costeña
Managua: tel. 263-1228 or 263-2142, fax 263-1281
Bluefields: tel. 572-2500
Corn Island: tel. 575-5131 or 575-5132
U.S./Canada: tel. 800/948-3770
LaCostena@centralamerica.com

FLIGHT TIMES
Managua-Bluefields
La Costeña: 6:30 A.M., 10 A.M. (except Sun.)
Atlantic: 6:45 A.M., 10:30 A.M., 2:10 P.M.

Bluefields-Managua
La Costeña: 7:40 A.M., 8:40 A.M., 11:20 A.M. (except Sun.), 4:10 P.M.
Atlantic: 9:10 A.M., 11:45 A.M., 4:35 P.M.

Managua-Corn Island
La Costeña: 6:30 A.M., 2 P.M.
Atlantic: 6:45 A.M., 10:30 A.M., 2:10 P.M.

Corn Island-Managua
La Costeña: 8:10 A.M., 3:40 P.M.
Atlantic: 8:35 A.M., 4 P.M.

Managua-Puerto Cabezas
La Costeña: 6:30 A.M., 10:30 A.M., 2:30 P.M.
Atlantic: 6:30 A.M., 10:30 A.M.

Bluefields-Puerto Cabezas
La Costeña: 12:10 P.M.

Puerto Cabezas-Bluefields
La Costeña: 11:10 A.M.

Nicaraguan puddle-jumpers fly daily between Managua and the Atlantic Coast.

being run in the "developed" world, the Atlantic coast is a breath of fresh air, slow and relaxed even by Nicaraguan standards. If the easygoing lifestyle doesn't sway your opinion, maybe a plateful of fresh lobster will. The Atlantic coast isn't for everyone by a long shot, but for intrepid souls willing to forgo a bit of luxury for a bit of adventure—and isolation—Nicaragua's Atlantic coast is unlike any other place in the country.

CLIMATE

Today's Atlantic coast forecast is "29–33°C (85–92°F) with high humidity and a chance of rain in the early afternoon." Tomorrow's too, and that's about how yesterday played out as well. The Caribbean sea moderates the rainy and dry seasons throughout the Caribbean, and while there is still somewhat of a dry season and somewhat of a rainy season, you're never too far away from an afternoon shower. That said, the driest months are December through February, but just barely. The humidity and the frequent rainfall will be apparent as soon as you step off the plane—the whole region is vaguely redolent of tropical vegetation and wet wood. And locals pay the rainfall no mind. Don't go far without your raincoat and don't travel with important papers and books that haven't been wrapped up in plastic. More than one unlucky soul has had to wring out a soggy passport after a tropical downpour, Bluefields style. And, um, for the record: Lots of expats who have lived or worked for the long term on Nicaragua's Atlantic coast have body fungus stories that will make your skin curl. Keep dry and keep clean, and a little talcum powder between the toes wouldn't hurt at all.

Bluefields and Pearl Lagoon

Bluefields itself is barely a tourist attraction, much less a place to call home, but as the economic heart of the Atlantic coast, it bears mentioning as a point of departure for more attractive destinations north and south along the coast: You cannot avoid Bluefields. Nearly 50,000 people call Bluefields their home, and with few exceptions these folks make their living off the sea catching, packing, and processing lobster, fish, shrimp, and oysters (not to mention the occasional endangered turtle). A number of Bluefileños have found work in the cruise ship industry, where their lower relative salary requirements and good command of English and Spanish make them valued crew members on the luxury liners that ply the waters of the Caribbean. Hardly a single family in Bluefields doesn't have somebody working somewhere on a ship.

THE LAY OF THE LAND

Like most of the Caribbean, Nicaragua's coastline is long and flat with only relatively minor changes in elevation. Don't go looking for any scenic overlooks around here! To the north, the nutrient-poor red sand feeds extensive but thin stands of Caribbean pine, which dominate the horizon

© JOSHUA BERMAN

floating into Bluefields

PRIME LIVING LOCATIONS

in all directions. South of Bluefields the extended rainy season makes the landscape more tropical and facilitates a wider diversity of flora that grows more variegated as you head south.

Bluefields Bay, Nicaragua's premier Atlantic coast port, has been polluted enough by the regular maritime traffic and sewage outflows of the city that it's better for looking at than for swimming in, but the bay is the lone exception to an otherwise unspoiled and crystalline turquoise sea and a coastline that alternates between sandy bays and mangroves for hundreds of kilometers. Much of the coastline is deserted. That makes for shady business in the most remote and unpoliced areas like Sandy Bay and Karawala, where itinerant drug traffickers exert an increasingly important influence over daily life (paradoxically, foreign investment is more important than ever in places like this because it provides an economic alternative, provided it is done correctly).

To the north of Bluefields at the end of a lovely 45-minute *panga* ride from the municipal dock lies quiet and clean Pearl Lagoon, a traditional Caribbean village whose well-laid-out streets and relative order are in pleasant contrast to cacophonous, chaotic Bluefields.

WHERE TO LIVE

In Pearl Lagoon, the locals live off the sea, as does the entire Atlantic coast, and several European aid organizations have been directly involved in helping the local fishing families connect to the world's seafood markets. Pearl Lagoon (Laguna de Perlas) makes a good jumping-off point for travelers interested in getting to know the region's Miskito communities, but expats interesting in making their home on the terra firma of the Atlantic coast ought to start their search here rather than in Bluefields, even though you will still find yourself returning to Bluefields to do your errands and shopping.

Pearl Lagoon is not immune to the socio-economic struggle going on between would-be drug traffickers and others who want to develop legitimate businesses or just keep fishing, but Pearl Lagoon's strong community and pleasant geography afford it better probability of becoming a charismatic tourist community than many points along the Atlantic shore. Nearby Greenfields Nature Reserve on the outskirts of Kukra Hill is a clever example of just that sort of endeavor: Owned and run by a Swiss couple who have lived in Nicaragua for more than 25 years, Greenfields is a privately managed eco-lodge boasting over 25 kilometers (15 miles) of trails, canoe routes, and more; they arrange group tours and excursions and host their guests in simple but comfortable guesthouses with all meals included.

If you decide Bluefields is where you would like to live, expect to pay US$60,000 for a single-family home in the better part of town. Take a close look at proximity to community garbage pits and streams that flood during stormy periods. Pearl Lagoon is healthier and cleaner but a little farther away, and provided you can identify somebody looking to sell out, you might be able to find a single-family home in the US$70,000 range, but this is wildly speculative. You are better off renting in either area, and can do so for US$400–600 per month.

GETTING AROUND

Bluefields is the maritime transportation hub for most of the southern half of Nicaragua's Atlantic coast: Passenger-boat traffic to Pearl Lagoon and elsewhere departs from the main municipal dock behind Bluefields' market. You pay a small entrance fee at the first window to be admitted to the wharf, then catch a boat to wherever you're going. While you could technically even get to Corn Island from this wharf, the semi-weekly diesel-belcher, *Captain-D*, makes for a slow and sun-drenched ride out to the island, so you're better off taking a flight from the Bluefields airport.

Once your *panga* deposits you on the docks of Pearl Lagoon, Kukra Hill, or elsewhere, your public transportation options are exactly nil. The Atlantic coast communities are linked by the sea, not by a road network, meaning not only will you find no transport out of town, you won't need it: Each community is somewhat of an outpost.

Corn Island

Eighty-three kilometers (52 miles) eastward into the Caribbean lies a little island named after the one thing you won't find growing there, surrounded on all sides by turquoise sea and reef, and awash in the fresh breeze of the Caribbean. Corn Island is less Nicaraguan than even the Caribbean coast, bound to Spanish-speaking Nicaragua only by history and chance, not by language or culture. Caribbean in theory but wholly Latin American in nature, to the 9,000 people who call Corn Island home, this is a place unique in the world.

Pirates on their way up the Río San Juan to sack Granada were the first Europeans to lay eyes on Corn Island and its little brother to the

EXPAT PROFILE: PHOEBE HAUPT

After eight years leading educational and community service trips on Nicaragua's Atlantic coast, Phoebe Haupt is now a full-time Latin American-based trip consultant who – along with her Nicaraguan counterpart Wendy Hamilton – works with North American and Nicaraguan universities and NGOs to design and carry out numerous trips each year. When we spoke with her, Phoebe had just brought 20 undergraduate students from the University of Virginia to spend two weeks with 20 students at the Bluefields Indian and Caribbean University Business School in a program entitled "The Impact of Globalization on People in Emerging Economies." Of her work, she says, "I am interested in trips that focus on learning, on exposing people from the United States to a different reality." Phoebe's reality in Bluefields is a relatively simple one: She lives with a local family, eats the meals they cook, walks everywhere she needs to go, and gets by on about US$300 per month. Her website is www.culturalcrossing.blogspot.com.

Why is the Atlantic coast a great place to live?
It's not a great place to live, but once you get the Atlantic coast in your veins, you're doomed. I fell in love with the hopes and dreams of Atlantic coast people. The music is beautiful, the dancing is out of this world, laughter is in the air. The Atlantic coast is home to incredible cultural, ethnic, and linguistic diversity. Despite, or perhaps because of this diversity, it is quite remarkable that Costeños maintain such a solid cultural identity, quite separate from a Nicaraguan identity. Costeños have a different history, different experiences, different stories, and a different reality than those who live in the Pacific and central regions of the country. Costeños love the coast, love their land, love their people, their food, their music; their hospitality is incredible.

What are the drawbacks to living there?
I think the hardest aspect of living in Bluefields is the large-scale unemployment and the demoralizing effect that this has on everyday people. It is sad to me to see a once largely self-sufficient people become so urbanized and dependent on cash and imports. With such high rates of

east, but the cannibalistic Kukra Indians (now long-assimilated by the Miskitos) called it home first. Today, Corn Island does a decent trade in seafood and particularly in shellfish, and is a rapidly developing tourist hot spot that draws enthusiastic visitors from all over Europe and North America. The Crab Soup Festival is without a doubt one of the draws, a gluttonous celebration of the islanders' August 27, 1841, emancipation from English slavery. Join islanders every August 27 and 28 for huge pots of delicious crab soups, stews, and chowders and all the merriment that accompanies the meal, like the crowning of Miss

unemployment, the amount of alcohol consumed is staggering and has only negative impacts as far as I can see. Also, the wet season is a huge challenge because it pours down rain a huge part of the day from May through October. The other challenge is that although I love the fact that the place is not overrun with tourists, at times that can feel isolating. Also, everything is more expensive on the coast because of the cost of transporting goods across the country, and vegetables are usually not in the best shape.

Phoebe Haupt (left) and Martha, one of her students, in Bluefields

What is the expat community like there and how is it different from those in other parts of Nicaragua?
The main difference is that there really isn't an expat "community" in Bluefields. I know there's a woman from Germany, a snake charmer from somewhere, and there are the women who volunteer with the Franciscan order of the Catholic church – but aside from a few researchers who come and go . . . not much else.

Any advice you'd give to someone thinking about living there?
You know, it's really hard to give generic advice about Bluefields for foreigners because if you like Bluefields, you love it. If you don't love it, you hate it. It's not like, say, Granada, that *most* people would like, it's a very personal, subjective thing. I think that just like most places, if you get to know people, you will come to love it.

Corn Island, Miss Coconut, and Miss Photogenic. But a bigger draw than the island culture and the great island cooking—coconut bread, fine lobster, and delicious crab meat—is the island itself: sun, sand, and gorgeous Caribbean sea.

Three distinct layers of reef, composed of more than 40 species of coral, protect the north side of the island. It's not world-class diving territory due to deterioration of the reef structure and sedimentation caused by island runoff, but there are a few decent shallow dives and, for the intrepid snorkeler, lots to see.

THE LAY OF THE LAND

Corn Island is about 1.6 kilometers (one mile) wide and eight kilometers (five miles) long and shaped like a pork chop. Most of the residents live along the perimeter of the island but are concentrated on the northern half, while the southern half, culminating in the evocatively named Barracuda Point, is less inhabited.

Three low-slung hills form the interior of the island. Mt. Pleasant Hill and Little Hill, forming the bulk of the north half of Corn Island, reach 90 meters (299 feet) and 54 meters (177 feet) in height, respectively, and are mostly wooded with dense vegetation and scrub wood. The southern half of the island is dominated by Queen Hill, which reaches 50 meters (164 feet) in height and boasts nothing fancier than a pair of foot trails up and over the peak.

The island's commercial area, barely a "town," nestles along the west coast in the protection of Brig Bay. You could spend days on end just watching the fishing boats cruise in and out of the harbor. Here's where the town dock is located, along with a handful of small hotels and guesthouses, and some restaurants. Just east of town—meaning one block away—is the municipal airstrip, receiving a half dozen single-prop planes in the course of the day, and just beyond that the island's popular baseball field is tucked at the base of Mt. Pleasant Hill.

The Corn Island coastline is rocky in some parts (or faces nearly adjacent reefs that don't facilitate easy access to deep water) and lush with broad, sandy beaches in others. The most attractive beaches are everything you've ever dreamed of in a holiday: soft, white sand, coconut palms, and a turquoise sea at your feet. These stretches of pleasure include the long and impressive beach that faces Southwest Bay, whose sole dirt track is lined with coconut palms on one side and mangroves on the other. Walk through the palm border onto an isolated beach whose primary caretaker is the much-loved Picnic Center hotel and club.

On the east side of the island is the less-visited but equally gorgeous Long Beach, characterized by long afternoons of gentle surf pulling in from the Atlantic. The sun can be surprisingly bright on either of these two beaches due to the bright reflective nature of the sand.

Corn Island's north shore is frequently rocky or difficult to walk on due to fragments of reef and scattered big stones. This shore is also more exposed to the ocean weather patterns, leading to rougher waves in the afternoon or when storms approach from the Atlantic. Still, a large part of Corn Island's inhabitants call it home, and a string of settlements, churches, and family homes press against the shoreline's single road, all the way from the estuary at the island's northwest knuckle eastward to the residential neighborhood of Sally Peaches. As the road turns to the south and circles slowly back along what's called the South End inland past the baseball stadium and to Brig Bay, it runs parallel to the island's eastern coast but stays a couple of hundred meters away from the water, leading to properties that face the ocean but are not placed directly against the road and enjoy more privacy than the roadside homes along the island's sociable north side.

WHERE TO LIVE

Your options on Corn Island are essentially two: You can live somewhere in town in the more developed area of Brig Bay, or you can live elsewhere on the perimeter of the island, trying to capture a piece of gorgeous Caribbean-side living. It's not all up for grabs, though. The mangrove swamps and estuaries that line several stretches of coastline are crucial to the island's water supply, and the more ecologically minded of the island's residents protect them with a passion. Also off-limits, with the exception of the narrow road that crosses from the airstrip past the ball field to the eastern side of the island, is anything inland for the same reason: Corn Island's aquifer won't hold out if the island is carelessly developed. Many islanders have taken this concept to heart, but certainly not all.

For that reason, an important part of your strategy for buying and developing land on Corn Island is to think about an ecologically friendly and sustainable strategy for living in this delicate ecosystem in a low-impact way. Catchment basements for rainwater, on-site primary treatment of sewage waste, solar or wind energy generation, and so on: A clever strategy for developing a piece of property without contributing to the aquifer's increasingly beleaguered ability to provide drinking water will go a long way to convince the locals you mean well, and convince the government bureaucracy that your case for investment is a good one. If you are an entrepreneur sort and can provide job opportunities for the locals, that wouldn't hurt your case either.

In town you'll deal with a bit more noise and traffic, particularly around the harbor, but there are more options and more properties, and much more to do.

Along the north side of the island you'll have more privacy and less traffic, as the bulk of the excitement is concentrated around Brig Bay. The north is clearly breezier and a bit more exposed to the elements, and you may find yourself on a piece of property whose beach is rocky, not sandy. More than one local has extended a long dock out over the reef in order to have a place to moor a boat. The community of Sally Peaches in the northeast corner of the island is truly that—a community. Homes tend to be nicely kept and well-decorated, and everybody knows everyone else (you could argue that's true of the whole island).

The southern half of the island is the most difficult to envision developing, as many of the estuaries and mangrove swamps are concentrated here and they are so fundamental to the island's ecological health. A possible exception to that rule might be the southern terminus of the island, Barracuda Point. But you'll have to do some smooth talking.

Regardless of where you purchase, expect prices on Corn Island to run above US$300,000, and possibly well above that. Nicaragua's Atlantic coast residents are wealthier than their compatriots back in Managua and Estelí, and they are well aware of the value of the land they're living on. They're also less interested in packing their bags and relocating to Miami, meaning they will drive a harder bargain. They might be interested in some kind of a joint venture, if what you have in mind is entrepreneurial. But that means sticking around long enough to become somewhat of a local, find your business partner, and proceed from there. It's not impossible, but it requires creativity, sensitivity to local concerns, and a lot of patience. Fortunately, while you are patiently developing your relationships and moving your plans forward, the scenery, the food, and the company are all top-notch. Consider the time you spend chilling out in a rental part of the experience, and budget about US$600 per month for rent while you're there. You can get a better deal by striking a monthly rate with one of the local hotels.

GETTING AROUND

From the airport it's a five-minute walk westward to the waterfront, town park, and municipal docks of Brig Bay (where you can find a *panga* to Little Corn Island). From there, a two-lane road built of concrete paving stones runs around the better part of the island. The southern half of the island is served by two dirt tracks that penetrate the mangroves and palm forest along the east and west littorals. The impatient can hail a taxi in Brig Bay—several taxis operate on the island, and their drivers tend to be Spanish speakers from the mainland—it costs about US$0.75 to get anywhere on the island, though prices double at night. Corn Island is also big enough to warrant bus service, however, though it is rather sporadic. Minibuses circulate around the island's circumference about twice an hour and cost US$0.35. It's a frustrating ride because the buses stop everywhere someone is—or might be—waiting, but keep your cool, you're on island time.

There is nowhere you could possibly rent a vehicle except by striking a deal with its particular owner, but hotels are increasingly learning to make bicycles available for guests. Ask if yours has one they can rent you by the day. Lastly, Corn Island is a safe enough place that you can hitchhike just about anywhere, though courtesy dictates you pay a couple of córdobas as a polite thank you, now that fuel prices are so expensive. While you could conceivably walk your way around the island, judge your distances carefully: Corn Island is small, but not *that* small, and the hike from Brig Bay up around the north side and down to Sally Peaches will take you close to two hours on foot.

Little Corn Island

Small enough to meet the island's several hundred inhabitants in your first week, large enough to lose yourself on the sand, near enough to Corn Island to pop back to run a couple of errands, far enough that you wouldn't want to do it every day—Little Corn Island is an outpost at the ocean's edge. To the east lie only Colombia's San Andrés (formerly Nicaraguan territory, as any Nica will be quick to point out) and the warm, wide Caribbean. Little Corn Island in the 21st century still remains free of roads, vehicular traffic, and most infrastructure. For that matter, shy of a dozen small guesthouses and a restaurant or two, a dive shop, and a fire tower in the center of the island, Little Corn doesn't have much of anything at all. But that's precisely its attraction, of course. With no roads there are no cars, with no real "town" to speak of there's little noise or distraction.

Still, it would be unfair to paint Little Corn as an island paradise. With simplicity comes lack of services, with isolation comes not just tranquility but sometimes boredom, and with "small town" comes insularity and gossip. Still, if you're anxious to put behind you the complexity and complications of the working world and spend your days in a truly simple, Caribbean atmosphere, Little Corn Island has a lot to offer. Between you and tomorrow morning is a lazy afternoon spent writing your memoir, reading the next book off your stash, or walking the sandy shore, followed perhaps by a long nap and a dip in the sea or a lap around the reef to look for colored fish.

© RANDALL WOOD

Little Corn Island is tiny indeed.

THE LAY OF THE LAND

Little Corn Island looks like a pork chop, too; it's only about three kilometers (two miles) long and one kilometer (three-quarters of a mile) wide. At its widest point you could walk from one coast to the other in under 20 minutes, but in the narrow southern part of the "chop" you could go from coast to coast in under 5. Its population is a couple of hundred people including the burgeoning community of laborers who have come over from the mainland to work in the thriving tourism industry.

To get there you take a bumpy ride across the sea in one of several fiberglass open boats that operate between Corn Island and Little Corn Island. It will deposit you on the soft sands of what locals call the "front side," which is to say, the western side of the island that faces toward the mainland and Corn Island. The front side isn't a town per se but rather a strip of a dozen small wooden and concrete restaurants, bars, and guesthouses, and it's the social and economic center of the island. The sidewalk that runs in front of the whole area heads north and peters out after about 100 meters; to the south it peters out before 20. When you find yourself standing in front of the Happy Hut and Dive Little Corn, the island's premier dive shop, you are standing right in the middle of the island's busiest intersection. Follow the sandy trail eastward past a couple of residences toward the eastern shore and you will find yourself at Casa Iguana, perched on the cliffs that overlook the wide Atlantic. The Casa Iguana anchors the entire southern shore of the island from the bluffs of Patch Point, and to its south the island remains—for the moment—uninhabited.

North of the hustle and bustle of the front side the excitement tapers off pretty quickly. At the north end of "town," take a right at Miss Bridget's place and follow the impossibly small foot trail across the narrow end of the island and northward through the palms and foliage that make up the northeastern coastline until you emerge from the woods at Derek's, a popular and outdoorsy backpacker's place. Following the coastline to the west you'll pass a couple more small lodgings, the Farm Peace and Love, and then the coastline turns wild again.

Most of the interior of the island remains uninhabited, from the wooded crown of the small hill that holds Little Corn's lighthouse against the horizon to the rough coastline that nestles against Cotton Tree Bay and Water Hole Beach. This area is increasingly home to the island's temporary labor community, and they don't live well. From the lighthouse and fire tower, a foot trail fords some of the small fields (in which locals grow a handful of simple crops) straight up to the fishing families' homes on the north coast, which number no more than a dozen.

WHERE TO LIVE

You are truly on the frontier here, so creativity, patience, and a keen ability to bargain will come in handy. The island's inhabitants have lived there for several generations and feel proud of their little island. Whether they'll be resentful that you'd like to purchase their homestead or grateful to you for providing them the cash with which to relocate to be with their families overseas depends in no small degree on their personal economic situation, their perception of you and your intentions, and the degree to which they feel connected to the island. You might try offering to rent someone's home for a couple of months to see if that gets you anywhere, or make it clear you are going to care for your island community as would a native Corn Islander and that you are in no way simply a scalper looking to buy cheap and resell the property at a profit. Remember, not everyone sees this island as real estate; they see it as their home, and while they might be persuaded to sell to someone who will appreciate the land and participate in the community, they do not want to feel they are being manipulated, pressured into selling, or tricked into letting go a piece of their "ancestry" to some wild-eyed foreigner just out to make a profit.

Its name says it all: This is not a big island, and everyone knows who owns what and what's for sale, so start by asking around. Word will spread quickly if you're looking to buy, and if there's anything on the market you'll know about it soon enough. In the meantime, get to know the island's geographic regions while simultaneously assessing your ability to build, maintain, or renovate a property so far away from the nearest department store or hardware depot, not to mention your ability to live a satisfying life so far away from civilization.

Bad weather comes from the east, but so does the fresh breeze. So any property on the east side is bound to enjoy, in addition to marvelous sunrises, fresh clean air and the brunt of any passing hurricane. That's not to say you can avoid hurricanes by hiding on the west side, but make no mistake about what being located on the upwind side of a hurricane will mean to you. On the other hand, the western side (the front side) is in the lee, meaning a glassier water surface and fewer waves, a bit less wind even in the afternoon, more flying insects, and the buzz of the island's business community at your side.

The island's north and northwest remain essentially undeveloped and little trafficked, and any land for sale here will require just about everything, including hacking out your own road. For that matter, much of the interior of the island remains undeveloped as well, though none of it is without an owner. By living inland you gain the storm protection offered by the island's thick tree cover, the legal risk of having to go to battle for wanting to live on top of the island's precious and meager aquifer, and a small hike to water's edge. It's all relative.

Lastly, let it be said: Until early 2006 this small island had neither fire department nor police department. The former means you are expected to be self-sufficient in every way while you make this island your home, including providing against disasters natural and otherwise. The latter means until very recently a certain sense of lawlessness pervaded the island. The new police presence is expected to greatly reduce crime in the area. We're not talking Wild West gunslinging, but petty crime against casual travelers is certainly on the rise, and there's no doubt that these islands—as well as the entire Caribbean coast of Central America—take unwilling part in the Colombia–United States illicit drug trade superhighway. Locals report night beachings of "go-fast" boats bound north with their cargo under wraps, and more than one local who has decided to participate has wound up in trouble or behind bars, including one popular boat owner who gave up the Corn Island–Little Corn Island passenger transport business to supply gasoline to drug runners and is now doing hard time in Bluefields's prison.

Prices depend on how well you can bargain and how close the property is to the sea. Expect to pay several hundred thousand dollars for most plots on Little Corn Island, just because there is so little land available to purchase in the first place. At least one popular hotel destination was selling at one point for US$900,000, which represents the higher end of the property market. Rumor has it that the powerful Pellas family owns a bit of land on the island's northeast shore and hopes to develop it into a resort, but this far out to sea things change with the winds. The rental market is thin indeed, but if you are lucky you might find a fishing family that would prefer to visit their cousins in Miami for a summer. If fortune smiles on you, expect to pay US$800–1,000 per month to rent on Little Corn Island, but on this little green island the issue isn't prices, it's availability. There's simply not much to rent. You can just as easily strike a deal with a hotel for a monthly rate.

GETTING AROUND

You are currently standing on the only source of transportation on the island. Little Corn Island has neither roads nor vehicles, no bus service, no air strip, and no helicopter pad. It is not wheelchair-friendly and makes no effort to accommodate you in any form. Everyone gets around by walking. Though this is not "live on a deserted tropical island" empty, as a small community does call Little Corn Island home, with the exception of a couple hundred neighbors, you are wholly, completely on your own out here, guaranteed only that the sun will rise every morning in the east. If you are poking around here at all, it's because that's the lifestyle you like. Cut yourself a good walking stick and throw a pair of *chinelas* (rubber flip-flops) and a bottle of water in your bag, and put one foot in front of the other.

Puerto Cabezas

The "other Atlantic coast" is equally isolated from both Managua and Bluefields, but it is a relatively self-contained and fascinating port city with some thriving industries and a culture all its own. Notably absent is the Bluefields Creole English, and in its place is Miskito, the indigenous language of the people who populate both sides of the Río Coco and call Puerto Cabezas their capital city. Puerto Cabezas is somewhat of a paradox. If it were connected to the rest of the country by a decent, paved road, it could quickly regain its position as a thriving port town, and more than one investor has eyed Puerto Cabezas with big plans, including one Louisiana company interested in renovating the municipal dock and making Puerto into a state-of-the-art port complex replete with silos, grain storage facilities, a power plant, container storage, industrial cargo cranes, and facilities for deep-water tankers. Until that plan comes together, Puerto is stuck with its antique wooden municipal dock and a whole lot of lobsters.

THE LAY OF THE LAND

Puerto Cabezas measures about five kilometers (three miles) from north to south and less than two kilometers (one mile) from east to west. The two streets that run parallel to the Caribbean form the economic heart and

© JOSHUA BERMAN

the beach at Puerto Cabezas

PRIME LIVING LOCATIONS

the old Catholic church in Puerto Cabezas

© RANDALL WOOD

PRIME LIVING LOCATIONS

soul of the city, and along this strip you'll find the health clinic, post office, and many of the city's better eateries and hotels. Puerto Cabezas has both a Moravian and a Catholic church, a supermarket, an open market, a pleasant town square, and a baseball stadium, none of which are any higher than about 10 feet above sea level: Puerto Cabezas is flat as a pancake.

From the central park the road westward leads out of Puerto Cabezas and into the hinterland, including points north along the Río Coco, and to the road west that leads painfully and eventually to Managua (that one is a true spine-crusher). South from the park you'll find the old wooden pier. At the northern extreme of Puerto Cabezas is the well-loved Kabu Payaska restaurant, which enjoys a stunning view of the coastline and a flotilla of wheeling gulls and pelicans pulling loops above the waves. You'll know when you hit the edge of town, though, as the city ends quickly and there is no such thing as a suburb. From the pier you can catch a *panga* to the myriad Miskito communities southward along the coast.

WHERE TO LIVE

In Puerto Cabezas, the homes are a bit nicer than you'd find in Bluefields or elsewhere on the Atlantic coast, and the streets are breezy and tree-lined. You could easily live in town somewhere and enjoy a quick walk to the water's edge, but for waterfront property you will quickly find yourself exiled to the outskirts of town. North of town enjoys a prettier beach than south of town, so start your search in that direction. But drop in on the mayor's office first. The mayor will have an idea of which properties are vacant and help you through the process of identifying and purchasing available property. This is one office where you ought to make friends fast (start with dinner and drinks on your tab) because you'll be dealing with the mayor's office through the entire buying process.

While just west of town land is more readily available, there's little point in investigating it unless you are planning on opening up a lobster-processing plant. The land there is broad and largely unfettered, but wholly uninspiring.

In town, single-family homes sell for about US$60,000 and up depending on proximity to the water, and outside of town, provided the property is at the water's edge, lots can cost anywhere from US$100,000–300,000 or higher, if the lot is large. There are lots of "ifs" though, and this far out into the wild you owe it to yourself to find a trusty Nicaraguan companion to help you with the due diligence necessary before plunking down money on land.

GETTING AROUND

The airport is at the north end of town, where you will find a decent number of the city's hundreds of taxis. At last count, 500 licensed and unlicensed taxis circulated the streets of Puerto Cabezas; they charge a set fare of US$0.50 anywhere in town with surcharges for extra cargo and luggage. Puerto is an elongated city but remains walkable nonetheless, and there is nowhere you can't feasibly reach on your own two feet if you've got a water bottle and the time.

RESOURCES

© JOSHUA BERMAN

Consulates and Embassies

Nicaragua does not maintain a consulate in Canada. For additional consulates in Europe and Latin America, please visit the Nicaraguan Institute of Tourism (INTUR) website: www.intur.gob.ni.

UNITED STATES
HOUSTON, TEXAS
8989 Westheimer R.D., Suite 103
Houston, TX 77063
tel. 713/789-2762 or 276/789-2781

LOS ANGELES, CALIFORNIA
3550 Wilshire Boulevard, Suite 200
Los Angeles, CA 90010
tel. 213/252-1171 or 213/252-1174
fax 213/252-1177

MIAMI, FLORIDA
8532 SW 8th Street, Suite 270
Miami, FL 33144
tel. 305/265-1415
fax 305/265-1780

NEW YORK, NEW YORK
820 2nd Avenue, 8th floor, Suite 802
New York, NY 10017
tel. 212/986-6562
fax 212/983-2646

SAN FRANCISCO, CALIFORNIA
870 Market Street, Suite 1050
San Francisco, CA 94102
tel. 415/765-6821, 415/765-6823, or 415/765-6825
fax 415/765-6826

WASHINGTON, D.C.
1627 New Hampshire Avenue NW
Washington, DC 20009
tel. 202/939-6531 or 202/939-6532
fax 202/939-6574
http://consuladodenicaragua.com

NICARAGUA
CANADA
Calle Nogal 25
Bolonia, Managua
tel. 268-0433 or 268-3323

GREAT BRITAIN
British Honorary Consul
Plaza Churchill
Reparto los Robles, Managua
tel. 254-5454 or 254-3839
fax 254-5295
taboada@taboadalaw.com

There is no British embassy in Nicaragua. The nearest embassy is in Costa Rica:

Edificio Centro Colón
Apartado 815-1007
San José, Costa Rica
tel. 506/258-2025 or 506/225 4049
(off-hours pager service)
fax 506/233-9938
britemb@racsa.co.cr
www.britishembassycr.com

UNITED STATES
Carretera Sur Km 4
Barrio Batahola Sur, Managua
tel. 266-6010, after hours tel. 276-0267
http://managua.usembassy.gov

Introduction to Nicaragua

GENERAL NICARAGUA WEB PORTALS

AMIGOS DE NICARAGUA
www.amigosdenicaragua.org
Amigos de Nicaragua is the official site for Returned Peace Corps Volunteers of Nicaragua.

BUBL LINK CATALOGUE OF INTERNET RESOURCES
http://bubl.ac.uk/link/n/nicaragua.htm
This academic portal covers Nicaragua facts, politics, history, etc.

DIRECTORY OF ONLINE EXPAT COMMUNITIES AND FORUMS
www.expatcommunities.com/nicaragua expatriates.html
This site has collected useful links.

GLOBAL JOURNAL OF PRACTICAL ECOTOURISM
www.planeta.com/nicaragua.html
Planeta's site includes a user forum and many resources.

LATIN AMERICAN NETWORK INFORMATION CENTER (LANIC)
www1.lanic.utexas.edu/la/ca/nicaragua
The LANIC website is very thorough and practical.

THE NICARAGUA PAGE
www.thenicaraguapage.com
Check here for a thorough and eclectic Nicaragua web resource.

TRAVEL CONCERNS

GLOBAL GAYZ
www.globalgayz.com/g nicaragua.html
This site has detailed resources on the gay community in Nicaragua.

HER OWN WAY: ADVICE FOR THE WOMAN TRAVELER
www.voyage.gc.ca/main/pubs/her_own_way-en.asp
Women should look at this excellent online safety resource.

INTUR
www.intur.gob.ni
The Nicaraguan government tourism agency's page maintains a list of active and licensed tour operators in Nicaragua.

PHOTOGRAPHY AND ESSAYS

RICHARD LEONARDI
www.nicaraguaphoto.com
Based in Managua, U.S.-born and -trained documentary photographer Leonardi is also the author of *Footprint Nicaragua;* this site features essays on Nicaragua's culture, history, and politics.

TOMÁS STARGARDTER
www.agstar.com.ni
Stargardter is a Nicaragua-based photojournalist whose website features a wide range of Nicaraguan images, from the natural to the extreme to the political.

AUTHOR WEBSITES

JOSHUA BERMAN
www.stonegrooves.net
Joshua's site celebrates Nicaragua, the world, and "Tranquilo Traveling."

MOON LIVING ABROAD NICARAGUA
www.gotonicaragua.com
For more information about this book, visit the authors' personal website for *Moon Living Abroad in Nicaragua.* It features additional content, updates, a lively forum, and the personal attention of authors.

RANDALL WOOD
www.therandymon.com
Randall's site features topical articles on Nicaragua, Africa, and more.

Making the Move

EXPAT STUFF
www.expatstuff.com
Check here for goods, services, information, and tools for expatriates and travelers.

VISA SERVICES
BRICEÑO ASSOCIATES TRANSLATION
www.briceno-associates.com
This Nicaraguan English/Spanish translation/interpretation company has experience in Nicaraguan legal documents.

BRINGING YOUR PETS
PET CHAUFFEUR
www.petride.com

PET AIR
www.flypets.com

INTERNATIONAL SHIPPERS
BERNUTH LINES
South River Drive
Miami, FL 33169
U.S. tel. 305/637-8901 or
Managua tel. 871-7465

PAXTON INTERNATIONAL MOVER
www.paxton.com/international
Paxton ships everything from household goods to vehicles and has locations across the United States.

Language and Education

SPANISH LANGUAGE SCHOOLS

Granada
CASA XALTEVA
Calle Real Xalteva 103
tel./fax 552-2436 or
U.S. tel. 505/254-7535 (in New Mexico)
communit@nmia.com
www.casaxalteva.com

COCIBOLCA SPANISH SCHOOL
Calle El Caimito
tel. 889-9375 or 865-1340
esc_cocibolca@yahoo.com
www.pages.prodigy.net/nss pmc

ONE-ON-ONE SPANISH TUTORING ACADEMY
Calle La Calzada
tel. 552-6771
oneonone@cablenet.com.ni
www.1on1tutoring.net

Laguna de Apoyo
PROYECTO ECOLÓGICO
Laguna de Apoyo Shoreline Road, Masaya
eco-nic@guegue.com.ni
www.gaianicaragua.org

San Juan del Sur
DOÑA ROSA SILVA'S SPANISH SCHOOL
50 meters west from the Mercado Municipal
tel. 621-8905
spanish_silva@yahoo.com
www.spanishsilva.com

LATIN AMERICAN SPANISH SCHOOL
half a block west of the central park
tel. 820-2252
info@latinamericanspanishschool.com
www.latinamericanspanishschool.com

SAN JUAN DEL SUR SPANISH SCHOOL
right on the beach, across from the BDF bank and Restaurante Lago Azul
tel. 568-2432
sjdsspanish@yahoo.com
www.sjdsspanish.com

SPANISH LESSONS SCHOOL
next to Cyber Leo
tel. 872-1645
lvl1948@yahoo.es

León

VA PUES TOURS
next door to Restaurante CocinArte,
across from Iglesia El Laborío
tel. 606-2276
info@vapues.com
www.vapues.com

Estelí

ESCUELA HORIZONTE NICA
two blocks east and a half block north of
INISER
tel. 713-4117 or 836-5943
horizont@ibw.com.ni
www.ibw.com.ni/u/horizont

Matagalpa

**CENTRO NICARAGÜENSE DE
APRENDIZAJE CULTURAL (CENAC)**
west side of the Pan-American Highway, 150
meters north of the Shell Esquipulas
tel. 713-5437
cenac@ibw.com.ni
www.ibw.com.ni/~cenac

**ESCUELA DE ESPAÑOL
MATAGALPA**
half a block from the Calle de los Bancos, across
from the Club Social
escuela@matagalpa.info
www.matagalpa.info

SPANISH SCHOOL GÜEGÜENSE
250 meters east of the Shell Esquipulas
tel. 713-7172

Managua

**NICARAGUA SPANISH SCHOOLS
(NSS)**
tel. 244-1699 or U.S. tel. 805/687-9941
nssmga@ibw.com.ni
http://pages.prodigy.net/nss pmc

RAUL GAVARRETTE
Raul is a private tutor and tour guide.
tel. 233-1298, cell 776-5702
aige@tmx.com.ni

VIVA SPANISH SCHOOL
Casa L16 (azul), Barrio La Luz (from FNI,
two block south)
tel. 877-7179 or 270-2339
vivaspanish@btinternet.com

www.vivaspanishschool.com
Viva caters to expats and short-term
visitors.

INTERNATIONAL SCHOOLS IN MANAGUA

Note: Most of these schools provide K–12
service, sometimes preschool as well.

AMERICAN NICARAGUAN SCHOOL
across from Club Lomas de Monserrat
tel. 278-0029 or 278-4508
fax 267-3088
www.ans.edu.ni

COLEGIO ALEMÁN NICARAGÜENSE
Carretera Sur Km 10.5
P.O. Box 1636
tel. 265-8449, 265-8107, or 265-8758
fax 265-8117
coalnic@ibw.com.ni
www.coalnic.com
www.dasan.de/ds_Managua

**COLLEGE NICARAGUAYEN VICTOR
HUGO (THE FRENCH SCHOOL)**
three blocks east and half block south of Velez
Paiz Hospital
Managua, Nicaragua
tel. 265-2410, 265-0526, and 088-27386
fax 265-2426
secretaria@cnf.edu.ni

**LINCOLN INTERNATIONAL
ACADEMY**
Las Colinas Sur, 600 meters south of the
military base
tel. 276-3000
fax 276-1700
mayela@lincoln.edu.ni
www.lincoln.edu.ni

NOTRE DAME SCHOOL
Km 81/2 Carretera Masaya
P.O. Box 6092
tel. 276-0353 or 276-0343
fax 276-0416
www.notredame.edu.ni

**ST. AUGUSTINE PREPARATORY
SCHOOL**
De Loteria Nacional 150 v. abajo
tel. 277-3440
fax 278-7849

joyangur@yahoo.com
http://staugustineprep.catholicweb.com

PRIVATE UNIVERSITIES
AVE MARIA COLLEGE OF THE AMERICAS
San Marcos, Carazo
U.S. tel. 800/559-1008
www.avemaria.edu.ni

HOMESCHOOLING AND DISTANCE-LEARNING WEB PORTALS
A TO Z HOME'S COOL HOMESCHOOLING WEBSITE
www.homeschooling.gomilpitas.com

YOUR VIRTUAL HOMESCHOOL
www.homeschool.com

OTHER STUDY OPPORTUNITIES
BIOLOGICAL FIELD STATIONS AT LA SUERTE
U.S. tel. 305/666-9932
U.S. fax 305/666-7581
info@lasuerte.org
www.lasuerte.org
At these scientific classrooms and group accommodations on the slope of Volcán Maderas, you can study flora, fauna, and ecology of the rainforest. University credit is available.

CLOUD FOREST ADVENTURES
U.S. tel. 203/856-1134
info@cloudforestadventures.com
www.cloudforestadventures.com

CULTURAL CROSSING
tel. 834-0434 or U.S. tel. 954/923-9227
phoebehaupt@yahoo.com or jahaila7@yahoo.com
www.culturalcrossing.blogspot.com
With Cultural Crossing you can organize or participate in learning trips to the Atlantic coast.

SCHOOL FOR INTERNATIONAL TRAINING (SIT) STUDY ABROAD
Kipling Road
P.O. Box 676
Brattleboro, VT 05302-0676 USA
tel. 888/272-7881
studyabroad@sit.edu
www.sit.edu/studyabroad/latinamerica/nicaragua.html

SPANISH THROUGH LEADERSHIP
Nicaragua Summer Exchange Program
4017 Tokay Boulevard
Madison, WI 53711
tel. 888/674-0408
info@highschoolspanish.org
www.highschoolspanish.org

Health

CENTERS FOR DISEASE CONTROL
U.S. tel. 404/332-4559 or 877/394-8747
www.cdc.gov/travel/camerica.htm

EXPATRIATE HEALTH INSURANCE
BOOTSNALL TRAVEL INSURANCE PORTAL
www.bootsnall.com/travel insurance

INTERNATIONAL MEDICAL GROUP
www.imglobal.com

HEALTH CARE
U.S. EMBASSY-RECOMMENDED MEDICAL RESOURCES
http://managua.usembassy.gov/
wwwhcon14.html
These listings include laboratories, specialists, OBs, dentists, and more.

Hospitals in Managua
HOSPITAL BAUTISTA
Barrio Largaespada, 24 hours daily
tel. 249-0967 or 249-7070
fax 249-7327

HOSPITAL METROPOLITANO VIVIAN PELLAS
Carretera Masaya, Km 9.75, 250 meters west
tel. 255-6900 or emergency tel. 255-5153, 255-5163
www.metropolitano.com.ni

Dentist in Managua
DR. ESTEBAN BENDAÑA
300 meters south of the Enitel Villa Fontana
tel. 270-5021 or 850-8981
estebanbm@hotmail.com

Employment and Volunteering

THE JOB HUNT
General Work Abroad Resource
TRANSITIONS ABROAD
www.transitionsabroad.com/listings/work
This is an enormous resource and information portal.

Finding a Job in Nicaragua
LOCAL NEWSPAPERS (CLICK ON "CLASIFICADOS")
www.elnuevodiario.com.ni
www.usa.laprensa.com.ni

PLAZA VIRTUAL NICARAGUA JOB LISTINGS
www.plazavirtual.com.ni/clasificados/empleos

PRESELECCIÓN EMPRESARIAL, HUMAN RESOURCE CONSULTANTS
Colonia Los Robles V Etapa #64
Managua
tel. 278-3951 or 278-0074
nicaragua@preseleccion.com
www.preseleccion.com
Nicaragua's closest thing to a headhunting firm, its posts are read by U.S. Embassy staff and others.

STARTING A BUSINESS
MINISTRY OF DEVELOPMENT, INDUSTRY, AND COMMERCE (MIFIC–MINISTERIO DE FOMENTO, INDUSTRIA Y COMERCIO)
Km 6 Carretera Masaya,
Frente al Camino de Oriente
Managua
www.mific.gob.ni

PRONICARAGUA INVESTMENT PROMOTION AGENCY

Km 4 Carretera Masaya Restaurante Tip-Top,
1 C. al Oeste, Edificio Cesar
Managua
tel. 270-6400
info@pronicaragua.org
www.pronicaragua.org

VENTANILLA UNICA DE INVERSIONES

Km 6 Carretera Masaya, Frente
al Camino de Oriente
tel. 277-3860
www.mific.gob.ni/VUI/index.asp
This is MIFIC's one-stop shop for
business registration.

VOLUNTEERING OPPORTUNITIES

Following is a list of programs, mostly
by nongovernmental organizations, offering community service/volunteer opportunities throughout Nicaragua. For
regional opportunities, see the contacts
listed under *Prime Living Locations.*

AYUDANICA

2932 Normandy Road
Ardmore, PA 19003
tel. 610/649-2811
info@ayudanica.org
www.ayudanica.org
Ayudanica offers several work and cultural tours to Nicaragua for teens and
adults.

BRIDGES TO COMMUNITY

95 Croton Avenue
Ossining, NY 10562
tel. 914/923-2200
info@bridgestocommunity.org
www.bridgestocommunity.org
This organization has various project
sites in Nicaragua; trips are short-term
(7–9 days).

EL PORVENIR

2508 42nd Street
Sacramento, CA 95817
tel. 303/520-0093
info@elporvenir.org
www.elporvenir.org

El Porvenir runs sustainable water, sanitation, and reforestation projects in rural
Nicaragua and offers one- to two-week
volunteer vacations; price includes lodging, meals, health insurance, bilingual
coordinators, in-country transportation,
activity fees, and the cost of the project
the participant works on.

GENERAL VOLUNTEER ABROAD PORTAL

www.transitionsabroad.com/listings/work/
volunteer
Click on "Nicaragua" for info.

HABITAT FOR HUMANITY INTERNATIONAL

121 Habitat Street
Americus, GA 31709-3498
tel. 800/HABITAT (800/422-4828)
habitworld@habitat.org
There are ongoing opportunities for
volunteers and career professionals.

NICARAGUA NETWORK

1247 E Street SE
Washington, DC 20003
tel. 202/544-9355
nicanet@afgj.org
www.nicanet.org/volunteer
Short-term, long-term, study, volunteer,
and work: The Nicaragua Network has
been organizing in solidarity with the
people of Nicaragua for over 26 years.

NICARAGUA SOLIDARITY CAMPAIGN

129 Seven Sisters Road
London, N7 7QG
U.K. tel. 20/7272-9619 or
U.S. tel. 610/649-2811
U.K. fax 20/7272-5476
nsc@nicaraguasc.org.uk
www.nicaraguasc.org.uk
This London-based organization or-
ganizes brigades, study tours, and delegations to Nicaragua, and also raises
awareness in the U.K. of social and economic issues affecting Nicaragua.

POTTERS FOR PEACE

2216 Race Street
Denver, CO 80205

tel. 303/377-7998
potpaz@igc.org
www.potpaz.org
Annually organized visits cover a very exciting itinerary, allowing potters from the United States and Nicaragua to converse.

SEEDS OF LEARNING
P.O. Box 429
Glen Ellen, CA 95442
tel. 707/939-0471
www.seedsoflearning.org
This group offers volunteers the chance to work together with rural communities to build schools.

VOLUNTEER ABROAD
www.volunteerabroad.com/Nicaragua.cfm
This site has more Nicaragua listings.

WITNESS FOR PEACE
707 8th Street SE
Washington, DC 20003
tel. 202/547-6112
hostetler@witnessforpeace.org
www.witnessforpeace.org/nicaragua/
actiontools.html
Witness for Peace has a variety of delegations and long-term volunteer opportunities.

Government-Sponsored Volunteer Programs
UNITED STATES PEACE CORPS
Paul D. Coverdell Peace Corps Headquarters
1111 20th Street NW
Washington, DC 20526
tel. 800/424-8580
www.peacecorps.gov

VOLUNTARY SERVICE OVERSEAS (VSO) CANADA
806-151 Slater Street
Ottawa, ON K1P 5H3
tel. 888/876-2911
inquiry@vsocan.org
www.vsocanada.org

VOLUNTARY SERVICE OVERSEAS (VSO) IRELAND
Carmichael Centre
Brunswick Street N
Dublin 7, Ireland
tel. 1/872-7173
info@vso.ie

VOLUNTARY SERVICE OVERSEAS (VSO) UNITED KINGDOM
317 Putney Bridge Road
London, SW15 2PN
tel. 20/8780-7200
www.vso.org.uk

Finance

BANKING AND CURRENCY
BANCENTRO NICARAGUA
Km 4 Carretera Masaya
Managua
tel. 278-2777
fax 278-6001

CENTRAL BANK OF NICARAGUA
www.bcn.gob.ni

SEGUROSSA
Centro Financiero LAFISE
Km 5 Carretera Masaya
Managua
tel. 270-3505, fax 270-3558

HOUSEHOLD HELP
LEY LABORAL WEBSITE
www.leylaboral.com

MINISTRY OF LABOR (MITRAB)
www.mitrab.gob.ni

INVESTING AND BROKERAGES
LAFISE NICARAGUA
Centro Banic, Piso 1, Km 5 Carretera Masaya
Managua
tel. 278-7140
fax 278-3984

NICARAGUAN STOCK MARKET
www.bolsanic.com

Financial Advisors
CALVET & ASSOCIATES
tel. 270-1320 or U.S. tel. 305/748-4947

fax 270-0438
info@rcalvet.com
www.rcalvet.com
An investment consultant performs market and/or financial analysis.

Communications

POSTAL AND COURIER SERVICES
CORREOS DE NICARAGUA
Nicaragua Postal System
atencion124@correosdenicaragua.com.ni
www.correos.com.ni

TRANSEXPRESS INTERNATIONAL COURIER
across the street the Mansión Teodolinda
Managua
tel. 222-2270
info@transexpress.com.ni
www.transexpress.com.ni
Send packages or buy your NicaBox in Miami.

CABLE AND INTERNET SERVICE PROVIDERS
CABLENET
500 meters west of the Rotonda Jean Poul Genie at the entrance to Reparto Planes de Puntaldía
Managua
tel. 255-7300
www.cablenet.com.ni
Cablenet provides cable broadband Internet.

DIRECTV
Hospital Monte de España, 70m al lago
Managua
tel. 270-6767
www.directv.com.ni
Satellite TV is available throughout Nicaragua.

ENITEL
Every city has its own ENITEL office, and Managua has several offices.
Telephone service: www.enitel.com.ni
Internet service: www.tmx.com.ni

ESTESA
Managua, Rotonda Jean Poul Genie 500m abajo, entrada al Reparto Planes de Puntaldía
tel. 255-7272 or 278-3300
www.estesa.com.ni
Estesa provides cable TV and cable broadband Internet.

IBW
Semáforos do ENITEL Villa Fontana 200m al norte #287, Managua
tel. 278-6328
www.ibw.com.ni
IBW offers Internet service via dial-up or broadband.

TELEPHONE SERVICES
ENITEL
www.enitel.com.ni

MOVISTAR
Carretera Masaya at the Rotonda Jean Paul Genie
Managua
www.movistar.com.ni

MEDIA
NICARAGUA MEDIA GATEWAY: IBW
www.ibw.com.ni

NICARAGUA TV CHANNEL 8
www.telenica.com.ni

RADIO PIRATA 99.9 FM: LA ONDA BARBARA
www.pirata.tk

Newspapers and Magazines
BETWEEN THE WAVES
www.turq.com/betweenthewaves
This publication has English-language

articles on tourism and real estate; it's available everywhere.

INVESTMENTS AND TOURISM
www.rcalvet.com
This English-language magazine for foreigners and the real estate crowd is available at many Realtors' offices.

EL NUEVO DIARIO
www.elnuevodiario.com.ni

LA PRENSA
www.usa.laprensa.com.ni

Travel and Transportation

GETTING TO NICARAGUA

By Air
MANAGUA INTERNATIONAL AIRPORT
Km 11 Carretera Norte
Managua
tel. 233-1624 or 233-1628
www.eaai.com.ni/flash.shtml

NATURE AIR
U.S./Canada tel. 800/235-9272 or Costa Rica
tel. 506/299-6000
info@natureair.com, reservations@natureair.com
www.natureair.com
This airline is based in Tobias Bolaños Airport, San José, and Costa Rica.

TACA AIR
Plaza España, Edificio Barcelona local 17
Managua
tel. 266-3136
www.taca.com

By International Bus
Note: All addresses are in Barrio Marta Quezada in Managua.

KING QUALITY/ CRUCEROS DEL GOLFO
Antiguo Cine Dorado, 2 cuadras al este
tel. 228-1454
fax 222-3065

TICA BUS
two blocks east of the Antiguo Cine Dorado
tel. 222-6094 or 222-3031
ticabus@ticabus.com
www.ticabus.com

TRANSNICA
Rotonda Metrocentro 300 meters north, 25 meters east, across from DGI
tel. 277-2104 or 882-7600
www.transnica.com

GETTING AROUND

By Air
ATLANTIC AIRLINES
tel. 222-3037 or 222-5787
reservaciones@atlanticairlines.com.ni
www.atlanticairlines.com.ni

LA COSTEÑA
tel. 263-2142 or U.S./Canada
tel. 800/948-3770
LaCostena@centralamerica.com

Rental Cars
ALAMO
Managua International Airport
tel. 233-1624, ext. 2433
alamo@cablenet.com.ni
www.alamonicaragua.com

BUDGET MANAGUA
Managua International Airport
tel. 263-1222
info@budget.com.ni
www.budget.com.ni/nicaragua/

DOLLAR
Managua International Airport
tel. 233-2192
gperez@casapellas.com.ni
www.dollar.com.ni

HERTZ (C/O POPULAR RENT A CAR)
Pista Juan Pablo II, Plaza Julio Martinez
tel. 260-1292
mail@lugorentacar.com.ni

Housing Considerations

PROPERTY TITLE RESEARCH AND INSURANCE

FIRST AMERICAN TITLE INSURANCE COMPANY
Latin America/Caribbean Operations
13450 W. Sunrise Boulevard, Suite 300
Sunrise, FL 33323
tel. 954/839-2900, ext. 188, or
877/641-6767
fax 954/838-9228
www.firstam.com

NICARAGUA CONSULTANT–PROPERTY INVESTMENT & LEGAL SERVICES
www.NicaraguaConsultant.com
Longtime Managua resident (and Boston native) Richard Leonardi offers unbiased property investment counseling; in-depth research of property title; custom land searches, legal help with purchase, selling, and legalization of property; also assistance in attaining residency and other legal docs.

CONSTRUCTION AND CONTRACTORS

CONSTRUCCIONES PACÍFICO, S.A.
San Juan del Sur
tel. 568-2544 or 568-2527, cell 846-7372
conpacsa@ibw.com.ni
A construction company based in San Juan del Sur that features North American quality standards, California seismic standards, and English-speaking administration.

LOCAL TREASURE INTERNATIONAL
San Juan del Sur
tel. 838-3808 or
U.S. tel. 415/290-9556, 877/360-633
www.localtreasureinternational.com
This is a consulting, construction, design, and development alternative in Nicaragua.

REAL ESTATE AGENTS

Granada and Environs

BRENES MORALES BIENES RAICES
Calle La Calzada
tel. 889-7045 or 613-0158
www.es.geocities.com/bmbienesraices

CENTURY 21 GRANADA
Calle Calzada
Granada
tel. 552-6458
www.century21granada.com

RANCHO MONTERREY
on the lip of the Laguna de Apoyo, in Catarina
www.nicaraguaproperty.com/rancho_monterrey.html

RE/MAX
Calle La Libertad
tel. 552-3199
www.nicaraguaproperty.com/developments.html

San Juan del Sur, Rivas, and La Isla de Ometepe
Note: Real estate agencies sprout and die like mushrooms in San Juan del Sur; this is not an exhaustive list, but it's a place to start.

ARENAS BAY
tel. 278-6888 or 270-3002
fax 278-8256
contact@arenasbay.com
www.arenasbay.com

AURORA BEACHFRONT REALTY
a half block east of Restaurant Timon
tel. 884-7141 or U.S. tel. 323/908-6730
aurorabeachfront@yahoo.com
www.aurorabeachfront.com
As of 2006, this was the only Nicaraguan real estate agent operating in San Juan del Sur.

BEACHFRONT REALTY
www.nicaland.com
This company focuses on surf-friendly plots for sale.

CENTURY 21
Reparto Pedro Joaquín Chamorro, one block north of Restaurant Timon on the water side
tel. 568-2283 or 872-3517, U.S./Canada tel. 888/522-0897
info@c21nicaragua.com
www.c21sanjuandelsur.com

NICADEV
tel. 820-8682 or U.S. tel. 858/945-7235
NicaDev focuses on ethical and environmentally sensitive real estate development, featuring the NicaDev Fund, which gives a percentage of profits back to the community.

NICARAGUA PROPERTIES
next to BDF, Apartado 25
tel. 568-2180 or 839-0157
nicaprop@ibw.com.ni
www.realestatenicaragua.com

PACIFIC BRISAS REALTY
tel. 568-2448, 882-9229 or
U.S. tel. 702/944-9702
pacificbrisasrealty@gmail.com
www.pacificbrisas.com

PARADISE DEVELOPMENT HOLDINGS
tel. 838-3877 or U.S. tel. 949/495-4142
www.pacificcoastparadise.com

PARQUE MARÍTIMO EL COCO
18 km south of San Juan del Sur
satellite tel. 892-0124
parquemaritimo@playaelcoco.com.ni
www.playaelcoco.com.ni

RE/MAX TIERRA NICA
Calle Frente al Mar
tel. 568-2253
www.nicaraguaproperty.com

SNIDERS REALTY
tel. 872-9776 or 839-7978
cunser@silk.net
www.sniderrealty.com.ni

WATER'S EDGE INTERNATIONAL REALTY
next to Hotel Estrella
tel. 885-7651 or U.S. tel. 786/206-4361
U.S. fax 305/675-0678
info@puntodeagua.com
www.puntodeagua.com

Managua

DISCOVER REAL ESTATE
70 meters south of Semáforos de Villa Fontana
tel. 270-4000 or 883-2200
info@discovernica.com
www.discovernica.com

EUROAMERICANA NICARAGUA
www.euram.com.ni/br/ofertas.asp
This site is especially good for rentals in Managua.

INMONICA.COM
nica@inmonica.com
http://209.15.138.224/inmonica/contenidos.htm (or Google for "Inmonica")
Buy or rent houses, apartments, ranches, etc.

León and the North
There are no real estate agencies that specialize in these areas or are based in the north, but numerous Granada and San Juan-based agents dabble in León, Poneloya, and beyond.

The Atlantic Coast
There are no real estate agencies that specialize in these areas or are based on the Atlantic coast, but you can start your search at inmonica.com (http://209.15.138.224/inmonica/contenidos.htm)

Prime Living Locations

GRANADA

General Resources
MAIN GRENADA WEBSITE
www.granada.com.ni

NICARAGUA SOJOURN
www.nicaraguasojourn.com
Try this site for yoga or Spanish classes, volunteer opportunities, lodging, and more.

Volunteer Opportunities in Granada
BUILDING NEW HOPE
hope@buildingnewhope.com
www.buildingnewhope.org
At Building New Hope there's a plethora of projects, collaborations, and opportunities; start on the website by shopping, buying coffee, donating miles, and learning more; continue by volunteering in Granada and joining the family.

LA ESPERANZA GRANADA
www.la-esperanza-granada.org
Various community education and health projects take place in several small villages outside the city. A one-month minimum commitment is required, but periodically there are short-term projects available; intermediate Spanish is desirable.

PUEDO LEER (I CAN READ)
Helen Kaye: helenkaye2003@yahoo.com
This project is dedicated to bringing books and reading programs to the children of Granada; it's always looking for books, donations, and volunteers.

SAN JUAN DEL SUR AND THE SOUTHWEST

General Resource
SAN JUAN DEL SUR'S WEBSITE
www.sanjuandelsur.org.ni

Services
RICARDO MORALES NARVAEZ, DEPENDABLE CAR AND DRIVER
three blocks south of Hotel Villa Isabella
tel. 882-8268
richardsjds@hotmail.com
Airport rides, Masaya/Granada transfers, and coast trips cost US$60–80.

SANO Y SALVO STORAGE SPACE
jaxtraw2@aol.com.
This company offers storage of Jet Skis, boats, automobiles, RVs, surfboards, vehicles, furniture, household goods, construction equipment and supplies, and retail business goods.

Volunteer Opportunities
A. JEAN BRUGGER EDUCATION PROJECT
De la Parroquia, 1 c. al Este
tel. 458-2110, 568 2511
Pelican@ibw.com.ni
www.sanjuandelsur.org.ni/community/brugger/index.htm
This project supports the education and training of San Juan del Sur youth, including environmental campaigns, scholarships, and school materials. Contact A. Jean Brugger and Chris R.A. Berry.

SAN JUAN DEL SUR BIBLIOTECA MOVIL (COMMUNITY LIBRARY PROJECT)
Apartado Postal 17, San Juan del Sur, Rivas
tel. 568-2338
janem101@aol.com
www.sjdsbiblioteca.com
The first lending library in Nicaragua seeks volunteers and Spanish books.

MANAGUA

General Resource
MANAGUA MAYOR'S OFFICE
www.managua.gob.ni

LEÓN AND THE NORTH

Services
MATAGALPA TOURS
across the street from the Club Social
tel. 847-2004
info@matagalpatours.com
www.matagalpatours.com
Services include hiking trips, tourist information, and a crafts shop.

VA PUES TOURS
next door to the Restaurante CocinArte, across from Iglesia El Laborío in León
tel. 606-2276
info@vapues.com
www.vapues.com
This is a good bet for area tours and general information.

THE ATLANTIC COAST

General Resources
ATLANTIC COAST WEB PORTAL
www.bluefieldspulse.com
This site's slogan is "Uniting the Caribbean Coast of Nicaragua at Home and Abroad."

BIG CORN ISLAND
www.bigcornisland.com
This site offers tips, links, and more.

Glossary

a mano derecha/izquierda on your right-hand/ left-hand side

abogado lawyer

abajo down, or to the west

"¡Adios amor!" "Goodbye, my love!"

agencias aduaneras customs agents

aguinaldo Christmas bonus, equal to one month's salary

aire acondicionado air conditioning

alcaldía mayor's office

alegría happiness

allí no más just over there

amueblado furnished

apartamento apartment

area de servicio maid's quarters

arriba up, or east

artesanía crafts

ayudante the guy on the bus who collects your fee after you find a seat

baño bathroom

"¡Barriga llena, corazón contenta!" "Belly full, happy heart!"

barrio neighborhood

bombero firefighter

bravo rough, strong, wild

cafetín light food eatery

calle street

campesinos country folk

campo countryside

carretera highway, road

casarse to get married

catastro property registry

cédula residency card

centro de salud public MINSA-run health clinic, there's one in most towns

centro recreativo public recreation center

cerro hill or mountain

cerveza, cervecita beer

chatarra junk, scrap

chele pale, light-skinned

chinelas rubber flip-flops

chofer driver

coca short for cocaina (cocaine)

colectivo a shared taxi or passenger boat

colegio high school

comedor cheap lunch counter

comida corriente plate of the day

confianza trust

contiguo a next to, adjacent to

cooperativa cooperative

córdoba Nicaraguan currency

corriente standard, base

coyote illegal immigrant smuggler or profit-cutting middleman

cuadras city blocks

cuajada white, homemade, salty cheese

Cuerpo de Paz Peace Corps

departamentos subsection of Nicaragua, akin to states or counties

domestica maid

don/doña terms of respect for elders

empalme intersection of two roads

entrada entrance

escuela elementary school

esquinera on the corner of two streets

expreso express bus

extranjero foreigner

felicidades congratulations

fiestas patronales patron saint's day festivals, celebrated annually

folklóricos folk dances or songs

frente a across the street from

fritanga street-side barbecue and fry-fest

gancho gap in a fence

garaje garage

gaseosa carbonated beverage

gringo North American, or any foreigner

gallo pinto national mix of rice and beans

guaro booze

guayabera formal/casual lightweight, short-sleeve shirt

guitarrón mariachi bass guitar

habitaciones rooms

"Hasta luegito" "See you in a little bit"

hospedaje hostel, budget hotel

Indio of indigenous origin (perjorative)

ingeniero engineer

inquilino renter

instituto high school

inversionista investor

el invierno winter

invito I'll pay for this; literally, "I invite you"

jalar to date (colloquial)

jardinero gardener

lago lake

lancha small passenger boat

lanchero lancha driver

lavandero concrete washboard for washing clothes

machismo cultural double standard between the genders

machista something following rules of machismo

mala maniobra moving violation, literally "bad driving"

malecón waterfront

manzana besides an apple, this is also a measure of land equal to 100 square *varas*, or 1.74 acres

mariachi Mexican country/polka music

maricón gay (perjorative)

mercado market

mesa/meseta geographical plateau

mestizaje mixing

mestizo descendant of Spanish and native mix

microbus minivan

mojado illegal immigrant in the U.S. (literally, "wet")

monte weed, marijuana

mota pot, marijuana

mosquitero mosquito net

muchachos/as boys/girls

muelle dock, wharf

no importa it doesn't matter

nuevo new

ordinario local bus (also *ruteado*)

panga small passenger boat

panguero panga driver

parqueo parking

pena embarrassment

permanente permanent

pila concrete cistern for storing water

pinche cheapskate

pinolero one who drinks *pinol,* i.e., a Nicaraguan

preservativo condom

primaria elementary school

primer año freshman year of high school (ages 12-14)

pueblo small town or village

pulpería corner store

putería whorehouse

puro cigar

quintal 100-pound sack

quinto año senior year of high school

rancheras Mexican drinking songs

rancho thatch-roofed restaurant or hut

rato a short period of time

Reparto a kind of urban neighborhood

residente resident

residente inversionista investor's residence visa

residente permanente residence visa

ruteada local (slow) bus

sala living room

salida exit, road out of town

salto waterfall

secundaria high school

selador watchman

semáforo traffic light (used for giving directions)

sin intermediarios without intermediaries (brokers)

suave soft, easy, quiet

suerte luck

suyo yours

taquezal form of adobe architecture prevalent in colonial Latin America

teja hard clay tile, for roofs

terreteniente landowner

universidad university

vara colonial unit of distance equal to roughly one meter

el verano summer

vigorón traditional food of pork rinds and boiled yucca

viviendo juntos seriously dating and probably (lit.) "living together"

voceo the use of *vos*

vos the informal second person

volcán volcano

zancudos mosquitoes

Spanish Phrasebook

PRONUNCIATION GUIDE

Spanish pronunciation is much more regular than that of English, but there are still occasional variations.

Consonants

c as "c" in "cat," before "a," "o," or "u"; like "s" before "e" or "i"

d as "d" in "dog," except between vowels, then like "th" in "that"

g before "e" or "i," like the "ch" in Scottish "loch"; elsewhere like "g" in "get"

h always silent

j like the English "h" in "hotel," but stronger

ll like the "y" in "yellow"

ñ like the "ni" in "onion"

r always pronounced as strong "r"

rr trilled "r"

v similar to the "b" in "boy" (not as English "v")

y similar to English, but with a slight "j" sound. When standing alone, it's pronounced like the "e" in "me".

z like "s" in "same"

b, f, k, l, m, n, p, q, s, t, w, x as in English

Vowels

a as in "father," but shorter

e as in "hen"

i as in "machine"

o as in "phone"

u usually as in "rule"; when it follows a "q," the "u" is silent; when it follows an "h" or "g," it's pronounced like "w," except when it comes between "g" and "e" or "i," when it's also silent (unless it has an umlaut, when it is again pronounced as English "w")

Stress

Native English speakers frequently make errors of pronunciation by ignoring stress. All Spanish vowels—a, e, i, o, and u— carry accents that determine which syllable of a word gets emphasis. Often, stress seems unnatural to nonnative speakers— the surname Chávez, for instance, is stressed on the first syllable—but failure to observe this rule may mean that native speakers may not understand you.

NUMBERS

0 *cero*
1 *uno (masculine)*
1 *una (feminine)*
2 *dos*
3 *tres*
4 *cuatro*
5 *cinco*
6 *seis*
7 *siete*
8 *ocho*
9 *nueve*
10 *diez*
11 *once*
12 *doce*
13 *trece*
14 *catorce*
15 *quince*
16 *dieciseis*
17 *diecisiete*
18 *dieciocho*
19 *diecinueve*
20 *veinte*
21 *veintiuno*
30 *treinta*
40 *cuarenta*
50 *cincuenta*
60 *sesenta*
70 *setenta*
80 *ochenta*
90 *noventa*
100 *cien*
101 *ciento y uno*
200 *doscientos*
1,000 *mil*
10,000 *diez mil*
1,000,000 *un millón*

DAYS OF THE WEEK

Sunday *domingo*
Monday *lunes*
Tuesday *martes*
Wednesday *miércoles*
Thursday *jueves*
Friday *viernes*
Saturday *sábado*

TIME

While Nicaraguans mostly use the 12-hour clock, in some instances, usually associated with plane or bus schedules, they may use the 24-hour military clock. Under the 24-hour clock, for example, *las nueve de la noche* (9 P.M.) would be *las 21 horas* (2100 hours).

What time is it? *¿Qué hora es?*
It's one o'clock. *Es la una.*
It's two o'clock. *Son las dos.*
At two o'clock. *A las dos.*
It's ten to three. *Son las tres menos diez.*
It's ten past three. *Son las tres y diez.*
It's three fifteen. *Son las tres y cuarto.*
It's two forty-five. *Son las tres menos cuarto.*
It's two thirty. *Son las dos y media.*
It's six A.M. *Son las seis de la mañana.*
It's six P.M. *Son las seis de la tarde.*
It's ten P.M. *Son las diez de la noche.*
Today *hoy*
Tomorrow *mañana*
Morning *la mañana*
Tomorrow morning *mañana por la mañana*
Yesterday *ayer*
Week *la semana*
Month *mes*
Year *año*
Last night *anoche*
The next day *el día siguiente*

USEFUL WORDS AND PHRASES

Nicaraguans and other Spanish-speaking people consider formalities important. Whenever approaching anyone for information or some other reason, do not forget the appropriate salutation—good morning, good evening, etc. Standing alone, the greeting *hola* (hello) can sound brusque.

Hello. *Hola.*
Good morning. *Buenos días.*
Good afternoon. *Buenas tardes.*
Good evening. *Buenas noches.*
How are you? *¿Cómo está?*
Fine. *Muy bien.*
And you? *¿Y usted?*
So-so. *Más o menos.*
Thank you. *Gracias.*
Thank you very much. *Muchas gracias.*
You're very kind. *Muy amable.*
You're welcome. *De nada (literally, "It's nothing").*
Yes *sí*
No *no*
I don't know. *No sé.*
It's fine; okay. *Está bien.*
Good; okay. *Bueno.*
Please *por favor*
Pleased to meet you. *Mucho gusto.*
Excuse me (physical). *Perdóneme.*
Excuse me (speech). *Discúlpeme.*
I'm sorry. *Lo siento.*
Goodbye. *Adiós.*
See you later. *Hasta luego (literally, "until later").*
More *más*
Less *menos*
Better *mejor*
Much, a lot *mucho*
A little *un poco*
Large *grande*
Small *pequeño, chico*
Quick, fast *rápido*
Slowly *despacio*
Bad *malo*
Difficult *difícil*
Easy *fácil*
He/She/It is gone; as in "She left" or "he's gone." *Ya se fue.*
I don't speak Spanish well. *No hablo bien el español.*
I don't understand. *No entiendo.*
How do you say... in Spanish? *¿Cómo se dice... en español?*

Do you understand English? ¿Entiende el inglés?
Is English spoken here? (Does anyone here speak English?) ¿Se habla inglés aquí?

TERMS OF ADDRESS

When in doubt, use the formal *usted* (you) as a form of address. If you wish to dispense with formality and feel that the desire is mutual, you can say, "*Me puedes tutear*" ("You can call me "tu").

I yo
You (formal) usted
you (familiar) tú
He/him él
She/her ella
We/us nosotros
You (plural) ustedes
They/them (all males or mixed gender) ellos
They/them (all females) ellas
Mr., sir señor
Mrs., madam señora
Miss, young lady señorita
Wife esposa
Husband marido or esposo
Friend amigo (male), amiga (female)
Sweetheart novio (male), novia (female)
Son, daughter hijo, hija
Brother, sister hermano, hermana
Father, mother padre, madre
Grandfather, grandmother abuelo, abuela

GETTING AROUND

Where is... ? ¿Dónde está... ?
How far is it to... ? ¿A cuanto está... ?
from... to... de... a...
Highway la carretera
Road el camino
Street la calle
Block la cuadra
Kilometer kilómetro
North norte
South sur
West oeste; poniente
East este; oriente
Straight ahead al derecho; adelante

To the right a la derecha
To the left a la izquierda

ACCOMMODATIONS

Is there a room? ¿Hay cuarto?
May I (we) see it? ¿Puedo (podemos) verlo?
What is the rate? ¿Cuál es el precio?
Is that your best rate? ¿Es su mejor precio?
Is there something cheaper? ¿Hay algo más económico?
Single room un sencillo
Double room un doble
Room for a couple matrimonial
Key llave
With private bath con baño
With shared bath con baño general; con baño compartido
Hot water agua caliente
Cold water agua fría
Shower ducha
Electric shower ducha eléctrica
Towel toalla
Soap jabón
Toilet paper papel higiénico
Air conditioning aire acondicionado
Fan abanico; ventilador
Blanket frazada; manta
Sheets sábanas

PUBLIC TRANSPORT

Bus stop la parada
Bus terminal terminal de buses
Airport el aeropuerto
Launch lancha; tiburonera
Dock muelle
I want a ticket to... Quiero un pasaje a...
I want to get off at... Quiero bajar en...
Here, please. Aquí, por favor.
Where is this bus going? ¿Adónde va este autobús?
Round-trip ida y vuelta
What do I owe? ¿Cuánto le debo?

FOOD

Menu la carta, el menú
Glass taza
Fork tenedor
Knife cuchillo

Spoon *cuchara*
Napkin *servilleta*
Soft drink *agua fresca*
Coffee *café*
Cream *crema*
Tea *té*
Sugar *azúcar*
Drinking water *agua pura, agua potable*
Bottled carbonated water *agua mineral con gas*
Bottled uncarbonated water *agua sin gas*
Beer *cerveza*
Wine *vino*
Milk *leche*
Juice *jugo*
Eggs *huevos*
Bread *pan*
Watermelon *sandía*
Banana *banano*
Plantain *plátano*
Apple *manzana*
Orange *naranja*
Meat (without) *carne (sin)*
Beef *carne de res*
Chicken *pollo; gallina*
Fish *pescado*
Shellfish *mariscos*
Shrimp *camarones*
Fried *frito*
Roasted *asado*
Barbecued *a la parrilla*
Breakfast *desayuno*
Lunch *almuerzo*
Dinner (often eaten in late afternoon) *comida*

Dinner, or a late-night snack *cena*
The check, or bill *la cuenta*

MAKING PURCHASES
I need... *Necesito...*
I want... *Deseo... or Quiero...*
I would like... (more polite) *Quisiera...*
How much does it cost? *¿Cuánto cuesta?*
What's the exchange rate? *¿Cuál es el tipo de cambio?*
May I see... ? *¿Puedo ver... ?*
This one *ésta/ésto*
Expensive *caro*
Cheap *barato*
Cheaper *más barato*
Too much *demasiado*

HEALTH
Help me please. *Ayúdeme por favor.*
I am ill. *Estoy enfermo.*
Pain *dolor*
Fever *fiebre*
Stomach ache *dolor de estómago*
Vomiting *vomitar*
Diarrhea *diarrea*
Drugstore *farmacia*
Medicine *medicina*
Pill, tablet *pastilla*
Birth-control pills *pastillas anticonceptivas*
Condom *condón, preservativo*

Suggested Reading

Although new books on Nicaraguan history and culture continue to trickle onto the shelves, there is an enormous number of out-of-print books about Nicaragua that you can seek out in your library, online (www.dogbert.abebooks.com/abe and www.powells.com are both excellent used-book sources), or in the Latin America section of your favorite independent used bookstore. As you'll see, the lion's share of literature on Nicaragua is nonfiction, mostly relating to the Sandinista period and its aftermath. For Nicaraguan literature (both Spanish and translated), visit the bookstores near Managua's University of Central America.

HISTORY, MEMOIR, AND NONFICTION

Babb, Florence. *After Revolution: Mapping Gender and Cultural Politics in Neoliberal Nicaragua.* University of Texas Press, 2001.

Barrios de Chamorro, Violeta. *Dreams of the Heart.* New York: Simon & Schuster, 1996. A very readable and human history of Nicaragua from the Somoza years through Doña Violeta's electoral triumph in 1990.

Belli, Gioconda. *The Country Under My Skin: A Memoir of Love and War.* New York: Knopf, 2002. A wonderful woman's-eye view from within the revolution.

Cabezas, Omar. *Fire from the Mountain (La Montaña es Algo Más que una Inmensa Estepa Verde).* New York: Crown, 1985. A ribald, vernacular account of what it's like to be a guerrilla soldier in the mountains of Nicaragua; one of the few books about the early stages of the revolution.

Cardenal, Ernesto, and Donald D. Walsh (trans.). *The Gospel in Solentiname.* Orbis Books, 1979. These are the transcripts of the masses on Solentiname that helped spawn the Liberation Theology movement.

Chomsky, Noam. *Turning the Tide: U.S. Intervention in Central America and the Struggle for Peace.* Boston: South End Press, 1985. Succinctly and powerfully shows how U.S. Central American policies implement broader U.S. economic, military, and social aims.

Colburn, Forrest D. *My Car in Managua.* Austin: University of Texas Press, 1991. An objective, often humorous description of the great difficulties and occasional pleasures of life in Nicaragua during the Sandinista revolution.

Davis, Peter. *Where Is Nicaragua?* New York: Simon & Schuster, 1987. Davis breaks down the revolution and Contra War, and ties it all into the country's history; he articulates the complexity of the situation in a graspable manner.

Dickey, Christopher. *With the Contras.* New York: Simon & Schuster, 1985. Dickey was the *Washington Post* correspondent in Honduras, and his book makes an excellent complement to Kinzer's, who spent much more time with the Sandinistas.

Kinzer, Stephen. *Blood of Brothers: Life and War in Nicaragua.* New York: Putnam, 1991. If you're only going to read one book, this is the one. Kinzer, the *New York Times* Managua bureau chief during the war, sensed that Nicaragua was "a country with more to tell the world than it had been able to articulate, a country with a message both political and spiritual."

Kruckewitt, Joan. *The Death of Ben Linder: The Story of a North American in Sandinista Nicaragua.* New York: Seven Stories Press, 2001. In 1987, the death of the first U.S. citizen killed by the U.S.-backed Contras ignited a firestorm of protests and debate. Investigative journalist Joan Kruckewitt tells Ben Linder's story, incorporating formerly classified CIA documents that reveal who killed Ben Linder and why.

Lancaster, Roger N. *Life is Hard: Machismo, Danger, and the Intimacy of Power in Nicaragua.* Berkeley, Calif.: University of California Press, 1992. Lancaster is an anthropologist, and this is an ethnography studying not current events but their effect on the Nicaraguan individual and family. It is intimate and offers details about Nicaraguan life that one can only get living with the people in their homes.

Marriott, Edward. *Savage Shore: Life and Death with Nicaragua's Last Shark Hunters.* New York: Owl Books, 2001. A curious and descriptive journey up the Río San Juan and beyond.

Plunkett, Hazel. *In Focus Nicaragua: A Guide to the People, Politics and Culture.* Northhampton: Interlink Books, 1999. A 100-page overview to Nicaragua, including Nicaraguans in the 1990s.

Randall, Margaret. *Risking a Somersault in the Air.* Willimantic, Conn.: Curbstone Press, 1990. Just as much about Nicaraguan literature as it is about the Revolution, this is a fascinating series of interviews with Nicaraguan authors and poets, most of whom were part of the FSLN revolution and government.

Randall, Margaret. *Sandino's Daughters.* Point Roberts, Wash.: New Star Books, 1981. Written about the role of feminism in the Sandinista revolution, via a series of interviews with participants.

Rushdie, Salman. *The Jaguar Smile.* New York: Picador Books, 1987. A poetic, passionate jaunt with the Sandinistas and short examination of their policies.

Squier, Ephraim George. *Nicaragua; Its People, Scenery, Monuments, and the Proposed Interoceanic Canal.* D. Appleton, 1852. This massive, multivolume tome by Squier (1821–1888), an anthropologist, is available for hundreds of dollars in rare book stores.

Zimmerman, Matilde. *Sandinista: Carlos Fonseca and the Nicaraguan Revolution.* Durham: Duke University Press, 2001. A captivating account of the life of the FSLN's founder.

Photography

Gentile, William Frank. *Nicaragua.* Photographs by William Frank Gentile; introduction by William M. LeoGrande; an interview with Sergio Ramirez Mercado. New York: W.W. Norton & Company, 1989. These are some of the deepest, most powerful photos you'll ever see, with fantastic juxtapositions of Contra and FSLN soldiers.

Kunzle, David. *The Murals of Revolutionary Nicaragua 1979–1992.* Berkeley, Calif.: University of California Press, 1995. Many murals were strictly political, but most intertwined the revolutionary process with cultural, historical, and literary themes, all celebrated in Kunzle's book, which has an 83-page introduction and 100 color plates.

Living, Working, and Traveling in Nicaragua

Berman, Joshua, and Randall Wood. *Moon Nicaragua.* Emeryville, Calif.: Avalon Travel Publishing, 2005. The authors of *Moon Living Abroad in Nicaragua* also wrote the most comprehensive and thoroughly enjoyable practical guidebook to Nicaragua.

Griffith, Susan, et al. *Work Abroad: The Complete Guide to Finding a Job Overseas.* Amherst, Mass.: Transitions Abroad Publishing, 2002. Arthur Frommer calls it "The definitive book on the subject."

Rupp, Rebecca. *Home Learning Year by Year: How to Design a Homeschool Curriculum from Preschool through High*

School. New York: Three Rivers Press, 2000. The author is one of the most respected home-schooling authorities in the world.

FICTION AND POETRY

Morelli, Marco. *Ruben's Orphans*. Managua: Painted Rooster Press, 2001. An anthology of contemporary Nicaraguan poets, with English translations.

Pope, Liston, Jr. *Living Like the Saints: A Novel of Nicaragua*. N.A. Gilbert & Sons, 1997. By charting the course of one family and its barrio neighbors as they lead an insurrection against the brutal government of Anastasio Somoza, the author of *Redemption* paints a dramatic and intimate group portrait of the Nicaraguan people during the Sandinista rebellion of the late 1970s.

White, Steven, ed. *Poets of Nicaragua: A Bilingual Anthology* 1918–1979. Sheffield, UK: Unicorn Press, 1982. An anthology of the most important Nicaraguan poets of the 20th century.

Suggested Films

Fire from the Mountain

The film version of the book by the same name (*La Montaña es Algo Más que un Inmensa Estepa Verde* in Spanish) provides powerful empathy for the Sandinista revolution and the young people that made it happen.

Karla's Song

Filmed in the mid-1980s at the height of the Contra insurgency, in this film a Scottish bus driver finds love and danger in Nicaragua. Still poignant 20 years later, it offers decent insight into the madness of the proxy war.

Metal and Glass

A gut-wrenching 20-minute short film that tells the story of a young boy, played by Giovanni Padilla, who forages in a garbage dump for bottles so that he can sell them. The movie deals with issues and ideas ranging from poverty, crime, and war to lost childhoods and childhood fantasies. Produced by a Nicaraguan cinematographer and probably tough to find.

The World Is Watching

Examines the unseen elements of news gathering, editing, and reportage that shaped our understanding of Nicaragua's Contra War.

The World Stopped Watching

The journalists who produced *The World is Watching* return to Nicaragua 14 years after their first film with two American journalists who appeared in the original to discover what became of the first revolution to be conducted in the glare of the world media. They question the role and responsibility of journalists and their employers, who first put Nicaraguans under the microscope and then rushed off to the next hot spot.

Index

Acknowledgments

This book represents much more than the combined experience and knowledge of the two authors; it is, in fact, the collaboration of a small army of friends and colleagues living throughout Nicaragua. We are grateful to each and every person who took the time to help us during our research, especially our five expat profilees: Olin Cohan, Donna Tabor, Chris Berry, Phoebe Haupt, and Monica Drazba. Richard Leonardi was especially gracious with his words and insight—thank you. Also, *mucho* respect to Jean Walsh, Chris Romano, Mark Lewis, and the *¡Va Pue!* archives.

The following folks helped enormously, whether responding to our survey, answering our ensuing barrage of questions, or just offering their own hard-won insight into so many aspects of living in Nicaragua: A thousand thanks to Tim Coone, Marliese Mendel, Jan Strik, Arjen Roersma, Andy and Inge, Helen Korengold, David Thomson, Terry Leary, Vikki Stein, Rich Castillo Pelón, Mary Helen Espinosa, Peter Christopher, Donn Wilson, Jamie Carson, Nadene Holmes, Mike Sabine, Tom Bardner, J. J. and Kimberly Yemma, Tyler Tibbs, Karol Dixon, Ruth Northey, Nick Cooke, Henry Morgan, Bryan McMandon, Barry Oliver, Julio Lacayo, Zach Lunin, Turalu Brady Murdock, and Tura Murdock-Rocha. In acknowledgment of the invaluable support of these people, a portion of the profits from the sale of this book will be donated to their favorite Nicaraguan charity organizations and NGOs.

Joshua would like to offer his *media naranja*, Sutay, a big ol' *beso* for her patience and support during the less-than-ideal timing of this project; Randall owes a big hug to his wife, Ericka, and to his in-laws in Managua, all of whom provided many patient hours of support, logistics work, and a good deal of running around after elusive bits of critical information—not to mention lots of great food and good times.

This book was written over the course of a year in which the authors lived and worked in over a dozen countries around the globe in addition to Nicaragua; for that reason we'd like to thank DARPA (the Defense Advanced Research Projects Agency), for creating the Internet, and also enterprising cybercafe owners around the world. Thanks as well to the many ingenious creators of open-source software (on which this book was entirely written) and to the folks at Apple, who (eventually) came through when Joshua's iBook went up in flames five days before deadline in Chiang Mai, Thailand. An enormous hug of gratitude to Carrie Stephens, who swooped in from Baltimore bearing a brand-new laptop.

Thank you to our editorial teammates in Emeryville: Rebecca Browning, Erin Raber, Tabitha Lahr, Kevin McLain, and Kat Smith, as well as publicist Hannah Cox and the rest of the Avalon Travel Publishing crew.

Finally, our appreciation extends way back to our own bumbling first efforts at living in Nicaragua, when, along with our Nica-15 brethren, we were shown the way by the first of numerous adopted Nicaraguan host families and by our original Peace Corps trainers, especially Naomi Till.

www.moon.com

For helpful advice on planning a trip, visit www.moon.com for the **TRAVEL PLANNER** and get access to useful travel strategies and valuable information about great places to visit. When you travel with Moon, expect an experience that is uncommon and truly unique.

 *HANDBOOKS • OUTDOORS • METRO • LIVING ABROAD*